Kaplan Publishing are constantly finding
difference to your studies and our exciti
offer something different to students lo

CW00664567

This book comes with free MyKaplan on
study anytime, anywhere. **This free online resource is not sold
separately and is included in the price of the book.**

Having purchased this book, you have access to the following online study materials:

CONTENT	ACCA (including FBT, FMA, FFA)		FIA (excluding FBT, FMA, FFA)	
	Text	Kit	Text	Kit
Electronic version of the book	✓	✓	✓	✓
Knowledge checks with instant answers	✓		✓	
Material updates	✓	✓	✓	✓
Latest official ACCA exam questions*		✓		
Pocket Notes (digital copy)	✓		✓	
Study Planner	✓			
Progress Test including questions and answers	✓		✓	
Syllabus recap Videos		✓		✓
Revision Planner		✓		✓
Question Debrief and Walkthrough Videos		✓		
Mock Exam including questions and answers		✓		

* Excludes BT, MA, FA, FBT, FMA, FFA; for all other papers includes a selection of questions, as released by ACCA

How to access your online resources

Received this book as part of your Kaplan course?
If you have a MyKaplan account, your full online resources will be added automatically, in line with the
information in your course confirmation email. If you've not used MyKaplan before, you'll be sent an activation
email once your resources are ready.

Bought your book from Kaplan?
We'll automatically add your online resources to your MyKaplan account. If you've not used MyKaplan before,
you'll be sent an activation email.

Bought your book from elsewhere?
Go to **www.mykaplan.co.uk/add-online-resources**
Enter the ISBN number found on the title page and back cover of this book.
Add the unique pass key number contained in the scratch panel below.
You may be required to enter additional information during this process to set up or confirm your account
details.

This code can only be used once for the registration of this book online. This registration and your online
content will expire when the examinations covered by this book have taken place. Please allow one hour from
the time you submit your book details for us to process your request.

Please scratch the film to access your unique code.

Please be aware that this code is case-sensitive and you will need
to include the dashes within the passcode, but not when entering
the ISBN.

KAPLAN
PUBLISHING

ACCA Diploma in Financial and
Management Accounting (RQF Level 2)

FA1

Recording Financial Transactions

STUDY TEXT

KAPLAN PUBLISHING'S STATEMENT OF PRINCIPLES

LINGUISTIC DIVERSITY, EQUALITY AND INCLUSION

We are committed to diversity, equality and inclusion and strive to deliver content that all users can relate to.

We are here to make a difference to the success of every learner.

Clarity, accessibility and ease of use for our learners are key to our approach.

We will use contemporary examples that are rich, engaging and representative of a diverse workplace.

We will include a representative mix of race and gender at the various levels of seniority within the businesses in our examples to support all our learners in aspiring to achieve their potential within their chosen careers.

Roles played by characters in our examples will demonstrate richness and diversity by the use of different names, backgrounds, ethnicity and gender, with a mix of sexuality, relationships and beliefs where these are relevant to the syllabus.

It must always be obvious who is being referred to in each stage of any example so that we do not detract from clarity and ease of use for each of our learners.

We will actively seek feedback from our learners on our approach and keep our policy under continuous review. If you would like to provide any feedback on our linguistic approach, please use this form (you will need to enter the link below into your browser).

https://docs.google.com/forms/d/1Vc4mltBPrfViy8AhfyKcJMHQKBmLaLPoa_WPqFNf4Ml/edit

We will seek to devise simple measures that can be used by independent assessors to randomly check our success in the implementation of our Linguistic Equality, Diversity and Inclusion Policy.

British Library Cataloguing-in-Publication Data

A catalogue record for this book is available from the British Library.

Published by:

Kaplan Publishing UK
Unit 2 The Business Centre
Molly Millars Lane
Wokingham
RG41 2QZ

ISBN: 978-1-83996-349-0

Acknowledgments

These materials are reviewed by the ACCA examining team. The objective of the review is to ensure that the material properly covers the syllabus and study guide outcomes, used by the examining team in setting the exams, in the appropriate breadth and depth. The review does not ensure that every eventuality, combination or application of examinable topics is addressed by the ACCA Approved Content. Nor does the review comprise a detailed technical check of a the content as the Approved Content Provider has its own quality assurance processes in place in this respect.

We are grateful to the Association of Chartered Certified Accountants for permission to reproduce past examination questions. The answers have been prepared by Kaplan Publishing.

CONTENTS

Quality and accuracy are of the utmost importance to us so if you spot an error in any of our products, please send an email to mykaplanreporting@kaplan.com with full details.

Our Quality Co-ordinator will work with our technical team to verify the error and take action to ensure it is corrected in future editions.

KAPLAN PUBLISHING

INTRODUCTION

This is the new edition of the Foundations in Accountancy study text for FA1, Recording Financial Transactions, approved by the ACCA and fully updated and revised according to the examiner's comments.

Tailored to fully cover the syllabus, this study text has been written specifically for Foundations level students. A clear and comprehensive style, numerous examples and highlighted key terms help you to acquire the information easily. Plenty of activities and self-test questions enable you to practise what you have learnt.

At the end of most of the chapters you will find multiple-choice questions. These are exam-style questions and will give you a very good idea of the way you will be tested.

ACCA SUPPORT

For additional support with your studies please also refer to the ACCA Global website.

SYLLABUS AND STUDY GUIDE

Position of this examination syllabus in the overall syllabus

No prior knowledge is required before commencing study for FA1. The syllabus content for FA1 provides the basic techniques required to enable candidates to prepare financial statements for various enterprises at a later stage. Candidates will, therefore, need a sound knowledge of the methods and techniques introduced in this examination syllabus to ensure they can employ them in later studies and examinations. The methods used in this syllabus are extended in FA2, *Maintaining Financial Records,* and further developed in FA, *Financial Accounting.*

Syllabus

A TYPES OF BUSINESS TRANSACTION AND DOCUMENTATION

1 Types of business transaction

(a) Describe a range of business transactions including:[K]

   (i) Sales

   (ii) Purchases

   (iii) Receipts

   (iv) Payments

   (v) Petty cash

   (vi) Payroll   **Ch 1**

(b) Define types of discounts including, where applicable, the effect that trade discounts have on sales tax.[K]   **Ch 4**

(c) Describe the processing and security procedures relating to the use of:[K]

   (i) Cash

   (ii) Cheques

   (iii) Credit and debit cards

   (iv) Digital payment methods   **Ch 5**

2 Types of business documentation

(a) Summarise the purpose and content of a range of business documents to include but not limited to:[K]

   (i) Sales invoice

   (ii) Supplier (purchase) invoice

   (iii) Credit note

   (iv) Debit note

   (v) Delivery note

   (vi) Remittance advice   **Ch's 2, 7, & 9**

(b) Prepare the financial documents to be sent to credit customers including:[S]

   (i) Sales invoice

   (ii) Credit note

   (iii) Statements of account.   **Ch's 2 & 9**

(c) Prepare remittance advice to accompany payments to suppliers.[S]   **Ch. 2**

(d) Prepare a petty cash voucher including the sales tax element of an expense when presented with an inclusive amount.[S]   **Ch 8**

3 Process of recording business transactions within the accounting system

(a) Identify the characteristics of accounting data and the sources of accounting data records, showing understanding of how the accounting data and records meet the business' requirements.[K]   **Ch 3**

(b) Describe the key features of a computerised accounting system, including the use of external servers to store data (the cloud).[K]

(c) Summarise how users can locate, display and check accounting data to meet user requirements and understand how data entry errors are dealt with.[K]   **Ch 3**

(d) Summarise the tools and techniques used to process accounting transactions and period-end routines and consider how errors are identified and dealt with.[K]   **Ch 3**

(e) Identify risks to data security, data protection procedures and the storage of data.[K] **Ch. 2**

(f) Explain the principles of coding in entering accounting transactions, including:[K]

   (i) describing the need for a coding system for financial transactions within a double entry bookkeeping system

(ii) describe the use of a coding system within a filing system. **Ch. 3**

(g) Code sales invoices, supplier invoices and credit notes ready for entry into the accounting system.(S) **Ch 3**

(h) Describe the accounting documents and management reports produced by computerised accounting systems and understand the link between the accounting system and other systems in the business.(K)
Ch 3

B DUALITY OF TRANSACTIONS AND THE DOUBLE ENTRY SYSTEM

1 Double entry system

(a) Define the accounting equation.(K) **Ch. 4**

(b) Demonstrate the accounting equation.(K)**Ch. 4**

(c) Describe how the accounting are entered in the accounting system. **Ch. 4**

(d) Explain how transactions from the books of prime entry into the double entry bookkeeping system.(K) **Ch 4**

2 Journal entries **Ch 4**

(a) Explain the use of the journal including the reasons for and format of the journal.(K)

(b) Prepare journal entries for various transactions.(K)

3 Elements of the financial statements **Ch. 4**

(a) Define and distinguish between the elements of the financial statements.(K)

(b) Identify the content of a statement of financial position and statement of profit or loss and other comprehensive income.(K)

C BANK SYSTEM AND TRANSACTIONS

1 The banking process **Ch. 5**

(a) Explain the differences between the services offered by banks and banking institutions.(K)

(b) Describe how the banking clearing system works.(K)

(c) Identify and compare different forms of payment.(K)

(d) Summarise the processing and security procedures relating the use of cash, cheques, credit cards, debit cards and digital methods.(K)

2 Documentation **Ch. 2**

(a) Explain why it is important for an organisation to have a formal document retention policy.(K)

(b) Identify the different categories of documents that may be stored as part of a document retention policy.(K)

D PAYROLL **Ch. 6**

1 Process payroll transactions within the accounting system

(a) Calculate and prepare entries in the accounting system to process payroll transactions including:(S)

(i) Calculation of gross wages for employees paid by the hour, paid by output and salaried workers

(ii) Accounting for payroll costs and deductions

(iii) The employers' responsibilities for taxes, state benefit contributions and other deductions

(b) Identify the different payment methods in a payroll system, e.g. cash, cheques, automated payments.(K)

(c) Explain why authorisation of payroll transactions and security of payroll information is important in an organisation.(K)

E GENERAL LEDGER ACCOUNTS

1 Prepare general ledger accounts

(a) Prepare general ledger accounts, clearly showing the balances brought forward and carried forward as appropriate.(S)
Ch's 4 – 14

F CASH AND BANK

1 Maintaining cash records **Ch. 7**

(a) Record cash transactions within the accounting system, including any sales tax effect where applicable.(S)

2 Maintaining a petty cash record **Ch. 8**

(a) Enter and analyse petty cash transactions in the accounting system, including any sales tax effect where applicable.(S)

(b) Demonstrate the use of the imprest and non-imprest systems of maintaining a petty cash record.(S)

(c) Reconcile the petty cash record with cash in hand.(S)

(d) Prepare and account for petty cash reimbursements.(S)

G SALES AND CREDIT TRANSACTIONS

1 Recording sales, customer account balances and trade receivables **Ch's. 9 & 10**

(a) Record sales transactions taking into account:(S)

(i) various types of discount

(ii) sales tax

(iii) the impact on the sales tax ledger account where applicable

(b) Enter invoices and credit notes issued to customers into the accounting system. (S)

(c) Prepare the trade receivables general ledger account by accounting for: (S)

(i) Sales

(ii) Sales returns

(iii) receipts from customers including checking the accuracy and validity of receipts against relevant supporting information

(iv) Discounts

(v) Contra entries

(d) Prepare entries in the accounting system to record cash sales, credit sales and receipts from customers. (S)

(e) Account for irrecoverable debts and allowances for irrecoverable debts. (S)

H PURCHASES AND CREDIT TRANSACTIONS

1 Recording purchases, supplier account balance and trade payables   Ch's.11 &12

(a) Record purchase transactions taking into account: (S)

(i) various types of discount

(ii) sales tax

(iii) the impact of the sales tax ledger account where applicable

(b) Enter supplier invoices and credit notes received from suppliers into the accounting system. (S)

(c) Prepare the trade payables general ledger account by accounting for: (S)

(i) Purchases

(ii) Purchase returns

(iii) payments to suppliers including checking the accuracy and validity of the payment against relevant supporting information

(iv) Discounts

(v) Contra entries

(d) Prepare entries in the accounting system to record cash purchases, credit purchases and payments to suppliers. (S)

I RECONCILIATION   Ch's 13

1 Purpose of reconciliations

(a) Describe the purpose of reconciliations to external documents as a checking device to aid management and help identify errors. (K)

(b) Explain why it is important to reconcile to external documents regularly and to deal with discrepancies quickly and professionally. (K)

2 Reconcile the cash records

(a) Reconcile the cash records to a bank statement and deal with any discrepancies. (S)

3 Reconcile individual supplier accounts

(a) Reconcile the balance on individual supplier accounts to supplier statements and deal with any discrepancies. (S)

J PREPARING THE TRIAL BALANCE   Ch. 14

1 Prepare the trial balance

(a) Extract an initial trial balance. (S)

2 Correcting errors

(a) Identify the types of errors that are revealed by extracting a trial balance. (K)

(b) Identify the types of error that are not disclosed by extracting a trial balance. (K)

(c) Prepare journal entries to correct errors in the trial balance. (S)

(d) Identify when a suspense account is required and clear the suspense account using journal entries. (S)

(e) Redraft the trial balance following correction of all errors. (S)

THE EXAMINATION

Format of the examination

	Number of marks
50 multiple-choice questions (2 marks each)	100
Time allowed: 2 hours	
This is a computer-based examination.	

Computer-based examinations

- Be sure you understand how to use the **software** before you start the exam. If in doubt, ask the assessment centre staff to explain it to you.

- Questions are **displayed on the screen** and answers are entered using keyboard and mouse. At the end of the examination, you are given a certificate showing the result you have achieved.

- **Multiple choice questions** may ask for numerical answers, but could also involve paragraphs of text which require you to select a narrative, rather than numerical, answer. This could be, for example, requiring you to select the correct definition from several possible answers.

- **Don't panic** if you realise you've answered a question incorrectly – you can always go back and change your answer.

Answering the questions

Multiple-choice questions – read the questions carefully and work through any calculations required. This examination comprises a mixture of narrative and computational questions.

If you don't know the answer, eliminate those options you know are incorrect and see if the answer becomes more obvious. Remember that only one answer to a multiple-choice question can be right!

If you get stuck with a question skip it and return to it later. Answer every question – if you do not know the answer, you do not lose anything by guessing. Towards the end of the examination spend the last five minutes reading through your answers and making any corrections.

Equally divide the time you spend on questions. In a two-hour examination that has 50 questions you have about 2.4 minutes per a question.

Do not treat multiple-choice questions as an easy option. **Do not skip any part of the syllabus** and make sure that you have **learnt** definitions, **know** key words and their meanings and importance, and **understand** the names and meanings of rules, concepts and theories.

STUDY SKILLS AND REVISION GUIDANCE

Preparing to study

SET YOUR OBJECTIVES

Before starting to study decide what you want to achieve – the type of pass you wish to obtain.

This will decide the level of commitment and time you need to dedicate to your studies.

DEVISE A STUDY PLAN

Determine when you will study.

Split these times into study sessions.

Put the sessions onto a study plan making sure you cover the course, course assignments and revision.

Stick to your plan!

Effective study techniques

Use the **SQR3** method

Survey the chapter – look at the headings and read the introduction, summary and objectives. Get an overview of what the text deals with.

Question – during the survey, ask yourself the questions that you hope the chapter will answer for you.

Read through the chapter thoroughly, answering the questions and meeting the objectives. Attempt the exercises and activities, and work through all the examples.

Recall – at the end of the chapter, try to recall the main ideas of the chapter without referring to the text. Do this a few minutes after the reading stage.

Review – check that your recall notes are correct.

Use the **MURRED** method

Mood – set the right mood.

Understand – issues covered and make note of any uncertain bits.

Recall – stop and put what you have learned into your own words.

Review – go over the material you covered to consolidate the knowledge.

Expand – read relevant articles and newspapers.

Digest – go back and reconsider the information.

While studying...

Summarise the key points of the chapter.

Make linear notes – a list of headings, divided up with subheadings listing the key points. Use different colours to highlight key points and keep topic areas together.

Try mind-maps – put the main heading in the centre of the paper and encircle it. Then draw short lines radiating from this to the main sub-headings, which again have circles around them. Continue the process from the sub-headings to sub-sub-headings, etc.

Revision

The best approach to revision is to **revise the course as you work through it**.

Also try to leave **four to six weeks before the exam for final revision**.

Make sure you **cover the whole syllabus**.

Pay special attention to **those areas where your knowledge is weak**.

If you are stuck on a topic find somebody (a tutor) to explain it to you.

Read around the subject – read good newspapers and professional journals, especially ACCA's *Student Accountant* – this can give you an advantage in the exam.

Read through the text and your notes again. Maybe put key revision points onto index cards to look at when you have a few minutes to spare.

Practise exam-standard questions under timed conditions. Attempt all the different styles of questions you may be asked to answer in your exam.

Review any assignments you have completed and look at where you lost marks – put more work into those areas where you were weak.

Ensure you **know the structure of the exam** – how many questions and of what type they are.

Chapter 1

BUSINESS TRANSACTIONS

This chapter introduces the common types of business transaction. Later chapters will look at how transactions are recorded, how accounting records are controlled and how the accuracy of these is scrutinised.

This chapter covers syllabus area A1.

CONTENTS

LEARNING OUTCOMES

At the end of this chapter, you should be able to:

- understand the main types of transaction that a business is likely to undertake

- distinguish between cash and credit transactions

- distinguish between transactions in goods and in services

- distinguish between receipts and payments and income and expenditure

- understand the need to document business transactions

- identify the key personnel involved in initiating, processing and completing transactions

- understand the need for effective control over transactions

- identify the timing of various transactions.

1 TYPES OF BUSINESS TRANSACTION

Every business sells goods or services to customers and should be paid for what it sells. Every business buys goods and services from suppliers, and must pay for what it buys.

For example, retail businesses such as department stores and supermarkets buy goods from suppliers for resale to shoppers, and a garage buys car parts and components to repair customers' cars. Businesses buy stationery and computers for their office work.

All businesses incur expenses for various services, such as the supply of electricity, telephone services, property rental costs and local taxation (business rates). Many businesses have employees, and have to pay for their labour in the form of wages and salaries.

In this publication, the tern 'business' is used to refer to an organisation or entity which undertakes trading activities, irrespective of the legal structure or characteristics of that business. The ACCA FA1 syllabus does not require any knowledge of different business structures such as a partnership or limited liability company. The focus is upon sole proprietors – individuals who both own and manage the business.

2 TERMINOLOGY

Precise terminology is important in bookkeeping and accounting. Key terms are given at the end of each chapter to highlight appropriate terminology. It is important to be clear on the following:

- **Sales** – the exchange of goods or services for money. Items such as commission and fees received are also used instead of sales for some services, perhaps by professional businesses such as accountants and lawyers.

- **Purchases** – goods and services obtained for resale to customers, or for use or consumption in the business.

- **Receipts** – money received, mainly from cash sales or from customers who have been allowed a period of credit before making payment.

- **Payments** – money paid out in cash or from the bank account by cheque or digital or electronic means.

- **Income** – a more general term than sales to also include interest received, rent received from letting part of the business premises and so on.

- **Expenses** – cash paid for rent, electricity for lighting, telephone charges and so on. This does not include purchases of goods for resale or the purchase of assets, such as machinery and equipment for use in the business.

- **Expenditure** – includes purchases, expenses and money spent on buying anything else for the business.

- **Petty cash** – relatively small amounts of cash in the form of notes and coins used to pay small, occasional expenses, such as office refreshments or travel expenses. Normally, the cost would be paid by an employee who would then receive a cash reimbursement.

- **Payroll** –is accounting for the costs of having employees, which includes all elements of gross pay (before any tax deductions) such as basic wage or salary, plus any bonus, commission and also additional employer costs.

3 CASH AND CREDIT TRANSACTIONS

Most business transactions for buying and selling goods or services are either cash transactions or credit transactions.

- With a **cash transaction**, the buyer pays for the item either upon exchange of goods/services or they pay in advance. For example, sales in a shop or supermarket are cash transactions, because the customer pays at the cash desk or check-out point.

- With a **credit transaction**, the buyer doesn't pay for the item on receipt, but is allowed some time (a 'credit period') before having to make the payment.

Example of a credit transaction

Velocity Book Publishers places an order with a printing company, Q Print, to print 5,000 copies of a new book they are publishing. Q Print agree to print the books and Velocity Book Publishers will be given up to 60 days to pay after the books have been printed. Q Print delivers the books into the warehouse of Velocity Book Publishers on 1 March, and submits a demand for payment (known as an invoice) for $15,000, payable on or before 1 May.

This is a credit transaction because Velocity Book Publishers does not have to pay for the purchased items when it orders the books, nor even when the books are received. Instead, it has been given time to pay after the goods have been received.

Most transactions between two businesses are credit transactions. In other words, businesses usually buy from other businesses and sell to other businesses on credit. The credit terms, such as how long the buyer has to pay, are agreed between the buyer and the supplier in advance.

	Cash	**Credit**
Sale	Goods are sold or a service provided and the customer pays immediately.	Goods are sold or a service provided and the customer pays at a later date.
Purchase	Goods are purchased or a service received and is paid for immediately.	Goods are purchased or a service received and paid for at a later date.

ACTIVITY 1

A client receives a haircut by a self-employed hairdresser. The client pays for this with $20 cash.

1 What kind of transaction is this from the client's perspective?

    A The sale of goods by the hairdresser

    B The sale of a service by the client

    C The purchase of goods by the hairdresser

    D The purchase of a service by the client

2 What kind of transaction is this from the hairdresser's point of view?

    A   A cash sale

    B   A credit sale

    C   A cash purchase

    D   A credit purchase

For a suggested answer, see the 'Answers' section at the end of the book.

Every purchase from one party's perspective is a sale from the other perspective of the other party to the transaction. The purchaser makes payment and seller receives it in exchange for the goods or services supplied.

3.1 METHODS OF PAYMENT

You need to understand the different methods of receiving payment from customers, or making payments to a supplier. Four common methods of receiving and making payments used in many businesses are:

- payments in 'cash', in other words, in notes and coins

- payments by debit and credit cards and electronic payment methods

- payments by cheque

- automated receipts and payments through the business bank accounts. Examples are standing orders and direct debits.

Receiving and making payments by each of these methods will be explained in subsequent chapters.

4 PETTY CASH

Most businesses prefer to make as few payments in notes and coins ('cash') as possible. It is more secure to pay by cheque or online because there is less risk of loss or theft. However, sometimes it is more convenient, or even necessary, to make payment in cash.

Examples of items for which a business may make payment in cash include the following:

- payment for small office expenses such as office refreshments, postage stamps etc

- payment for taxi fares for business purposes

- payment for travel costs such as rail and bus for business purposes

- payment for flowers to send to an employee who is absent due to illness.

A small amount of cash is held on business premises for such purposes. In a business that rarely makes cash transactions, such as a large engineering business, this is convenient. In businesses that regularly handles cash such as a restaurant, it is useful to retain a small amount of petty cash separate from income received from sales. This makes it easier to reconcile the cash received with the records of meals and drinks served and to investigate any discrepancies than it would be if a number of employees were able to take cash from the sales receipts to use to meet expenses at any time.

5 PAYROLL

Many businesses have employees who are paid by the business for the work they do. Most businesses will have a set day on which employees should be paid, and it is the payroll department's responsibility to ensure that wages are paid on the correct due dates. Weekly paid employees (wage earners) will be paid at least once a week, normally on the same day each week. Commonly the pay day will be either Thursday or Friday if the working week is from Monday to Friday.

Monthly paid employees (salary earners) will be paid once a month, and there will be a formula for determining the pay day. For example, this may be:

- the last day of the calendar month
- the last Thursday or Friday of the calendar month
- the same date each month, such as the 26th.

Employees may be paid their wages in several ways:

- in cash or by cheque
- by bank transfer
- through the Banks Automated Clearing System (BACS).

Making payments by these methods will be described in subsequent chapters. The payroll department also makes payments to outside agencies, such as tax and social services authorities and pension schemes.

ACTIVITY 2

1   Which of the following terms would be used to classify a payment for electricity to heat the business premises of a firm of plumbers?

    A   Expense

    B   Purchase

    C   Receipt

    D   Sales

2   Which of the following would be paid for by petty cash?

    A   Car repairs on the business owner's private vehicle

    B   Packet of envelopes at local store

    C   Paying a supplier for goods bought on credit

    D   Wages and salaries

3   Which of the following transactions are associated with payroll?

    A   Income from cash sale of computer used to calculate salaries

    B   Postage and stationery, office expenses

    C   Taxes on employee income, pension scheme payments, wages

    D   Credit purchase of safety equipment for delivery staff

For a suggested answer, see the 'Answers' section at the end of the book.

6 KEEPING A RECORD

A business maintains detailed records of its sales, purchases, receipts and payments. There are several reasons for keeping records.

- A business needs to keep track of how much it owes to its suppliers and how much it is owed by credit customers.

- Records of transactions, such as sales and purchases, are useful in the event of a query or dispute with a customer or supplier.

- Keeping records of transactions enables checks to be carried out to ensure that they have been properly processed, and that there have been no errors or omissions for any reason, including fraud.

- Keeping records of sales, purchases and other transactions enables a business to monitor how well it is performing, and whether it is making a profit or a loss.

Similar reasons apply to maintaining petty cash records. Payroll records must also be maintained to ensure that employees are properly rewarded for their work and to ensure that the correct deductions (e.g. for taxation) are made.

Transactions are recorded in ledger accounts. The system of recording transactions is therefore called the accounting system or the bookkeeping system. The system organises transactions into sets of structured ledger accounts. Accounting records will be explained in subsequent chapters.

To maintain records, it is important to retain documents that provide evidence of transactions. Chapter 2 reviews these documents in some depth.

7 KEY PERSONNEL

In most businesses it is likely that a different employees will be involved in different types of business transaction.

For example, in a department store, the sales will be made by the shop floor or retail assistants. The purchases of goods for resale will be made by the departmental buyers. The general expenses will be paid by the accounts department, the wages by the payroll department and any purchases of equipment will probably be made by the store manager.

In a large business the number of people involved in entering into, recording and authorising transactions may be considerable, so it is important to have a system of control over the amount they spend or authorise to prevent the business getting into financial difficulties. Senior management authorise the larger items of expenditure because they have greater knowledge of business policies and objectives and understand the financial circumstances of the business.

8 CONTROL OVER TRANSACTIONS

If many people in a business are involved in entering into and authorising a range of transactions then it is important that these transactions are properly controlled. This has two aspects:

- only properly authorised employees can enter into transactions on behalf of the business. For example only properly trained sales assistants can make sales to customers and only the departmental buyer can enter into a transaction to buy goods for the store.

- transactions are carried out in the correct manner and following the correct procedures. For example, each time a shop assistant makes a sale the amount of the sale must be entered into the till or cash register and the money received placed into the till.

When a transaction takes place in a business, the systems that the business operates should ensure the correct recording of that transaction.

For example when money is received for a cash sale this receipt must be recorded as part of the monies received during the day and also as a sale. The accounting systems should ensure that the cash received is recorded in the till and recorded on the till roll. This receipt should then also be recorded in the accounting system as a sale.

However, on occasions, errors may be made when transactions are recorded. Businesses will therefore usually have a variety of internal checks or controls in order to identify any errors made so that they can be corrected.

8.1 EXAMPLES

Depending upon the size and structure of a business, it may operate a number of internal checks and controls including:

- reconciliations of cash in the till or cash register to the till roll records

- checking of the addition of cheque listings used to complete paying in slips

- reconciliations of amounts of petty cash held to the petty cash records

- checking of accounting entries

- checking of bank payments made or petty cash authorisations, and

- reconciliations of bank and cash records to bank statements received.

9 TIMING OF TRANSACTIONS

The timing and frequency of business transactions will vary. Some, such as sales, may take place on a daily basis whilst others, such as salary payment, are paid monthly. Items such as electricity and gas bills may be paid on a quarterly basis. Purchases of equipment will probably be occasional, but infrequent.

Whenever transactions occur they should be promptly recorded in the accounting records on the day that they occur. This is important in order to ensure that the business records are complete and up to date. It is also necessary, as you will see in your later studies, to ensure that the annual financial statements show a true and fair view of the business to management, owners and other interested parties, such as banks and providers of finance.

ACTIVITY 3

The manager of the research and development department of a large chemical business has been given control of the investigation of the potential healing properties of a naturally occurring compound found in the Amazonian rainforest.

1   State why the manager will need to ensure careful records are maintained of the receipts and payments associated with this project.

2   Explain why the manager will need to set up a system of authorisation and control for expenditure.

3   Explain why timing is important when dealing with financial transactions under such a project.

For a suggested answer, see the 'Answers' section at the end of the book.

CONCLUSION

All forms of business are set up to provide goods and/or services to their customers or to benefit the public (i.e. charitable work). In order to facilitate the provision of such goods and services they will need to engage in a series of transactions. These transactions need to be recorded in the accounting system so that the individuals who manage and control the business can produce and review reports to help them understand the financial performance and position of the business. This information will help them operate the business in a more effective and efficient manner.

Cash and credit transactions are used in the sale and purchase of goods and services and in the receipt of income and payment of expenditure.

Small, day-to-day transactions are commonly paid in cash. Larger transactions tend to be paid for by cheque or other payment made from the business bank account, such as automated payments. Such expenditure is authorised at different levels in the business and within a system of financial control.

Payments to employees are also controlled and authorised and made regularly and in a timely manner.

KEY TERMS

Expenses – Money spent for rent, electricity for lighting, telephone accounts and so on. This does not include purchases of goods for resale or the purchase of assets for use in the business on a continuing basis.

Income – A more general term than sales to also include items such as interest received, rent received from letting part of the business premises.

Ledger account – A record of similar financial transactions in a business.

Payroll – List of employees and the wages or salaries due to each.

Petty cash – A small amount of notes and coins held to reimburse employees for small payments made on behalf of the business.

Purchases – Buying goods and/or services for use in the business or for resale to customers.

Receipt – Written statement of an amount of money that has been paid/received.

Sales – The exchange of goods or services for money. Terms such as commission and fees are also used instead of sales for some services.

Till roll – Printed listing of all payments received through a till/point of sale desk in a retail outlet.

SELF TEST QUESTIONS

		Paragraph
1	Explain the difference between a customer and a supplier.	1
2	What is a cash transaction?	3
3	What is a credit transaction?	3
4	Give examples of purchases and expenses.	3
5	When would petty cash be used?	4
6	Name three payments made by the payroll department.	5
7	Give two reasons why a business keeps a record of business transactions.	6
8	Senior personnel should authorise major expenditure in a business. Why?	7
9	Give one reason for maintaining a system of internal checks or controls.	8
10	Why is it important for a business to pay expenses, such as wages, on time?	9

EXAM-STYLE QUESTIONS

1   A business buys goods on credit. When will this require the accounting records to be updated?

   A   Only when the goods are received

   B   Only when the goods are paid for

   C   When the goods are received and again when they are paid for

   D   When the goods are received, again when they are paid for and when the goods are resold

2   Which of the following describes the receipts generated by an Internet Service Provider?

   A   Income from sale of goods

   B   Income from giving a service

   C   Payments for employees

   D   Payments for share capital

3   How would you describe petty cash?

    A   Cash for some small everyday expenses

    B   An overdraft arranged by the bank

    C   Spare cash invested in a separate bank account

    D   Money in the current account

4   A stationery business sold computer supplies to a customer for payment in one month. Which of the following are true in respect of this transaction?

    (i)   It is a cash transaction

    (ii)   The expenditure must be authorised by the stationery business

    (iii)   A record of the transaction must be kept in case of future query by the stationery business

    (iv)   The stationery business will need to ensure that it receives payment in one month

    A   (i) only

    B   (ii) and (iii)

    C   (iii) and (iv)

    D   All of the above

5   Which section of a grocery business pays salaries?

    A   Accounts department

    B   Payroll

    C   Sales

    D   Store manager

For suggested answers, see the 'Answers' section at the end of the book.

Chapter 2

TYPES OF BUSINESS DOCUMENTATION

In the first chapter you looked at the different transactions that take place in business which need to be properly documented and recorded. This chapter looks at the documents which underlie those business transactions. It covers the syllabus content on types of business documentation.

This chapter covers syllabus areas A2.

CONTENTS

1   Documents for business transactions

2   Processing a cash transaction

3   Credit transaction procedures

4   Processing a credit transaction: a credit sale

5   Processing a credit transaction: a credit purchase

6   Statements of account

7   Returns, credit and debit notes

8   Petty cash claim

9   Document retention policies

10   Data protection

LEARNING OUTCOMES

At the end of this chapter, you should be able to:

- distinguish between different types of business documentation

- outline the purpose and contents of a range of business documents

- describe the documentation and the flow of documentation for different transactions including internet transactions

- identify the personnel involved in preparing and authorising documents.

1 DOCUMENTS FOR BUSINESS TRANSACTIONS

When a business enters into a transaction, such as a sale or purchase, each stage of the transaction is documented. Some businesses use electronic documents in their computer systems and that electronic information can be sent from the computer of suppliers to customers without the need for a paper trail or record. Nevertheless, depending upon the size and nature of a business, many transaction documents may still be produced in paper form.

Documents for business transactions need to be produced for several reasons.

- It is evidence of the transaction and its details. For example, suppose that Charu buys some flower pots from Gopi, which Gopi delivers. Charu may complain to Gopi that 250 flower pots had been ordered but only 200 were delivered, and that the agreed price was $1.50 per pot, whereas Gopi was now asking for $1.75 for each pot. If the original order has been documented, the dispute could be resolved by checking the order details.

- It is evidence of the stage that the transaction has reached. Documents are produced at different stages in a transaction. You may have had some experience of this yourself. Suppose that you buy a new set of chairs for your house from a local store. The sales assistant will record the details of your order in the store, and ask you to sign it as evidence that you have placed the order. The document you sign is called a sales order. Some weeks later, the chairs may be delivered to your house by a delivery van, and you will be given a document by the van driver, which you may have to sign as evidence that you have received the chairs. This document is called a delivery note. Sometimes you may receive a letter first containing an **advice note** which will advise you that the delivery will be made on a specific day and will list the items to be delivered. When you order the chairs, or after they have been delivered, you will be required to pay. The store will confirm the payment to you when the payment occurs, by giving you a **receipt**. A receipt is a document providing evidence that you have paid.

- Documents enable checks and reviews to take place. In business, it is difficult to keep track of every transaction. Documents can be used to check details and confirm that everything appears to be correct. For example, a business may receive an invoice from a supplier demanding payment for goods delivered by the supplier. Before the business makes the payment, there should be a check that everything is in order, and that the goods were ordered and have been delivered properly (as the supplier has claimed) and that the amount asked for in payment is correct. This checking process is carried out by reviewing at the relevant documents.

- Documents enable transaction details to be captured and for them to be recorded in the accounting system, which is explained in subsequent chapters. Briefly, details of all the sales and purchase transactions entered into by a business are recorded in its 'accounts' or 'books'. To maintain accounting records, a business needs a record of the transaction details. These details come from the documents relating to each transaction.

You need to know: **what** the main business documents are and what details they contain; **why** they are needed; **who** produces and authorises them; and **when** they are needed.

2   PROCESSING A CASH TRANSACTION

Cash transactions are fairly straightforward. The buyer orders goods or services and pays for them immediately at the time of receipt of goods or performance of the service. The seller delivers the goods or provides the service, and often gives the customer a **receipt** as evidence of payment.

You probably have been the buyer yourself in many cash transactions, such as the purchase of a newspaper or magazine from a local retailer, but let's look at a number of different cash transactions from the viewpoint of the seller.

Example 1: Over-the-counter sale

Sales in a shop are 'over the counter'. The customer selects the goods required, takes them to a sales desk or check-out point, pays for them, and takes them away. The seller gives the customer a **receipt**, as evidence of the transaction and the payment. If the customer then wants to return the goods, because there is something wrong with them, the seller can ask to see the receipt, to confirm that the customer did actually buy the items recently in the shop. Sales are also recorded automatically by the seller's cash register, and at the end of the day, a **till roll** may be produced by the cash register, listing all the items sold through the check-out point during that day.

Example 2: Verbal order

Another type of transaction involving a face-to-face verbal order occurs when the goods or services are not available immediately. Instead, the customer orders them for future receipt or delivery. In many cases, the customer may be asked to pay a deposit with the order, and make the rest of the payment ('pay the balance') when the goods or services are delivered or provided.

Suppose, for example, that you go to a car dealer to buy a new car. The salesperson will show you a demonstration model, and talk to you about all the optional extras you can buy with the car. The salesperson will then record the details of your order on a **sales order form**, which you will sign. This form will include the name and address of seller and purchaser together with the full details of the order and agreed costs. You will probably have to pay a deposit, which could be, say, 10% of the purchase price. The car dealer uses this order form to process your order, by asking the manufacturer to supply a car to your specification. You will be given a copy of the sales order form as evidence of your order, and as a receipt for your deposit. (Alternatively, you may be given a separate receipt for the deposit.) When the car is delivered to the car dealer, you will be issued with an **invoice**, stating the full purchase price and the deposit you have already paid, and asking you to pay the balance of the purchase price. When you have paid, you will go to the car showroom and receive a **receipt** for your payment, and then you can drive the car away.

Sometimes the extent of an order is not completely clear. For example, if your heating or air conditioning system breaks down you would call an engineer to fix the problem. Usually the engineer will examine the equipment and then provide you with a **quotation**. This will contain details of the work needed including a list of replacement parts and labour and an indication of the amount the repair will cost. Sometimes the quotation will be preceded with an **estimate** which may be provided verbally at the time the engineer calls. The **quotation** is a more formal document, which may be relied on by the prospective purchaser and which is provided in writing to confirm agreement of the estimate.

Example 3: Telephone order

The procedures for taking orders by telephone can vary from organisation to organisation, but may be as follows.

Suppose that you want to buy a book and contact the seller by telephone with your order. The details of your order will be taken, and entered on a **sales order form**. A sales order form may be a paper document, but more likely to be entered into a computerised system which displays an order form on screen. Payment details will usually be taken at this time.

The sales order is then used to create a **dispatch note**, which is an instruction to the warehouse to send the book to the address you have given. A copy of the dispatch note will be attached to the package containing your book, and this copy is called a **delivery note**. When you receive the book, you will also receive the delivery note, as evidence that the item has been delivered to you. (Some businesses use two copies of a delivery note, which the customer is asked to sign. One copy is then retained by the supplier, as evidence that the customer has taken delivery of the goods.)

You will also be given a receipt, as documentary evidence that you have paid for the book. The receipt could either be a separate document, or included along with the delivery note.

Example 4: Written order

A common example of a written order in a cash transaction is buying goods from a mail order or catalogue business, using an order form within the catalogue.

Suppose, for example, that you have a sales catalogue from Postal Fashions, a mail order firm that sells items of clothing. You might place an order for some shirts by filling in the form, indicating which shirts you want and how many, and signing it. This order form may be called a **purchase order**. You would send the form, together with your cheque payment or credit card details, to Postal Fashions. Postal Fashions would copy the order details on to a **dispatch note**. (In practice, order details are usually keyed into a computer system from the order form, and the computerised system then produces a dispatch note and delivery note automatically.) The shirts would then be posted to you with a **delivery note**, which will probably also include a statement that you have paid for the items in full. In other words, for this type of transaction, the delivery note also acts as a receipt.

Example 5: Internet order

Increasingly, customers are using the internet to make orders. A common way of selling on the internet is for a business to have a website that allows customers to select the goods or services they want to buy, by placing them in an electronic 'shopping basket'. Usually, the customer enters credit card or debit card details with the order, to pay for the purchased items. If the customer wants to purchase books, they enter their requirements on an electronic **order form** which may involve simply ticking a box or specifying the quantity they wish to purchase. They will then be taken through a secure buying system which results in a paid invoice and/or a **receipt** which can be printed out at the end of the transaction. A copy may also be emailed to the purchaser. The books are then despatched with a **delivery note**.

ACTIVITY 1

What do you think is the difference between a sales order form and a purchase order form?

For a suggested answer, see the 'Answers' section at the end of the book.

The cash transactions above are those you will recognise as taking place between individuals and businesses. Businesses may also buy from other businesses using cash, rather than bank, transactions. Purchases must be properly agreed and authorised within the purchasing business.

2.1 CHEQUE REQUISITION

Internal cheque requisition forms may be completed by a junior member of staff to be authorised by more senior management. They contain details of proposed purchases, including: the nature of the goods, their cost and the chosen supplier. The cheque requisition form is then sent to the cashier (or other authorised person having control of the business cheque book). A cheque is drawn up and provided for the purchase.

Many businesses maintain a system whereby a cheque requisition form is required for any abnormal expense, any item of capital expense and any payment request not supported by a relevant invoice.

Given below is an example cheque requisition form for payment of balance on the sales director's company credit card.

J Forrester
Wholesales Supplies Ltd

CHEQUE REQUISITION FORM

Date: _____17 July 20X7_____

Please draw a cheque on the company's bank account as follows:

Payable to: _____Bankcard_____

Amount: _____$848-23_____

Explanation: _____Settlement of June 20X9 Company credit card_____

_____(statement attached)_____

Signature: _____Sales Director_____

Approved: _____Managing Director_____

Note the following details:

- The requisition form should include enough detail of the payee (person to be paid, Bankcard in this case) and amount of the cheque to be prepared.

- The explanation should explain clearly the reason for the payment.

- Although there is no invoice, any supporting documentation, such as the statement in this case, should be attached to the requisition form.

- The requisition should be signed by the person requesting it and approved or authorised by an appropriate senior person within the business.

3 CREDIT TRANSACTION PROCEDURES

The procedures for credit transactions are a little more complex than for cash transactions. Here, we shall focus on credit transactions where both the buyer and the seller are a business. We shall begin by looking at a credit transaction from the viewpoint of the seller. Then we shall look at the same type of transaction from the viewpoint of the buyer.

For any credit transaction, both parties to the transaction, buyer and seller, must agree what the **credit terms** should be.

- For regular customers, a supplier will agree credit terms for **the period of time the customer will be given before payment is required** and, in addition, will set a **credit limit** for the customer. A credit limit is the maximum amount that the customer will be permitted to have outstanding, based upon the value of all unpaid purchases at that time. For example, suppose that Dilip's Deli is a food store that buys frozen pizzas on credit from a supplier, Tuscan Pizzas. Tuscan Pizzas may agree to allow Dilip's Deli 60 days to pay for deliveries of its pizzas, but set a credit limit of $2,000 on the account. This means that Dilip's Deli must pay for deliveries within 60 days and, in addition, the total amount it owes to Tuscan Pizzas at any time cannot exceed $2,000.

- For 'one off' credit transactions, the buyer and seller will agree credit terms for the individual order. This will consist simply of how much time the customer will be given to pay for the items purchased.

- The credit terms are agreed by the credit controller or a senior manager in the selling business. Transactions above agreed limits and other transactions on credit need to be separately authorised.

4 PROCESSING A CREDIT TRANSACTION: A CREDIT SALE

Businesses usually like to receive an order in writing for a credit transaction. It helps to have a written order in the event of any subsequent disagreement with the customer. Even when a customer makes the order by telephone, the supplier usually asks the customer to confirm the order in writing, or will make a written or computerised record of the order.

Since the customer initiates the written order, the order document is a **purchase order**.

On receipt of the order, a member of the sales team or order processing team must check the order details, to ensure that they are valid and correct. At this stage, it may be necessary to check that the customer has enough credit left, and that the order would not exceed the customer's credit limit.

If the order is for the purchase of goods that the supplier already has in available e.g. in its warehouse, the supplier will produce a dispatch note for the warehouse and a **delivery note**. (In practice, it is likely that the order details will be keyed into a computer system, which then produces a dispatch note and delivery note automatically.)

The goods are then delivered to the customer, who signs the delivery note. A copy of the delivery note is returned to the supplier, as evidence that the customer has taken possession of the goods. The delivery note is matched with the purchase order.

The purchase order details are also used to produce an invoice. For the seller, it is called a **sales invoice**. One copy goes to the customer. One or more copies are kept by the supplier. An invoice can be used, when the customer eventually pays, to check that the payment is correct. The invoice might even be stamped 'PAID' to show that the customer no longer owes the money. (In practice, invoice details are usually held on computer, and when a customer pays, the computer record is used to check that the payment is correct, and is updated to record the fact that the customer has now paid.)

When a customer pays, the payment might be accompanied by a **remittance advice**. This is a document containing details of the payment, including the sales invoice number. A remittance advice can be valuable in helping the supplier to recognise what the payment is for, and which invoice or invoices is/are being paid.

4.1 THE SALES INVOICE

Invoices are particularly important source documents used to record credit sales and credit purchases.

An example of a sales invoice is shown below with along with a description of its contents. The contents will be explained in more depth in a subsequent chapter.

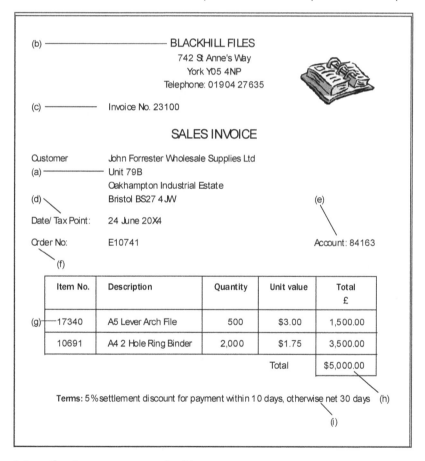

(a) Customer name and address

(b) Name of your business, business address and telephone number

(c) Invoice number

(d) Invoice date

(e)   Customer account reference

(f)   Order number

(g)   Quantity, description and price of goods

(h)   Final total value

(i)   Settlement terms – these state when the invoice should be paid

5   PROCESSING A CREDIT TRANSACTION: A CREDIT PURCHASE

It is important that purchases are properly authorised. If they are not, anyone could order whatever goods they want for any reason. For example, a junior office clerk may decide to order a new computer from a supplier because they want a machine that is faster and more powerful than the one they currently have. However, this should be properly authorised by a suitably responsible person, such as a senior manager. The manager may decide that the computer used by the clerk is sufficiently good enough and therefore refuse to authorise the purchase.

5.1   PURCHASE REQUISITION

To authorise a purchase, it is usual to complete a form known as a **purchase requisition**. The form is prepared by the person requesting the goods, and is then signed by another person who has the authority to agree to the order being placed. (In much the same way, if an individual wants to obtain an item that is held in the warehouse, they may need to prepare a **stores requisition**, and have it authorised by an appropriate person.)

The authorised purchase requisition is then given to a person whose job it is to place the order with a supplier. Larger businesses may have a purchasing department, with buyers whose job is to place orders with suppliers on the best financial and credit terms available. In smaller businesses, orders may be authorised and placed by a senior manager.

5.2   PURCHASE ORDER

A **purchase order** is prepared and sent to the chosen supplier, after the details have been discussed with the supplier, and the sales price and credit terms agreed. Purchase orders should have a unique identification number (the purchase order number).

An example of a purchase order is shown below together with a description of its contents.

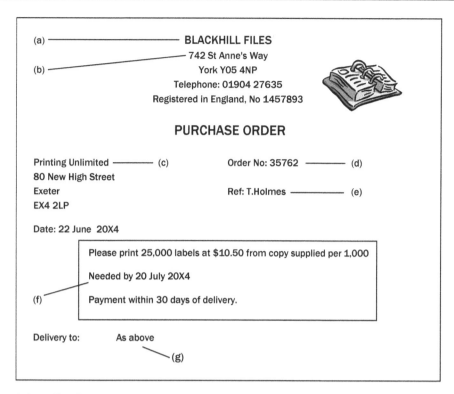

(a)
This is the business name of the buyer.

(a) **Business name**

This is the business name of the buyer.

(b) **Registered office and business registration number**

Most countries have legal requirements relating to disclosure of specified information. For example, in the United Kingdom, whenever a limited company uses its name on business letters or on documents, such as a purchase order, it must state its registered office and registration number. This disclosure is voluntary on invoices and credit notes. Note that individual countries may have slightly different requirements.

(c)/(g) **Supplier name and address**

This is where the purchase order is sent.

(d) **Purchase order number**

Each purchase order has a unique identification number.

(e) **Business contact**

This information allows a supplier to contact a named individual in the event of a query.

(f) **Delivery date**

It is important to specify the delivery date on a purchase order as it is possible that a supplier may not be able to send the goods when they are needed.

The purchase order is sent to the supplier, but a copy is retained by the buyer. Until the goods are delivered, this copy may be held in the purchasing department.

5.3   DELIVERY NOTE AND GOODS RECEIVED NOTE

When the goods are delivered, the supplier provides a **delivery note**. The employee taking the delivery, who may be a member of the stores or warehouse staff, should immediately check the delivery note details against the physical items that have been delivered. For example, if the delivery note states that 40 boxes of photocopier paper have been delivered, the boxes should be counted to make sure there are 40, and not just 39.

Delivery notes are not in a standard format, because each supplier has a different design of form, often in different paper sizes and colours. It is therefore quite common for the details of a delivery to be copied from the delivery note on to a **goods received note**. Extra details can be added on to a goods received note, such as the inventory identity numbers of the items delivered.

The next step is to check that the items delivered were actually what were ordered. This is done by comparing the details on the goods received note with the purchase order. If the supplier has supplied the wrong items, or the wrong quantity, the problem should be identified and resolved as soon as possible after delivery has been made – and certainly before the goods are paid for.

5.4   PURCHASE INVOICE

The supplier issues an invoice to the customer when the goods are delivered, or soon after; this is a **purchase invoice** which will be needed in the accounts department.

A purchase invoice is similar to a sales invoice, except that it is an invoice received from a supplier instead of an invoice issued to a customer. In fact, for the supplier of the goods or services, it is a sales invoice. This means that a purchase invoice is likely to have the words 'sales invoice' printed on it. A business receives invoices from many different suppliers, and so purchase invoices will be in different designs, sizes and colours, and the information they contain is set out differently by each supplier. An example of a purchase invoice is shown below.

A purchase invoice is missing some items of information that the buyer needs to add. This additional information is added when the invoice has been received and when it is checked. In many cases, the information is added by stamping a grid-like box on to the invoice, or adding a stick-on label on the invoice. The box or label is used to add items of information such as:

- the signature or initials of the person who has checked the invoice, for example by checking the details against the purchase order and goods received note

- a code identifying the nature of the expense

- a code identifying the supplier

- the signature or initials of the person who approves the invoice for payment.

ACTIVITY 2

A purchase invoice for a business that buys goods from a supplier is the sales invoice from the supplier. A business receives purchase invoices from its suppliers, and it keeps a copy of sales invoices that it sends to customers.

If you were shown a batch of sales invoices for your business and a batch of purchase invoices, how might they look different?

For a suggested answer, see the 'Answers' section at the end of the book.

5.5 PAYMENT AND REMITTANCE ADVICE

A member of the accounts department will check the details on the invoice against the purchase order. To do this, the purchase order and the invoice have to be matched together. If the purchase invoice shows the buyer's purchase order number, the task of matching the documents is made much easier and quicker.

If the invoice details appear to be correct, the invoice should be submitted for authorisation by a responsible person, possibly a senior manager. Usually, authorisation is given by means of adding a signature to the invoice.

The details of the authorised invoice are then recorded in the accounting system, and payment is made when the agreed credit period comes to an end.

When paying a purchase invoice, some businesses send a remittance advice with their payment. A remittance advice is a document giving details of the invoice that is being paid (or possibly, of several invoices that are being paid at the same time), including the supplier's invoice number. If any prompt payment discount has been deducted from the invoice amount in making the payment, this will also be detailed on the remittance advice. This will help the supplier to identify what the payment is for.

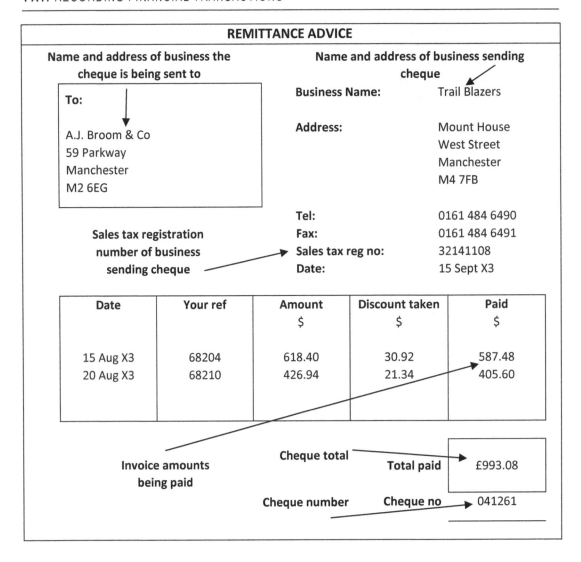

ACTIVITY 3

Explain the purpose of the following sales documents, and list them in the order in which they are produced:

- sales invoice
- delivery note
- remittance advice
- sales order.

Also, explain the purpose of the following purchase documents, and list them in the order in which they are produced:

- goods received note
- purchase order
- purchase invoice.

For a suggested answer, see the 'Answers' section at the end of the book.

6 STATEMENTS OF ACCOUNT

Instead of issuing a remittance advice to customers with each invoice, a business may, instead, choose to issue a statement of account to each customer at regular intervals, typically every month.

A statement of account shows how much the customer still owes. It may show the total amount owed by the customer at the date of the previous statement of account, the new invoices issued to the customer since then, the amounts the customer has paid, and, finally, the total amount still owed by the customer.

An example of a statement of account is shown below. This has been issued by a business called Disks and Labels Ltd to its customer, J Forrester Wholesale Supplies Ltd.

DISKS AND LABELS LTD

76 Wood End Road
Newcastle Upon Tyne
NE4 9AJ
Tel: 0141 839 4444

J Forrester Wholesale Supplies Ltd
Unit 79b
Oakhampton Industrial Estate
Bristol BS27 4JW

VAT Reg No. 341 5079 584

Date: 5 June 20X3

STATEMENT OF ACCOUNT

Date	Description	$	$	Balance owing ($)
14 May	Balance B/f			1,729.46
26 May	Invoice 314/X5	397.42		2,126.88
29 May	Invoice 386/X5	927.04		3,053.92
3 June	Cheque rec'd		1,729.46	1,324.46
4 June	Invoice 019/X5	1,062.96		2,387.42
			Amount now due	**2,387.42**

A customer may return the statement of account with the next payment. If so, the statement of account may also be used in a similar way to a remittance advice.

When the customer receives the monthly statement of account, the customer will reconcile it against the record held of the previous transactions. Any discrepancies are queried with the supplier. Because the statement is produced by a supplier, it acts as a useful external check of the internal records of the customer.

Statements of account represent the ledger account of the customer in the supplier's books of account.

7 RETURNS, CREDIT AND DEBIT NOTES

7.1 SALES RETURNS AND CREDIT NOTES TO CUSTOMERS

It is quite common in business for a customer to return goods to a supplier, perhaps because some of the goods are faulty, or not what the customer ordered. Sometimes, goods are sold to a retailer on a 'sale or return' basis, which means that if the retailer doesn't resell the goods within an agreed period of time, they can be return the goods to the supplier.

Suppose for example that a book publisher sells 100 copies of a book on credit to a book distributor at a price of $15 per book on a 'sale or return' basis. The publisher will initially send an invoice to the distributor for $1,500. Some weeks later, the distributor may send back 20 of the books because they were not needed and there is a sale or return agreement in place. The amount owed by the distributor is now just $1,200, not $1,500.

It might seem logical to suppose that the publisher will issue a new invoice for $1,200 to replace the original invoice for $1,500. However, if the book distributor is a regular customer of the publisher (an 'account customer'), this isn't what happens. Instead of issuing a new invoice to replace the old invoice:

- the original invoice for $1,500 remains valid

- the publisher issues a document called a credit note. In this example, the credit note will be for $300 (20 books at $15 each). A credit note could be described as a negative invoice. It is a statement that the supplier (the book publisher in this example) is reducing the amount owed by the customer. Here, the effect of the credit note is to reduce the amount owing on the book distributor's 'account' by $300, so the net amount owed by the book distributor is just $1,200 ($1,500 − $300).

- A credit note looks similar to a sales invoice. An example of a credit note is shown below. This has been issued by a supplier of office stationery, to an account customer who has returned some items of stationery that had been purchased but had been damaged in transit.

BLACKHILL FILES
742 St Anne's Way
York Y05 4NP
Telephone: 01904 27635

Credit note No: C456

CREDIT NOTE

Customer   J Forrester Wholesale Supplies Ltd
Unit 79B
Oakhampton Industrial Estate
Bristol BS27 4JW

Date/Tax Point: 24 June 20X4

Order No: E10741   Account: 84163

Item No.	Description	Quantity	Unit value	Total $
17340	A5 Lever Arch File	50	$3.00	150.00
10691	A4 2 Hole Ring Binder	100	$1.75	175.00
			Total	$325.00

Reason for return: Damaged in transit

7.2 CREDIT NOTE FOR PURCHASE RETURNS

Credit notes arise with purchases as well as sales, and for the same reasons. If the buyer is dissatisfied with the goods, and the seller agrees to take them back, the seller will issue a credit note for the items returned. The amount owed to the seller is then the amount of the original invoice less the value of the credit note.

7.3 DEBIT NOTE

A debit note is a document raised by a customer and issued to a supplier to request a credit note for goods returned because, for example, they were faulty.

ACTIVITY 4

1   Which document is used to correct an overcharge in an original invoice?

     A   Credit note

     B   Debit note

     C   Dispatch note

     D   Goods received note

2   Which document provides a summary of the credit transactions between a customer and supplier during the previous month?

     A   Advice note

     B   Internal cheque requisition

     C   Invoice

     D   Statement of account

For a suggested answer, see the 'Answers' section at the end of the book.

8 PETTY CASH CLAIM

The petty cash system within a business also has its own documents.

The initial record of any petty cash claim is a petty cash voucher. Blank petty cash vouchers are obtainable from stationery suppliers in pads, and each voucher is torn off the pad when it is used. An example of a blank voucher is shown below.

Petty Cash Voucher	No. _____	
Date _____		
For what required	AMOUNT $	¢
Signature _____		
Authorised _____		

Notes on completing a voucher

- Petty cash vouchers should be given a unique identification number. For control purposes, they should be numbered sequentially by the person with responsibility for accounting for petty cash.

- Each voucher should be dated (with the date it is completed and authorised).

- The details of the expenditure and the amount should be entered. If there is a receipt, this should be attached by a staple or paper clip.

- The person claiming the petty cash should sign the voucher.

- The person authorising payment of the claim should also sign the voucher.

8.1 SUPPORTING DOCUMENTATION

To ensure that a petty cash claim is a valid business expense, each claim must normally be supported by documentation demonstrating that the expense is genuine. Before the petty cash claim is authorised, this supporting documentation must be checked.

Most types of petty cash claim are for straightforward office expenses such as the purchase of office refreshments, postage stamps, or local train, bus or taxi fares to attend meetings. In these cases, a simple receipt is sufficient evidence of the payment for the expense. For train fares, the ticket itself may be used as the evidence.

However, if the payment includes sales tax (such as 'value added tax' or 'VAT' in the UK), a proper receipt showing the supplier's name and the sales tax registration number is required. Most till roll receipts do show this information.

In each case the supporting documentation should be attached to the petty cash claim.

Many of the examples throughout this publication use VAT as an example of the sales tax that may be included within relevant documents.

9 DOCUMENT RETENTION POLICIES

The documents used to process a transaction are not discarded, but are retained on file for some years. For sales transactions, the customer's order, the delivery note and the sales invoice may all be stapled together and filed. Similarly, for purchase transactions, a copy of the purchase order, delivery note, goods received note and purchase invoice may be stapled together and filed.

The documents should be filed in a way that will make it possible to easily locate them if they are needed at some future date, for example, in case of a disagreement between the customer and the supplier, documents could be produced that confirm goods had been supplied and what price had been charged for them. In addition, retention of business documents enables a business to prepare accounting information and to prepare annual financial statements.

There are good commercial reasons for retaining documents and there are also some legal requirements. Some countries also have legal requirements for business documents to be retained for a minimum number of years (usually between three and six years). Some business tax and sales tax laws, for example, require that documents are retained for a number of years in case of enquiry and investigation.

Documents can occupy a considerable amount of space so businesses often store images of old documents on microfiche or on a digital medium long after the original documents have been destroyed. Computerisation allows digital information to be stored on discs, tapes and so on almost permanently.

Any important records should be securely stored safely away from fire, water and other risks that could damage or corrupt the information. Duplicate files are generally maintained for computerised data at locations away from the main business premises.

Documents that should be part of a retention policy include the following:

- records of cash received and paid – petty cash, cash and bank transactions

- amounts owed to the business by customers, such as trade receivables records

- amounts owed by the business to suppliers, such as trade payables records

- records of the inventory count at the year-end

- records of assets used in the business e.g. items of plant and equipment.

ACTIVITY 5

Suppose that, for filing purposes, a business staples together:

- the customer's order, the delivery note and a copy of the sales invoice for all sales transactions

- a copy of the purchase order, delivery note, goods received note and purchase invoice for all purchase transactions.

In what order do you think these documents should be filed, for ease of future reference?

For a suggested answer, see the 'Answers' section at the end of the book.

10 DATA PROTECTION

A completely different aspect of business transactions is the need for a business to keep records and information about persons. The law attempts to provide some protection for individuals:

- to prevent businesses holding data about them, when there isn't a legitimate reason for doing so

- to require businesses to make sure that the data is not inaccurate

- to allow individuals the right to inspect any personal data about them that is retained by a business.

The data protection rules affect businesses. This is because businesses hold personal data records, for example about their customers and employees, mostly on their computer systems. Businesses find personal data useful for marketing and other purposes.

Personal data is data relating to a specific individual. It could include not just the name and address, but age and date of birth, education details, annual salary, family details, and so on. Personal data about a customer may include not just how much the customer owes, but how much was purchased in the past and details of those purchases. In other words, a personal data record could include a history of the customer's purchasing history.

As an example of relevant legislation, businesses in the UK that hold files of personal data about individuals are required to comply with the Data Protection Act 2018 which introduced the General data Protection Regulations (GDPR). Many other countries have similar legal requirements relating to obtaining, using, managing and retaining personal data.

First, they must register with the Data Protection Commissioner as a user of personal data. As a user of personal data, a business must comply with certain data protection principles. These include the following:

- information in personal data files must be obtained and processed lawfully and fairly

- personal data should be held only for specified lawful purposes

- personal data should not be used or disclosed in any way except for those purposes

- the amount of personal data held should be sufficient and relevant for its purpose, but should not be excessive

- personal data should be accurate and, where necessary, should be kept up-to-date

- personal data should not be held for longer than is necessary

- an individual is entitled to know that a data user is holding personal data relating to them. The individual has the right to look at this data and, where appropriate, to insist that it should be corrected or deleted.

If the personal data about an individual is inaccurate, or if there has been an unauthorised use or disclosure of that information by the data user to someone else, the individual has a right of legal action against the data user.

Processing personal data is not permitted except under certain conditions, such as:

- with the consent of the individual

- as part of a contractual arrangement between the data user and the individual

- for legal reasons.

Some personal data does not come within the scope of the Act, such as:

- personal data about employees for payroll purposes

- personal data about customers and suppliers for the purpose of maintaining accounting records.

Risks to data security and storage include the following issues:

- accidental loss or corruption of data due to poor business practices and procedures

- deliberate loss or destruction of data due to criminal or other inappropriate behaviour

- unauthorised access to data leading to misuse of data for an improper purpose.

The risks to data security and storage may be managed in a number of ways, including:

- recruitment of appropriate staff who act with honesty and integrity

- training of staff so that they understand the risks associated with data security and storage and how to effectively manage those risks

- good business practices regarding data management, processing and updating

- effective segregation of duties between employees to minimise the risks of undetected errors and similar problems

- physical controls regarding management of risk of damage to data from fire, smoke and other hazards.

ACTIVITY 6

You are employed in an accounts office and receive a telephone call from a person who says that they are the bank manager of North Bank in the local High Street. The bank has been approached by a customer of your employer, for a loan to pay off the debt they still owe your employer. The bank manager would like to know how much the customer owes, and would also like to check the marital or relationship status of your customer.

What should you do in this situation?

For a suggested answer, see the 'Answers' section at the end of the book.

CONCLUSION

In this chapter you reviewed a variety of documents used by a business as evidence of transactions. You will appreciate that they differ depending on their purpose and are often issued in order to indicate different stages of, for example, the sale or purchase of goods and/or services as indicated below.

DOCUMENT FLOW

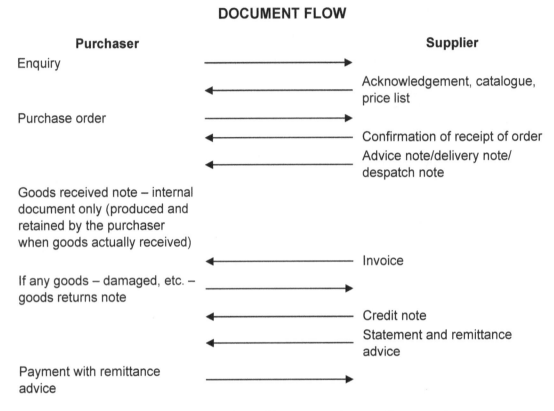

Documents, particularly associated with making payments, must be properly authorised. Generally this takes the form of the signature of an authorised person. Documents are used throughout a business to record transactions and the financial implications of those transactions.

Key documents used in recording financial transactions are invoices, credit notes, receipts and petty cash vouchers. Statements and payslips are useful summaries which can be used as a check of transactions.

KEY TERMS

Advice note – Document issued to a customer or received from a supplier, advising that a delivery will be made on a specific day and listing the items to be delivered.

Credit note – Document issued to a customer or received from a supplier, indicating that the amount owed is being reduced for sales returns/purchase returns.

Debit note – A debit note is a document raised by a customer and issued to a supplier to request a credit note for goods returned because, for example, they were faulty.

Delivery note – Document sent with items delivered to a customer. One copy is retained by the customer, one copy signed by the customer and retained by the supplier.

Internal cheque requisition – Form for use within a business, properly authorising payment to be made to a supplier.

Payslip – Document given to each employee giving details of pay and deductions from pay.

Petty cash voucher – Document giving details of money paid out from petty cash and the reasons for the expense.

Price quotation – Document sent to a potential customer quoting the price for some goods or a service. If signed and accepted by the customer, it becomes a purchase order from the customer.

Purchase invoice – Written request for payment from a supplier, giving details of items delivered.

Purchase order – Order from a customer on a form or document produced by the customer.

Purchase requisition – Request for an item to be purchased for the business. It should be authorised before being acted on.

Quotation – Indication of the costs of a specific contract or job. **See also** price quotation.

Personal data – Data about a specific individual.

Receipt – Written statement of an amount of money that has been paid/received.

Remittance advice – Document sent with payment, listing the items/invoices that are being paid.

Sales invoice – Written request to a credit customer for payment, giving details of items sold.

Sales order form – Order from a customer on a form produced by the seller.

Statement of account – A list of invoices, credit notes, settlement discounts received and payments made for a given period of time, sent by a supplier to a credit customer. The statement also shows the current amount owed by the customer.

Till roll – Printed listing of all payments received through a till/point of sale desk in a retail outlet.

SELF TEST QUESTIONS

		Paragraph
1	What is an advice note?	1
2	Explain the purpose of a receipt.	1
3	What is the difference between an estimate and a quotation?	2
4	What is the difference between a dispatch note and a delivery note?	2
5	Give two examples of when a cheque requisition form would be used.	2
6	State the purpose of a credit limit.	3
7	Give four items that would appear in a sales invoice.	4
8	What is the difference between a purchase requisition and a purchase order?	5
9	What are the benefits of using a goods received note?	5
10	Explain the main features of a purchase invoice.	5
11	What is a debit note?	7
12	Draw up a petty cash voucher.	8
13	Why should a business have policies for the retention of documents?	9
14	What are the main data protection principles?	10

EXAM-STYLE QUESTIONS

1   The types of documentation that may accompany a complex transaction for a machine includes three of the following. Which is the odd one out?

   A   Invoice for outstanding amount from manufacturer

   B   Initial enquiry letter from manufacturer

   C   Price quotation for machinery from manufacturer

   D   Deposit remittance from purchaser

2   Which of the following does not contain any monetary amounts?

   A   Delivery note

   B   Quotation

   C   Payslip

   D   Receipt

3   Which of the following lists is in the correct chronological order?

A   Sign petty cash voucher, spend money, obtain receipt, authorise voucher

B   Quotation, purchase order, purchase invoice, cheque requisition

C   Invoice, credit note, debit note, delivery note, remittance advice

D   Receipt, purchase invoice, statement, despatch note

4   Which document is used by a supplier to correct an earlier overcharge?

A   Advice note

B   Credit note

C   Debit note

D   Invoice

5   From the following list of situations where an invoice has been issued, choose one that would **not** require a credit note to be raised:

A   A customer has returned some or all of the goods because they are damaged or faulty.

B   A customer has returned some or all of the goods because they are not the items ordered.

C   A customer has never received the goods although an invoice was issued.

D   Postage and packaging charges were omitted from the original invoice.

6   Which of the following describes a goods received note?

A   It is a formal request, sent by a business to a supplier requesting the delivery of the goods specified on the purchase order.

B   It is an internal check document that serves as a record of the quantity and condition of goods that have been delivered to the business.

C   It is a discount that is offered to a customer if the invoice is paid by a certain date.

D   It is a means of identifying a transaction as being of a particular type by allocating to it an appropriate reference number.

7   Which of the following documents would not be entered in the accounting records after it has been raised?

A   A credit note

B   A debit note

C   A quotation

D   A payslip

For suggested answers, see the 'Answers' section at the end of the book.

Chapter 3

PRINCIPLES AND PROCESS OF BOOKKEEPING

This chapter explains the fundamental principles and process of basic bookkeeping. As part of this, the use of computerised accounting systems, including external servers, to store and process data is explained. The chapter concludes with a review of how financial data is coded as a basis for recording and processing in an accounting system.

This chapter covers syllabus area A3.

CONTENTS

1   The process to record transactions in the accounting system

2   Computerised accounting

3   Coding of transactions

4   Processing transactions

LEARNING OUTCOMES

At the end of this chapter, you should be able to:

•   explain the process to record transactions in the accounting system

•   show an understanding of how financial data may be used to meet the needs of the business and also external users of financial information

•   explain the key features, advantages and disadvantages of computerised accounting

•   explain the key features of using external servers to store data

•   explain the principles of coding transactions as a basis for recording transactions in a computerised accounting system

•   explain the difference between batch processing and real-time processing of accounting transactions.

---

1 THE PROCESS TO RECORD TRANSACTIONS IN THE ACCOUNTING SYSTEM

1.1 INTRODUCTION

The following diagram summarises the process to prepare the annual financial statements, from entering into transactions and recording those transactions in the accounting system and then progressing to preparation of the annual financial statements. The recording of transactions is performed using the principles of double-entry bookkeeping.

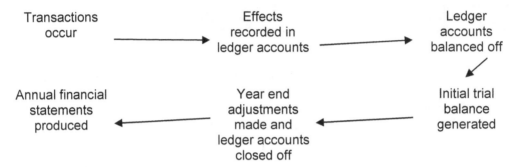

The remaining part of this chapter will focus upon accounting systems and processes and, in subsequent chapters, progress to recording transactions and the preparation of the trial balance and the correction of errors.

Note that the ACCA FA1 syllabus and exam includes year-end adjustments such as the correction of errors in the trial balance. The ACCA FA1 syllabus and exam does not include preparation of the annual financial statements.

When an accounting transaction has occurred, it must be recorded in the accounting system using double-entry bookkeeping principles. This requires a source document that provides evidence or information about the transaction to be recorded. Source documents will be referenced with account names or codes, along with monetary amounts, to enable transactions to be recorded appropriately in the accounting system.

Depending upon the nature of the transaction, data recorded is likely to include the following:

- transaction date

- nature of the transaction e.g. purchase on credit or cash sale

- service provided or product quantity plus description or code

- monetary value, including any sales tax element if applicable

- any trade or early settlement discount applicable, and

- the due date of payment or credit terms.

Note that not all business documentation referred to in chapter 2 is a source document for recording transactions in the accounting system and this is considered in the following section. We can now move on to explain the process to record those transactions in the accounting system as a basis for preparing useful accounting information and the trial balance.

In most businesses, classification and recording of each transaction is allocated to specific ledger accounts. For example, there will be a separate ledger account for each source of income (such as sales and interest received) and each type of expense (such as purchases, rent, wages and insurance).

There will also be asset accounts (for items such as property, plant and equipment and amounts due from credit customers) along with liability accounts (such as amounts outstanding to suppliers, bank loans and sales tax due). There is no rule or limit as to how many general ledger accounts a business should have but the system should enable effective and efficient accounting and control.

Before we look in detail at how transactions are recorded and processed in the accounting system some terminology should be explained.

The term **'general ledger'** refers to the complete set of ledger accounts used by a business in which transactions are recorded. It may also be referred to as a 'nominal ledger' or 'chart of accounts'. It forms the basis of financial accounting information used to produce a trial balance and, subsequently, the annual financial statements.

A **ledger account** contains a record of transactions assigned to a specific asset, liability, source of income or expense, along with a capital account for a sole proprietor. It will identify increases and decreases in that item during an accounting period. Collectively, the ledger accounts contain the record of accounting entries relating to all transactions and events during an accounting period. They are the principal books or files for recording, summarising and totalling monetary transactions by account item or type. The trial balance and annual financial statements of a business are generated from summary totals in the ledger accounts contained in the general ledger.

1.2 ACCOUNTING SYSTEMS

Irrespective of the size and complexity of a business, an accounting system has three components as illustrated below.

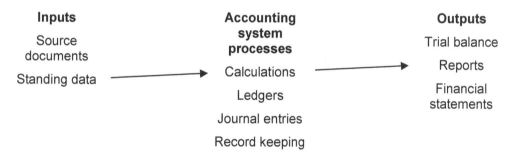

Inputs	Accounting system processes	Outputs
Source documents	Calculations	Trial balance
Standing data	Ledgers	Reports
	Journal entries	Financial statements
	Record keeping	

Inputs

Source documents include sales and purchase invoices, credit notes, payroll totals, petty cash summaries, summaries of bank receipts and payments and journals.

Standing data is data used repeatedly to assist with the processing of recurring or regular transactions and will include data such as price lists, wage rates, sales tax rates, customer account details and supplier account details.

Source documents must be referenced with the general ledger account codes to be updated as appropriate. A source document will normally require a minimum of two general ledger account codes. More than two general ledger codes may be required if, for example, sales tax needs to be accounted for, or a purchase invoice includes more than one item purchased.

In a computerised system, source documents are also be referenced or coded to enable simultaneous update of 'memorandum only' accounting information. Examples of 'memorandum only' accounting information include inventory usage reports and payroll analyses. Consequently, this means that when 'memorandum only' accounting information is recorded, it will match exactly the information recorded in the general ledger accounts.

Although these records are updated simultaneously when the general ledger accounts are updated, it is important to remember that 'memorandum only' information does not form part of the double-entry bookkeeping system. 'Memorandum only' information is used to enable managers to monitor and control the business, for example, to ensure that credit customers pay the amount due within the agreed credit period.

Not all of the business documents explained in chapter 2 are source documents used to update the accounting system. For example, a supplier statement provides a summary of transactions recorded by a supplier within the previous month and issued to a customer. It is not a source document used by either the supplier or the customer to update their respective accounting systems. Similarly, a remittance advice provides information relating to a payment made, although it is not the payment itself.

As you progress through this chapter, examples of how documents are coded so that they can be recorded in the accounting system will be explained and illustrated.

Processes

The key process is to record transactions, which may be done in real-time so that updating takes place at the time the transaction takes place, or batch processing at appropriate intervals e.g. daily, weekly as required.

In addition, systems will also perform tasks of calculating, classifying and summarising data, such as the monetary total of sales invoices issued during a specified period, or providing an analysis of expenses incurred during a specified period.

Finally, processing includes the updating general ledger accounts and the 'memorandum only' accounting information to provide management information.

Outputs

The primary outputs of an accounting system are the trial balance and financial statements (or selected extracts as required).

Reports, such as aged analysis of receivables' ledger accounts, payroll summaries and payslips, inventory usage summaries, analysis of expenses and exception reports can normally be obtained from most computerised accounting systems. This is useful financial information to help manage and control the activities and operations of the business.

Historically, it would have been a manual process to record transactions in handwritten books or ledgers. Although the components of the system have not changed, as the size and complexity of businesses have increased and manual accounting systems have largely been replaced by computerised systems.

The ACCA FA1 syllabus and exam assumes that computerised accounting systems and processes are used, although knowledge of specific computer packages and programs is not required.

1.3 USEFUL FINANCIAL INFORMATION

In addition to preparing the trial balance and annual financial statements, the accounting system is also used to monitor the effectiveness of the business and to help review and conclude relevant transactions. For this reason, additional data is recorded in the accounting system. The 'memorandum only' data is summarised and classified to provide information in a form useful for management decision-making and control of the business.

Examples of such information include:

- individual ledger accounts to record transactions with each credit customer, often referred to as receivables' ledger accounts

- individual ledger accounts to record transactions with each individual credit supplier, often referred to as payables' ledger accounts

- inventory usage reports, and

- payroll analyses.

In the case of credit sales, credit controllers require information from the accounting system to identify which customers have not settled their debts and, for that reason, who should be contacted to remind them that payment is due. Equally, for suppliers who have granted a period of credit to the business, there is a need to review which account payables are due for payment, and how much that payment should be.

Therefore, for goods purchased or sold on credit, individual customer or supplier accounts need to be set up within the accounting system, and each will have an individual supplier or customer account code. These accounts will be created using a standardised procedure and done under the supervision of a suitably responsible person such as a senior member of the accounting department. They will normally be subject to controls and checks to ensure that they are valid accounts.

2 COMPUTERISED ACCOUNTING

Although some businesses still use manual accounting records and processes, a significant number have now adopted computerised systems. A fully computerised system will operate using the same principles as a manual system except that all the records will be stored in one place i.e. the hard disk of the computer, or on cloud servers. This does not necessarily mean that all accounting personnel have access to all accounting records. The system will be broken down into sections in very much the same way as the manual system, with access configured and controlled by controls such as individual login credentials and the use of passwords. For example, payroll data should be accessible only to employees with payroll-related responsibilities, rather than being accessible by all employees.

Another difference in a computerised system is that when the data is reviewed on screen or printed the format of that information may appear different from a manual system particularly with regard to general ledger accounts. Whereas in a manual system the general ledger is a collection of 'T-accounts', the general ledger in a computerised system will probably appear as an arithmetic listing of debits and credits. This does not mean, however, that the system is not performing double-entry bookkeeping – it is; it is simply that the ledger accounts may take the following format:

Motor van account

Date	Details	Dr ($)	Cr ($)	Balance ($)
	Cash at bank	22,000		22,000 Dr

Computerised accounting systems make it easier to extract information and reports for accounting staff and managers to assist with management and control of business activities. Examples of reports that many accounting systems normally produce include the following:

- a summary of amounts due from customers, normally broken down by how long amounts have been outstanding from individual customers

- a register of items of property, plant and equipment owned by the business

- a listing of purchase invoices received from suppliers

- a summary of amounts due for payment, so that payments can be prepared and processed

- employee wages and salary payslips, along with a summary of the total of gross pay, deductions and net pay for the workforce as a whole, or by department

- an inventory usage report which summarises receipts and issues into and from inventory during a period of time e.g. each week or month.

2.1 ADVANTAGES OF COMPUTERISED ACCOUNTING

(a) **Speed**. Computer processing is very fast – much faster than a clerk or any other type of office machine. This speed can be of value to the business in two ways:

(i) high volumes of work can be handled by a computer

(ii) rapid turnaround and response times can be achieved.

For example, one business may value a computerised system primarily for its ability to cope with a large volume of orders, whilst another may be more interested in the speed of processing orders.

(b) **Stored programs**. Once the programs have been written and tested (or standard programs purchased), a computer can perform significant amounts of work with the minimum of labour costs. Only small teams of operators are needed for the most powerful and efficient machines. This is possible because a computer runs under the control of its stored programs, and operator activity is limited to loading and unloading peripherals and indicating what work or processing is to be done.

(c) **Decision-making.** The computer can be programmed to undertake complicated decision-making processes. It can handle work to a much higher degree of complexity than other office machines – and often more than a manager.

(d) **File storage and processing**. Large files of data can be stored on digital or magnetic media, which require very little space. More importantly, stored files can be reviewed and updated at speed, and information can be retrieved from them very quickly.

(e) **Accuracy and reliability**. Computers are very accurate (provided always that its programs are free from faults) and reliable processors of data.

2.2 DISADVANTAGES OF COMPUTERISED ACCOUNTING

(a) **Inability to detect human errors**. The computer is a machine. It cannot recognise human errors made in its programs or notice that data is incomplete or incorrect. It may, however, ensure that an equal value of debits and credits are posted when recording a transaction, but not that the account numbers selected by the accounts clerk are the correct codes. It could be programmed to incorporate conditional requirements relating to which account codes may or may not be used to prevent some posting errors. Errors that may be detected by clerks in a manual system may go unnoticed in a computer-based system. It is therefore necessary to devote the utmost care to the development of computer-based systems in order to foresee every contingency and to test every instruction. Thus, system development may be both prolonged and costly.

(b) **Quantifiable decisions**. The program can only take decisions that can be quantified, for example, that can be expressed as two numbers or amounts that can be compared with each other. It cannot make value judgements such as selecting personnel or deciding whether to take legal action if debts are overdue. The solution indicated by the program may have to be modified because of intangible factors known to the manager but incapable of being quantified or expressed in the program.

(c) **Initial costs**. Historically, costs of hardware, software, site preparation, training and so on were high, particularly for customised systems for complex entities. However, the cost of standard, user-friendly hardware and software packages has fallen over time and are now affordable for most small entities.

(d) **Inflexibility**. Owing to the care and attention to detail needed in systems along with program development and maintenance, computer systems tend to be inflexible. They take longer and cost more to alter than manual systems.

(e) **Vulnerability**. Computerised systems do have vulnerabilities, such as the risk of hacking or unintentional loss or corruption of data. However, there are protocols and procedures that can be put in place, such as the use of firewalls and software to detect malware, along with data back-up procedures or the use of cloud accounting, that can be used to mitigate those risks.

2.3 DEVELOPMENTS IN ACCOUNTING SYSTEMS

The initial introduction of computerised systems provided little more than the facility to have faster and more reliable summarisation and totalling of monetary values but with limited analysis of the data input. Now, there is an extensive range of 'off-the-shelf' relatively inexpensive accounting software packages available.

One benefit of these packages is that they are developed by experienced people and therefore regarded as reliable and robust. One potential downside is that any standard package may not meet the precise information needs and requirements of an individual business user. These packages are normally subject to regular software updates as the package is modified over time.

Accounting software systems have developed to meet the needs of businesses, such as multi-site operations. More recent developments include the availability of integrated systems. These systems are able to handle, not only accounting data, but also other systems and processes relevant to other parts of the business that may include:

- inventory management, linked to purchasing and requisitions and also sales invoicing and despatch of finished goods

- human resource management, which may include allocation of employees to jobs or activities, request and approval of annual leave, training and development activities and appraisal records

- payroll operations to ensure that employees are paid the correct amount on the due date and linked with human resource management to ensure that new starters and leavers are managed appropriately.

Many larger businesses have customised systems with software tailored to meet their particular specifications. One benefit of this is that it should meet the precise information needs of the business. However, any customised or tailored system may be at increased risk of operational problems if not properly designed, tested, installed and operated.

Many businesses with computerised systems utilise **'record-to-report' (R2R)** processes which involves collecting, processing, and presenting financial information in the form of documents that are used by management to perform analysis and review.

The first part of the process is to record transactions and events. This then leads on to data and information collated and presented in the form of management reports. For example, if a sales order is received, it is then input into the sales system which is linked to the inventory management system to confirm that goods are available or when they are expected to be available for despatch. Upon despatch to the customer, and confirmation of delivery to the customer, the inventory system updates the sales system to raise the sale invoice.

As the sale invoice is generated, the general ledger accounts for sales and receivables are updated. There will also be simultaneous updating of the memorandum information including the individual customer ledger account and the aged analysis of receivables. In due course, there should be a receipt from the customer which will be used to update the detailed listing of bank receipts along with the bank and receivables general ledger accounts. The memorandum information of the individual customer ledger account and the detailed analysis of aged receivables is also updated at the same time.

Many businesses use **'peer-to-peer' (P2P)** networks which enable files to be accessed, shared or transferred between those authorised on the network. Each user requires a personal user account to access the network and to use and share files. It facilitates flexible and collaborative working arrangements between those on the network.

In a computerised system, accounting information is more likely to be presented either in a columnar format, or perhaps by the use of +/- notation, rather than presented in the more traditional ledger or T-account format. The key point to remember is that the fundamental principles of double-entry bookkeeping are maintained and applied. The only difference is the format in which the information is presented.

Some, computerised accounting systems also include an integrated bank account. Note, however, that the bank account is assumed not to be integrated into the accounting system in the ACCA FA1 syllabus and exam.

2.4 CLOUD COMPUTING AND CLOUD ACCOUNTING

One of the more recent developments in accounting software is that of cloud computing and cloud accounting.

Cloud computing is access to software and data storage that is hosted on remote servers and is accessed via the internet. Cloud computing enables data and information stored to be accessed from any location at any time by multiple users if the user has an internet connection and can log in.

Cloud accounting is the application of cloud computing to accounting systems and processes.

Advantages of cloud accounting

- The business does not have to pay for, install, manage or protect software on individual machines.

- Capacity for the cloud to store more data and to share it more easily. This will also enable the business to easily scale up or scale down its cloud accounting capacity as circumstances change.

- It is accessed 'on demand' where and when needed which aids flexibility of working practices, particularly for businesses with multiple locations and multiple employees requiring access to stored data and information.

- Easier sharing of data and information within a business, but also with external parties who may be granted access to part of the system e.g. for customers to place an order.

- The absence of a physical server will reduce maintenance costs and the risk of physical damage.

- Disaster recovery and data security is likely to be improved. For example, loss or damage to a laptop with commercially sensitive or confidential data stored on it is a significant business risk. Cloud accounting means that the data is stored on a remote server, so loss or damage to the laptop has a reduced business impact.

Disadvantages of cloud accounting

- The business is reliant upon the financial stability of the cloud service provider to the extent that it will continue to operate and provide the services required.

- The business is reliant upon the cloud service provider not suffering a cyber-attack or that its servers go down for any reason.

- In common with any other system, there is a risk of unauthorised access by the server provider staff, or by those staff permitting access to unauthorised persons.

- The cloud service provider must comply with relevant regulations such as data protection law. The business will need to satisfy itself that the service provider has the necessary controls and procedures in place and can be relied upon to avoid any breach of relevant regulation. It is the responsibility of the cloud service provider to ensure that it complies with data protection regulation. However, if there is a breach of that law, along with unauthorised disclosure of confidential data (perhaps relating to employees) the entity suffer a loss of reputation, even though it was the responsibility of the service provider.

Examples of how cloud accounting is used

This relates particularly to allowing external parties access to part of the data and information.

- A payroll bureau may be granted limited access to data such as employees' working hours and pay rates, along with other information such as personal tax codes, to enable production of the payroll. The payroll bureau would not have access to other parts of the accounting system.

- An accountant may be granted access to information that enables the annual financial statements to be prepared and, perhaps, to the sales and business tax data to complete returns if they have responsibility to prepare those documents. Access to the system would be granted only to the extent it was required for the accountant to complete the work required.

3 CODING OF TRANSACTIONS

3.1 PRINCIPLES OF CODING TRANSACTIONS

How are transactions input into a computerised system?

Every account must be separately identifiable. One method of identification is to give each ledger account its own unique name or title. However, it is often quicker and more convenient to also give each ledger account its own unique code number.

- A code number is usually quicker to write than an account name, so using code numbers can save time.

- Using unique code numbers can reduce the risk of errors, where several different accounts have similar names so that there is a risk that a transaction is recorded in the wrong account.

- In computerised accounting, it is easier for a computer to process code numbers than account names.

Account codes can be designed to have some significance. For example, a business may have account codes consisting of four digits. If so, it may allocate the code number 1000 to the owner's capital account, give all asset accounts a code beginning with the number 2, all liabilities a code beginning with a 3, all income accounts a code beginning with 4 and all expense accounts a code beginning with 5. In this way, it is possible to tell immediately from the code whether the account is a capital, asset, liability, income or expense account.

It is usual to record the account codes on source documents before recording the transactions in the accounts. It is important to identify and apply the correct codes to avoid errors in the recording of transactions and financial information.

3.2 CODING SYSTEMS

Inputting transactions into the accounting system is normally organised using a system of codes. In most accounting systems all the general ledger accounts, suppliers, customers, inventory items and documents such as cheques and invoices are referenced using codes. This makes it easier to ensure that data input is allocated to the correct account and enables the business to conduct additional analysis of data in order to extract useful management information.

Sequential codes

In a sequential system, codes are allocated to items in strict numerical order. This means that there is no obvious connection between a code and what it represents.

For instance in the following system you can have no idea what code 62 would represent.

63   Baked beans
64   Kitchen towels
65   Batteries

Faceted codes

A faceted code is one that is broken down into a number of facets or fields, each of which signifies a unit of information. For instance:

*   The first digit:

1 Fresh foods
2 Frozen foods
3 Canned foods
etc...

*   The second digit:

1 Meat
2 Pulses
3 Fruit
etc...

*   The third and fourth digits:

01   Heinz
02   Crosse & Blackwell
03   Own brand
etc...

A can of Heinz baked beans would therefore have a code of 3201.

Mnemonic codes and significant digit codes

Mnemonic codes are usually in alphanumeric form and incorporate some descriptive element that makes it easy to identify the correct code. For example, a customer named 'Robertson' might have a code beginning ROB, e.g. ROB052.A similar concept can be used where items can be distinguished by some kind of measurement.

Significant digit codes incorporate digits that are part of the description of the item. For example:

500000 – Jeans
502828 – Jeans – 28" waist, 28" leg
503028 – Jeans – 30" waist, 28" leg

Block codes and hierarchical codes

Block/hierarchical codes commonly form the basis of general ledger coding systems, for instance:

0000 to 0999 – Non-current assets
1000 to 1999 – Current assets
etc…

The first 'block' is allocated to only non-current assets. This means that it is possible to have up to 1,000 different non-current asset ledger accounts.

A hierarchical code structure is a type of faceted code whereby each digit represents a classification, and each digit further to the right represents a smaller subset than those to the left. This makes it even easier to find items in a list of codes because related accounts are grouped together.

For instance within the 0000 – 0999 non-current assets block, the range 0300 to 0399 may be office furniture asset accounts and 0400 to 0499 may be motor car asset accounts.

3.3 CHART OF ACCOUNTS

When an accounting system is coded using the block/hierarchical method it is called a chart of accounts. An extract from the default chart of accounts in the widely-used Sage® bookkeeping package is as follows:

Category	Sub-category	Code range		
Non-current assets	Property	0010	to	0019
	Plant and Machinery	0020	to	0029
	Office Equipment	0030	to	0039
	Furniture and Fixtures	0040	to	0049
	Motor Vehicles	0050	to	0059
Current assets	Inventory	1000	to	1099
	Receivables	1100	to	1199
	Bank Account	1200	to	1209
	Deposits and Cash	1210	to	1239
	Credit Card (payables)	1240	to	1240
	Credit Card (receivables)	1250	to	1250

Within each of these sub-divisions there are a number of further default accounts. For instance the Professional Fees account codes range 7600 to 7699 has the following accounts already set up:

7600	Legal Fees
7601	Audit and Accountancy Fees
7602	Consultancy Fees
7603	Professional Fees

3.4 FEATURES OF A GOOD CODING SYSTEM

An efficient and effective coding system, whether manual or computerised, should incorporate the following features:

- Each general ledger account item should have a unique code.

- The coding system should have scope for additions and expansion. Codes need to be long enough to allow for the suitable identification of all items, but it should also be as brief as possible to save typing time, processing time and storage space.

- Codes should be uniform: for instance if one customer code has three letters and three numbers then all other customer codes should be of the same length and format. This helps to detect missing characters and makes analysis of data easier.

- The use of characters such as dots, dashes, colons is not recommended. A well designed system should avoid confusion between numbers and letters such as I and 1, O and 0, S and 5 and so on by only allowing letters or numbers in specific positions (e.g. characters 1 to 3 must be letters; characters 4 to 6 must be numbers).

- The coding system should be significant (in other words, the actual code should signify something about the item being coded). If the code consists of alphabetic characters, they could be derived from the item's description or name.

- Controls are needed over the creation and allocation of new account codes: for instance this may need to be authorised by the department manager.

- In a manual system, there should be an index or reference book of codes. Within a computerised system, this will maintained automatically.

4 PROCESSING TRANSACTIONS

4.1 INTRODUCTION

Processing of transactions may be done either in batches or in real-time.

4.2 BATCH PROCESSING

Batch processing of transactions (e.g. purchase invoices) may take place either at predetermined intervals such as daily or weekly or when a predetermined number of transactions are ready to be processed, for example 25 invoices.

In such a system, there is clearly a delay between the point at which a transaction occurs and the point at which processing of the transaction takes place. This means that accounting information available may not be up-to-date or complete as transactions may have taken place but not processed.

Batch processing of transactions is primarily associated with manual accounting systems and processes.

4.3 REAL-TIME PROCESSING

Real-time processing of transactions relates to computerised systems whereby processing of transactions is immediate. As soon as a transaction has occurred, the accounting system is updated.

Integrated computerised accounting systems will update all aspects of the accounting records and broader management information system as a transaction is processed. For example, as a sale to a credit customer has occurred, the accounting system is updated, and there will be simultaneous update of the individual customer account records.

This has the advantage that users of the accounting system and the information it generates will have access to the most up-to-date information available. This helps accounting staff and others employed in the business to make appropriate decisions to control and manage the business.

Note that the ACCA FA1 syllabus and exam assumes that businesses will be using an integrated computerised accounting system and no knowledge of any particular computerised accounting packages is assumed or required. The focus of the syllabus and exam is upon the processing of accounting transactions.

CONCLUSION

This chapter introduced and explained what an accounting system is, along with the key features, advantages and disadvantages of computerised systems. Recent developments in computerised accounting, including cloud accounting were also considered. The chapter concluded with a review of the principles of coding accounting transactions as a basis for recording transactions in the accounting system.

You are now ready to progress on to developing your knowledge and understanding of recording broad range of transactions and events in the general ledger accounts.

KEY TERMS

Accounting system – the inputs, processes and outputs of a system to record, process and manage accounting data.

Batch processing – the processing of transactions at either predetermined intervals or when a predetermined number of transactions are ready to be processed.

Block codes – a coding system commonly used as the basis of general ledger coding systems which allocate a block of codes to particular account headings so that the coding system can be added to in a logical manner if required.

Hierarchical codes – are a type of faceted code whereby each digit represents a classification, and each digit further to the right represents a smaller subset than those to the left.

Cloud accounting – the application of cloud computing to accounting systems and processes.

Cloud computing – access to software and data storage that is hosted on remote servers and is accessed via the internet. Cloud computing enables data and information stored to be accessed from any location at any time by multiple users if the user has an internet connection and can log in.

Faceted codes – codes that are broken down into a number of facets or fields, each of which signifies a unit of information.

General ledger – the complete set of ledger accounts used by a business in which transactions are recorded. It may also be referred to as a 'nominal ledger' or 'chart of accounts'.

Ledger account – a record of transactions assigned to a specific asset, liability, source of income or expense, along with a capital account for a sole proprietor. It will identify increases and decreases in that item during an accounting period.

Mnemonic codes – a code in alphanumeric form and incorporate some descriptive element that makes it easy to find the correct code.

Real-time processing – the processing of transactions in a computerised system whereby, as soon as a transaction has occurred, processing of that transaction is immediate.

Sequential codes – codes that are allocated to items in strict numerical order.

Significant digit codes – codes that incorporate digits that are part of the description of the item.

SELF TEST QUESTIONS

Paragraph

1   State four items of data that would normally be captured when a
transaction is recorded.   1.1

2   State the three components of an accounting system, and give one
example of each component.   1.2

3   State three advantages of computerised accounting.   2.1

4   State three disadvantages of computerised accounting.   2.2

5   What is cloud accounting?   2.4

6   Explain what block and hierarchal coding systems are.   3.2

7   What is a chart of accounts?   3.3

8   What is the difference between batch processing and real-time
processing of transactions?   4.1, 4.2

EXAM-STYLE QUESTIONS

1   Which of the following is a disadvantage of computers?

   A   Speed

   B   Accuracy

   C   Vulnerability

   D   File storage and processing

For suggested answers, see the 'Answers' section at the end of the book.

Chapter 4

DOUBLE-ENTRY BOOKKEEPING

The purpose of this chapter is to introduce and demonstrate the principles of double-entry bookkeeping. It begins defining the elements of the financial statements and progresses to defining and explaining the accounting equation, which makes use of the definitions. The components of a set of financial statements are also illustrated and explained.

The chapter then explains how accounting transactions are recorded in the general ledger, including journal adjustments, and how to balance and close a ledger account.

It then progresses on to defining and explaining the different forms of discount and how to account for then. The chapter concludes with defining, explaining and illustrating how to account for sales tax.

This chapter covers syllabus areas A1, B1, B2, B3.

CONTENTS

1   The elements of the financial statements

2   The accounting equation

3   Components of a set of financial statements

4   Ledger accounts and the division of the general ledger

5   The journal

6   Balancing and closing a ledger account

7   Trade and settlement discounts

8   Accounting for sales tax

LEARNING OUTCOMES

At the end of this chapter, you should be able to:

- define the elements of the financial statements

- explain and apply the accounting equation

- explain the components of a set of financial statements

- define the general ledger and explain how transactions are recorded in ledger accounts

- define the journal and explain how it is used to record accounting transactions

- explain how ledger accounts are balanced and closed off

- calculate and account for trade and settlement discounts

- calculate and account for sales tax.

1 THE ELEMENTS OF THE FINANCIAL STATEMENTS

1.1 INTRODUCTION

As an introduction to this chapter, it is helpful to begin with some definitions. The definitions of what constitutes an asset, liability, capital, income and expense bring consistency to how accounting transactions are recorded, classified and summarised. This helps to provide a foundation for the preparation of the trial balance and, ultimately, the financial statements.

In order to report the financial performance and financial position of a business the financial statements must summarise the five key elements. The statement of financial position consists of assets, liabilities and capital which are, in effect, the accounting equation (see later in this chapter). The statement of profit or loss consists of income and expenses.

1.2 THE ELEMENTS DEFINED

An **asset** is a present economic resource which the business controls as a result of a past event. It is used to generate future economic benefits for a business. An asset could either be sold for cash or could help the business to generate income and profits. Examples of an asset used to generate future economic benefits is plant and equipment used by a business to produce goods to sell to customers, or inventory held for sale to customers .

A **liability** is a present obligation to transfer an economic resource as a result of a past event. This could be a bank loan or overdraft outstanding, or amounts owed to suppliers for goods and services received but not yet paid for.

Equity or capital is the amount due to the owner of a business after all liabilities have been paid. The owner has the residual interest in the assets of the business after all liabilities have been settled. The term 'equity' is normally used in relation to a limited company, whereas 'capital' is the term normally used for an unincorporated business such as a sole proprietor or a partnership.

Income arises through increases in assets or decreases in liabilities that result in an increase in equity or capital, other than changes relating to contributions from the business owners in the form of capital introduced. The principal source of income for a business is the amount generated from the sale of goods or services to customers during an accounting period. Other forms of income include bank interest received and fees or commission earned by a business.

Expenses consists of decreases in assets or increases in liabilities that result in a reduction of capital due to the owner. Examples of expenses include wages paid to employees, repairs and maintenance, insurance and charges for heat, light and power.

2 THE ACCOUNTING EQUATION

2.1 INTRODUCTION

The accounting equation is a simple expression of the fact that, at any point in time, the assets of a business will be equal to its liabilities plus capital, where capital is the residual interest in the assets after all liabilities have been settled and which is due to the owner(s).

Note that, like any equation, it can be rearranged and presented in a different way as illustrated below.

$$\text{Assets} = \text{Capital} + \text{Liabilities}$$

$$\text{Assets} - \text{Liabilities} = \text{Capital}$$

$$\text{Liabilities} = \text{Assets} - \text{Capital}$$

Note that any gains or losses made by a business are due to the business owner(s). Using this simplified approach, losses or expenses incurred will reduce capital and profits or gains made will increase capital.

Over time, the assets, liabilities and capital of a business change continually, but the relationship between the components of the accounting equation is always true. This is because of the way assets, liabilities and capital are defined and because of the way in which changes in the three elements are recorded. The reason this equality is maintained is that the assets controlled by the business had to be financed in some way, either by the owner and/or lenders. Conversely, input of finance from the owner and/or lenders must be represented by an asset or assets to the same monetary value. Note that all transactions are always recorded from the perspective of the business, rather than the owner(s).

2.2 A WORKED EXAMPLE

Situation

Day 1   Sam Green (a sole proprietor) invests $5,000 of own funds to set up a garden design business. The $5,000 contributed to the business becomes the business's capital and the $5,000 in the business bank account represents the only asset of the business.

This situation has two effects – assets (cash at bank) increase by $5,000 and capital increases by $5,000. The business has $5,000 more cash than before and the owner is owed $5,000 from the business. There are no liabilities. The resulting accounting equation is as follows:

Assets (cash at bank) $5,000 = **Capital** $5,000

Day 2   The business pays cash for inventory of plants, flowers and seeds (goods for resale) costing $2,000. The capital remains the same, but there are now two assets.

The purchase of inventory results in two effects – assets (cash at bank) decreases by $2,000 and a new asset, (inventory), increases by $2,000. There are no liabilities. The resulting accounting equation is:

Assets (cash at bank $3,000 + inventory $2,000) $5,000 = **Capital** $5,000

Day 3   So far, all finance has come from the owner in the form of capital. In the next step, the business will borrow $4,000 from a bank to buy a van at a cost of $4,000. The capital remains the same, but there are now three assets and a liability.

Capital $5,000 **= Assets** $9,000 **– Liabilities** $4,000 (loan)

The assets are $3,000 (cash at bank) + $2,000 (inventory) + $4,000 (van)

Day 4   So far, capital has remained unchanged. This means that neither a profit nor a loss has been made. As soon as trading starts, profits (or losses) will be generated which will increase (or decrease) capital.

We will now assume that all inventory of plants, flowers and seeds, is sold for $3,500 cash, generating a profit of $1,500 ($3,500 – $2,000 cost of inventory).

Capital + Profit $6,500 **= Assets** $10,500 **– Liabilities** $4,000 (loan)

Capital is $5,000 (capital introduced) + $1,500 (profit).

The assets are Cash at bank $3,000 + Cash $3,500 + $4,000 (van)

Day 5   The business paid $480 cash to meet sundry expenses, reducing its profit to $1,020. The sundry expenses could be for casual labour, equipment hire, motor expenses and so on.

The accounting equation now becomes:

Capital + Profit $6,020 **= Assets** $10,020 **– Liabilities** $4,000 (loan)

Capital is $5,000 (capital introduced) + $1,500 (profit) – $480 sundry expenses.

The assets are Cash at bank $3,000, Cash of $3,020 (3,500 – 480) + $4,000 (van)

Day 6   Owners must obviously withdraw some cash from the business in order to pay their daily living expenses. All cash withdrawn from a business by its owner is referred to as drawings. This will decrease the amount of capital due to the owner. (Any other asset taken out of the business by the owner, such as inventory, will also be classified as drawings.) We will end this example with Sam Green withdrawing $350 from the business bank account for personal use.

Capital + Profit – Drawings $5,670 **= Assets** $9,670 **– Liabilities** $4,000

Capital is $6,020 (as before) – $350 (drawings).

The assets are $10,020 (as before) – $350 withdrawn from the bank as drawings.

2.3 EXPANDING THE ACCOUNTING EQUATION

The accounting equation helps you to understand the basic nature of accounting transactions. The accounting equation can be expanded to provide additional information and understanding as follows:

Capital = Assets – Liabilities, or rearranged as: Assets = Capital + Liabilities

Capital can be expanded to show more detail of any increases or decreases:

Capital = Opening net assets + Profit – Drawings

In a similar manner:

Assets – Liabilities = Capital introduced + Revenue – Expenses – Drawings

From this, it follows that:

- if a business makes a profit its capital and net assets increase

- if a business makes a loss its capital and net assets decrease

3 COMPONENTS OF A SET OF FINANCIAL STATEMENTS

3.1 INTRODUCTION

A set of financial statements for a sole trader consist of a statement of financial position and a statement of profit or loss. There may also be additional notes or disclosures of information that helps to explain the items in the financial statements. The financial statements are based upon the elements discussed in the previous section. The principal reason for preparing financial statements is to provide useful information to the different user groups who need to make decisions about their dealings with the business, such as managers and employees in the business, customers, suppliers and providers of finance such as banks.

You need to understand what comprises a set of financial statements, along with definitions of the statements and what they contain. However, the compilation or preparation of the annual financial statements is not included in the ACCA FA1 syllabus or exam.

3.2 THE STATEMENT OF FINANCIAL POSITION

The statement of financial position is a statement of assets, liabilities and capital of a business as at a specific point in time, usually the end of an accounting period.

Classification or grouping of assets, liabilities and capital in a consistent manner helps users of financial statements to understand that information and enable identification of information that is of particular relevance to them. Consistent presentation of information also helps users to make comparison and undertake analysis of that financial information.

A specimen statement of financial position for sole trader is presented below.

Statement of financial position at 30 June 20X7

	$	$
Non-current assets		
Land and buildings		×
Plant and equipment		×
Current assets		
Inventories	×	
Trade receivables	×	
Cash at bank	×	×
	———	———
Total assets		×
		———
Proprietor's capital account:		
Balance brought forward at 1 July 20X6		×
Add: capital introduced		×
Add: net profit for the year		×
Less: drawings		(×)
		———
Balance carried forward at 30 June 20X7		×
Non-current liabilities		
6% bank loan (20X9)		×
Current liabilities		
Trade payables	×	
Bank overdraft	×	×
	———	———
Total capital and liabilities		×
		———

Note that there is a standard format to the statement of financial position to provide consistency in the way in which financial statements are prepared and presented.

A **non-current asset** is an asset purchased for use within the business to help generate revenues and profits over more than one accounting period, such as buildings, plant and machinery, equipment and motor vehicles.

Current assets are assets that are expected to be converted into cash as part of the normal operating activities of the business within twelve months of the accounting year end. They will include items such as inventories available for sale and trade receivables, which are amounts due from credit customers.

A **non-current current liability** is a liability that is not required to be settled until at least twelve months after the accounting year end. An example of this is a long-term bank loan.

A **current liability** is a liability that will be settled within twelve months following the accounting year end. Examples include trade payables, which are amounts owing to suppliers not yet paid and sales tax owing to the tax authorities.

Capital is the residual difference between the assets and liabilities of the business. It represents the owner's net investment in the business as at that date. Note that the owner is entitled to the net profit for the period, may make additional capital contributions during the period (perhaps to expand business activities) or make withdrawals from the business ('drawings') to meet personal expenses.

3.3 THE STATEMENT OF PROFIT OR LOSS

The statement of profit or loss summarises the revenues earned and expenses incurred by a business during an accounting period, usually one year.

Revenue is income earned from the sale of goods and services by a business.

Revenue is matched against cost of sales to arrive at gross profit. Cost of sales is the cost of providing the goods and services sold during the accounting period, which has several components. Opening inventory is Inventory purchased or manufactured and unsold in the previous accounting period. It is still available to be sold in the current accounting period. Added to this is the cost of purchases (less any returned items to suppliers) which are also available to be sold in the current accounting period. At the end of the accounting period, there will be items of inventory purchased, but not yet sold and therefore available to be sold in the next accounting period. These items are excluded from cost of sales as they will not generate revenue until the next accounting period.

Other expenses, such as heat and light, repairs and renewals and loan interest are then deducted from gross profit to arrive at net profit for the year. The net profit (or loss) for the year is then transferred to the proprietor's capital account in the statement of financial position.

A specimen statement of profit or loss is presented below.

Statement of profit or loss for the year ended 30 June 20X7

	$	$
Revenue		×
Less: sales returns		(×)
Cost of sales:		
Opening inventory	×	
Plus: purchases	×	
Less: purchase returns	(×)	
	×	
Less: closing inventory	(×)	
		(×)
Gross profit		×
Less: Expenses:		
Heat and light	×	
Wages	×	
Repairs and renewals	×	
Interest on bank loan	×	
Sundry expenses	×	
		(×)
Net profit for the year		×

3.4 NOTES TO THE FINANCIAL STATEMENTS

The notes to the financial statements comprise additional explanation, clarification and detail to support the information in the financial statements. For example, the notes may include a summary of movements in non-current assets during the accounting period, or a summary of closing inventory.

4 LEDGER ACCOUNTS AND THE DIVISION OF THE GENERAL LEDGER

4.1 INTRODUCTION – A REMINDER

In most businesses, classification and recording of each transaction is based upon the elements of the financial statements (asset, liability, income, expense and capital) and is allocated to specific general ledger accounts. For example, there will be a separate general ledger account for income and expense accounts (such as sales, purchases, rent, insurance costs), asset accounts (such as property, plant and equipment and amounts due from credit customers) and liability accounts (such as amounts outstanding to suppliers, bank loans and sales tax due). There is no rule or limit as to how many general ledger accounts a business should have but the system should facilitate effective and efficient accounting and control.

The term **'general ledger'** is used to refer to the complete set of ledger accounts used by a business to record transactions. It may also be referred to as a 'nominal ledger' or 'chart of accounts'. It forms the basis of financial accounting information used to produce a trial balance and, subsequently, a set of financial statements.

A **ledger account** contains a record of transactions assigned to a specific asset, liability, source of income or expense. There is normally one capital account for a sole proprietor. It will identify increases and decreases in that item during an accounting period. Collectively, the ledger accounts contain the record of accounting entries relating to all transactions and events. They are the principal books or files for recording, summarising and totalling monetary transactions by account item or type. A business's financial statements are generated from summary totals in the ledger accounts contained in the general ledger.

Ledger accounts contain entries of transactions relevant to a particular item based upon the elements of the financial statements. For example, invoices for the purchase of fuel or motor repairs and maintenance on credit are recorded in the motor expenses ledger account. At the same time, a liability is also recorded, which will be reduced or cleared as subsequent payments are made to the suppliers. At the end of an accounting period, a balance is stuck on each ledger account. There will be a debit balance for the total of motor expense incurred during the accounting period. There may be a credit balance outstanding on the liability account if there are unpaid invoices.

The table below summarises the relationship between the elements of the financial statements, how three of the elements are arranged in the accounting equation, and how all five elements they are classified to produce the financial statements. Finally, the link with ledger accounting in which transactions are recorded and summarised is noted.

Elements	Elements of the financial statements				
	Assets	**Liabilities**	**Capital**	**Income**	**Expenses**
Accounting equation	Assets =	Liabilities +	Capital		
Financial statements	Statement of financial position			Statement of profit or loss	
Ledger accounting	Debit =	Credit +	Credit	Credit	Debit

The following section moves on to explain and demonstrate the format of a ledger account and how individual transactions are recorded in the ledger accounts using the principles of double-entry bookkeeping.

4.2 RECORDING TRANSACTIONS

Debits and credits

Individual transactions are recorded in the relevant general ledger accounts using double-entry bookkeeping.

An Individual general ledger account may simply be referred to as a 'ledger account' or 'T-account'. Traditionally each ledger account was presented as an enlarged 'T' that had two sides which, by established convention, the left-hand side and right-hand side are referred to as the debit side and credit side respectively.

An example ledger account is illustrated as follows:

Debit (Dr)   **Credit (Cr)**

Name of account e.g. Purchases, Wages

Date	Narrative	$	Date	Narrative	$

The duality concept means that each transaction will affect at least two ledger accounts. One account will be debited and the other credited. Whether an entry is made to the debit or credit side of a ledger account depends upon the type of account and the nature of the transaction. To increase an asset or an expense, the ledger account would be debited. To increase an income account or a liability, that account would be credited.

This can be summarised as follows:

DEBIT (increases)	**C**REDIT (increases)
Expenses (SP&L)	**L**iabilities (SOFP)
Assets (SOFP)	**I**ncome (SP&L)
Drawings/**D**ividends (SOFP)	**C**apital (SOFP)

Consequently, it follows that:

- **a decrease** in an expense, asset or drawings requires a **credit** entry in that account, and

- **a decrease** in a liability, income or capital requires a **debit** entry in that account.

You can use the mnemonic **'DEAD CLIC'** to help you remember this vitally important double-entry rule.

Summary of steps to record a transaction

- Determine the individual ledger accounts that are affected. account, and

- Consider whether each account balance is being increased or decreased.

- Decide which account should be debited or credited as applicable.

- Check that a debit and a credit entry have been made for the same monetary amount (i.e. the entries balance).

The following rules of double-entry accounting apply:

- An asset is recorded as a debit entry in an asset account.

- A liability is recorded as a credit entry in a liability account.

- Owner's capital is recorded by a credit entry in the capital account.

- Income is recorded as a credit entry in an income account, such as the sales account.

- Expenses are recorded as a debit entry in an expense account.

If more than two accounts are used to record a transaction (for example, to record sales tax on a transaction), the total value of the debit entries and the total value of the credit entries for the transaction must still be equal. In the ACCA FA1 exam, you may be presented with accounting information presented in the form of a T-account, and be asked to complete it or to identify and rectify missing or erroneous information.

EXAMPLE

A summary of some of the most common transactions entered into by a business are presented below.

Transaction	Debit	Credit
Purchases for cash	*Purchases*	*Cash at Bank*
Purchases on credit	*Purchases*	*Payables*
Cash sales (making profit on sale)	*Cash*	*Sales*
Credit sales (making profit on sale)	*recid*	*Sales*
Obtain a bank loan	*Cash*	*Bank Loan*
Bank payment for wages	*Wages*	*Bank*
Bank interest received	*Bank*	*Int recid*
Bank receipt from credit customer	*Bank*	*receivables*
Bank payment to credit supplier	*Payables*	*Cash*

Which accounting entries are required to record the transactions noted in the general ledger?

SOLUTION

Transaction	Debit	Credit
Purchases for cash	Purchases	Cash at bank
Purchases on credit	Purchases	Payables
Cash sales (making profit on sale)	Cash at bank	Sales
Credit sales (making profit on sale)	Receivables	Sales
Obtain a bank loan	Cash at bank	Loan liability
Bank payment for wages	Wages	Cash at bank
Bank interest received	Cash at bank	Interest received
Bank receipt from credit customer	Cash at bank	Receivables
Bank payment to credit supplier	Payables	Cash at bank

EXAMPLE

These basic rules can be illustrated using the transactions noted below for a business started by Hopper as a coffee trader.

Transaction 1: Hopper set up the business with $5,000 cash.

Here there is an increase in capital and assets. The asset is cash in the bank, which is recorded in an account called 'Bank'.

Capital

	$		$
		Bank	5,000

Bank

	$		$
Capital	5,000		

Commonly there is a folio or reference column in the T-account. This provides a reference so that the transaction can be traced through the accounting records if required.

The reference column is used to indicate the other account in the general ledger where the 'other side' of the double-entry can be found. So here, there is a reference to 'Bank' or 'Cash' in the Capital account and a reference to the Capital account on the Bank or Cash account.

Transaction 2: Purchase furniture for $1,500 using a bank payment.

Here, there is an increase in one asset (furniture) and a reduction in another (cash in the bank).

Furniture

	$		$
Bank	1,500		

Bank

	$		$
Capital	5,000	Furniture	1,500

In the bank account, the **debit entry exceeds the credit entry** by $3,500 ($5,000 – $1,500). We therefore say that there is a **debit balance** on the account. The debit balance is $3,500, showing that the business has $3,500 cash in the bank.

Transaction 3: Purchase equipment for $2,000 and tableware for $800 by bank payment.

Here we actually have two transactions, similar to the one above and are recorded as follows:

Equipment

	$		$
Bank	2,000		

Tableware

	$		$
Bank	800		

Bank

	$		$
Capital	5,000	Furniture	1,500
		Equipment	2,000
		Tableware	800

The total value of the credit entries in the bank account is now $4,300. The debit entry exceeds the credit entries by $700, so there is a debit balance on this account of $700, indicating that the business still has $700 in its bank account.

Transaction 4: Hopper takes out a business bank loan of $1,000.

A bank loan creates a new liability, but also adds to cash in the bank (an asset). The balance on the bank account now rises from $700 to $1,700, which is the amount by which total debit entries ($6,000) exceed total credit entries ($4,300).

Bank loan

	$		$
		Bank	1,000

Bank

	$		$
Capital	5,000	Furniture	1,500
Bank loan	1,000	Equipment	2,000
		Tableware	800

Transaction 5: Purchases of $700.

Purchases of materials are recorded in a purchases account, which is an expense account. Since the purchases are paid for by bank payment, there is a credit entry in the bank account and a reduction in the bank balance to $1,000.

Purchases

	$		$
Bank	700		

Bank

	$		$
Capital	5,000	Furniture	1,500
Bank loan	1,000	Equipment	2,000
		Tableware	800
		Purchases	700

Note that purchases of materials or goods are recorded in the purchases account. Sales of materials or goods are recorded in a sales account. Only the start and end of year balance of goods or materials is recorded in an inventory account. There are no accounts called 'materials' or 'goods' and these terms should not be used in the bookkeeping system.

Transaction 6: Sales of $1,050 which was banked.

Sales are recorded in a sales account, which is an income account. Since the income is all in cash, there is a debit entry in the Bank account for the increase in the bank balance of $1,050.

Sales

	$		$
		Bank	1,050

Bank

	$		$
Capital	5,000	Furniture	1,500
Bank loan	1,000	Equipment	2,000
Sales	1,050	Tableware	800
		Purchases	700

Transaction 7: Rent payable of $200

Rent payable is a type of expense. It will therefore be recorded in an expense account, just like purchases, with a debit entry. Since the amount is paid by a bank payment, there is also a credit entry in the bank account.

Rent payable

	$		$
Bank	200		

Bank

	$		$
Capital	5,000	Furniture	1,500
Bank loan	1,000	Equipment	2,000
Sales	1,050	Tableware	800
		Purchases	700
		Rent payable	200

Transaction 8: Stationery of $50 bought on credit from Green Supplies

This is another type of expense. A business will have many different types of expenditure that it needs to record in separate T-accounts, for management accounting purposes, financial reporting purposes and tax purposes. The stationery costs will therefore be recorded in a T-account by a debit entry. This time, however, there is no cash payment and therefore another T-account needs to be set up for the liability due to the supplier, referred to as a 'payable', which will be credited with $50. (Note that there will be a separate memorandum record maintain in a payable ledger to identify which credit supplier is owed $50.)

Stationery

	$		$
Payables (Green)	50		

Payables

	$		$
		Stationery	50

Transaction 9: Credit purchases of $1,000 from Blue Supplies

We saw in transaction 5 that purchases require debit entries in expense accounts. The only difference with these purchases for $1,000 is that they are made on credit, rather than paying for them in cash. Therefore, we need to debit purchases with $1,000 and record the liability in the payables general ledger account. (Note that there will be a separate memorandum record maintain in a payables' ledger to identify that Blue is owed $1,000.)

Purchases

	$		$
Bank	700		
Payables (Blue)	1,000		

Payables

	$		$
		Stationery (Green)	50
		Purchases (Blue)	1,000

Transaction 10: Credit sales of $2,000 to Grey

We saw in transaction 6 that sales are recorded in an income account, with a credit entry. The only difference with these sales is that they are made on credit, rather than the cash being received immediately. Therefore, we will post the credit entry to the sales account in the usual way, but this time we will set up a general ledger account to record amounts owed by credit customers, referred to as 'receivables'. There will also be a separate memorandum receivables' ledger to record amounts owing by individual credit customers.

Receivables

	$		$
Sales (Grey)	2,000		

Sales

	$		$
		Bank	1,050
		Receivables (Grey)	2,000

Transaction 11: Wages of $50

Hopper decides to employ a part-time worker. In the first week, Hopper pays the employee $50 from the business bank account. Again, wages are simply another type of expense account. The double entry is therefore to debit wages with the $50 and credit bank.

Wages

	$		$
Bank	50		

Bank

	$		$
Capital	5,000	Furniture	1,500
Bank loan	1,000	Equipment	2,000
Sales	1,050	Tableware	800
		Purchases	700
		Rent payable	200
		Wages	50

Transaction 12: Full payment of $2,000 received from Grey

When a credit customer pays the balance or part of the balance owing on their account, cash is received into the business. This increase in an asset (cash) is reflected by debiting the bank account with the $2,000. At the same time, there is a reduction in another asset, the receivables'. This reduction is reflected by a credit entry to the receivable account for $2,000.

Bank

	$		$
Capital	5,000	Furniture	1,500
Bank loan	1,000	Equipment	2,000
Sales	1,050	Tableware	800
Receivables (Grey)	2,000	Purchases	700
		Rent payable	200
		Wages	50

Receivables

	$		$
Sales	2,000	Bank	2,000

Transaction 13: Full payment by Hopper of $50 to Green Supplies and $1,000 to Blue Supplies

When a business pays an account payable, it reduces a liability – the payables' account and reduces an asset – cash at the bank. Reduction of a liability is a debit entry and reduction of an asset is a credit entry. Therefore, we need to debit the payables' general ledger account with $50 and $1,000 respectively, and we also need to credit the bank account with these two amounts. (Note, that the memorandum payables ledger accounts for Green and Blue will also be updated.)

Payables

	$		$
Bank (Green)	50	Stationery (Green)	50
Bank (Green)	1,000	Purchases (Blue)	1,000

Bank

	$		$
Capital	5,000	Furniture	1,500
Bank loan	1,000	Equipment	2,000
Sales	1,050	Tableware	800
Receivable (Grey)	2,000	Purchases	700
		Rent payable	200
		Wages	50
		Payable (Green)	50
		Payable (Blue)	1,000

Transaction 14: Partial repayment of $100 against loan

Hopper makes the first loan repayment of $100, which reduces the liability due to the bank by $100. It also reduces an asset, bank by $100. A reduction in a liability is a debit and a reduction in an asset is a credit. Therefore, we need to debit the loan account with $100 and credit the bank account with $100.

Bank loan

	$		$
Bank	100	Bank	1,000

Bank

	$		$
Capital	5,000	Furniture	1,500
Bank loan	1,000	Equipment	2,000
Sales	1,050	Tableware	800
Receivable (Grey)	2,000	Purchases	700
		Rent payable	200
		Wages	50
		Payable (Green)	50
		Payables (Blue)	1,000
		Loan	100

The memorandum receivables" ledger and payables' ledger accounts are not part of the double-entry bookkeeping system maintained in the general ledger. In an integrated computerised accounting system, these accounts are updated simultaneously with the general ledger accounts. For information, here are the updated individual accounts for each individual credit supplier and credit customer.

Payable ledger – Green Supplies

	$		$
Bank	50	Stationery	50

Payable ledger – Blue Supplies

	$		$
Bank	1,000	Purchases	1,000

Receivable ledger – Grey

	$		$
Sales	2,000	Bank	2,000

ACTIVITY 1

Record the following transactions in general ledger accounts.

Balance off the 'Cash at bank' account.

Transaction	Details
1	Set up the business by introducing $150,000 in cash.
2	Purchase property costing $140,000. Pay in cash.
3	Purchase goods costing $5,000. Pay in cash.
4	Sell goods for $7,000. All cash sales.
5	Purchase goods costing $8,000. Pay in cash.
6	Pay a sundry expense of $100, by cheque.
7	Sell goods for $15,000. All cash sales.
8	Pay wages of $2,000 to an employee.
9	Pay postage costs of $100 by cheque.

Note: A payment by cheque = a payment in cash.

Tip: Remember there is no such account as 'goods'.

For a suggested answer, see the 'Answers' section at the end of the book.

5 THE JOURNAL

5.1 INTRODUCTION

Any transaction can be recorded in the form of a journal. Indeed, in a computerised system, it is probably the easiest way to think of how transactions are recorded and processed in the general ledger. In this context, a journal is the recording of a transaction using the principles of double-entry bookkeeping. Examples of the double-entry required to record transactions are as follows:

- Cash sale

    Debit: Cash at bank   Credit: Sales

- Credit purchase

    Debit: Purchases   Credit: Payables

- Insurance of premises

    Debit: Insurance   Credit: Cash at bank

- Irrecoverable debt written off

    Debit   Irrecoverable debts   Credit   Receivables

The recording of non-routine transactions and the correction of errors in the general ledger can also be presented as journal entries to note the accounting entries required for situations such as the following:

- accruals and prepayments

- disposals of non-current assets

- closing inventories at the end of the accounting year

Journals are a clear way of setting out the required double-entry to record a transaction or adjustment in the general ledger.

The use of journals is illustrated as you progress through this study text. Note that, in the ACCA FA1 exam, you may be required to identify or prepare the journal entry for a transaction. It is a method of testing your knowledge and understanding of double-entry bookkeeping in an examination setting, such as those illustrated at the beginning of this section.

5.2 PRESENTATION OF A JOURNAL TRANSACTION

An example of a journal transaction is presented below:

Date	19/08/X3	Journal No. 2341	General Ledger Code Ref	$
Debit	Irrecoverable debts written off		4231	3,000
Credit	Receivables		7583	3,000
To write off the amount due from DFG Co which is subject to insolvency proceedings.				
Initiator: WE	Authorised: JR	Receivables' ledger account ref		DFG01

This clearly states the double-entry required, the monetary amount plus, for reference, a brief explanation or cross reference to other documents evidencing the reason for the transaction. As illustrated here, the journal document may also include references to identify the initiator of the transaction and the person approving or authorising the processing of the transaction. The presentation of the accounting entries required to record transactions is covered throughout this study text.

The document may not be for a single transaction as illustrated above, it could be a document that supports the posting of multiple transactions, such as all receipts from credit customers received and banked during the day. In this situation, along with the general ledger account references, there will be multiple coding references to e.g. the receivables' ledger records of individual credit customers.

ACTIVITY 2

State the journals required to record the following transactions in the general ledger:

(i)   the purchase of a delivery van for $10,000 with payment to be made one month later

(ii) the payment of wages of $2,750; and

(iii) the sale of goods to a credit customer for $1,500.

For a suggested answer, see the 'Answers' section at the end of the book.

6 BALANCING AND CLOSING A LEDGER ACCOUNT

6.1 INTRODUCTION

When all transactions for an accounting period have been recorded, it is necessary to establish the balance on each general ledger account. In many computerised accounting systems, this is done automatically, along with generation of a trial balance. However, it is important to understand the procedure involved and what happens to the general ledger account balances after the trial balance has been generated.

The procedure to strike a general ledger account balance is as follows:

1 Total both sides of the T-account and find the larger total.

2 Insert the larger total in the total box on both the debit and credit side.

3 Insert a balancing figure to the side of the T-account which does not currently add up to the amount in the total box. Call this balancing figure 'balance c/f' (carried forward) or 'balance c/d' (carried down).

4 Carry the balance down diagonally and call it 'balance b/f' (brought forward) or 'balance b/d' (brought down).

EXAMPLE

Balance the following general ledger account:

Cash at bank

	$		$
Capital	10,000	Purchases	200
Sales	250	Rent	150
		Electricity	75
	———		———
	———		———

SOLUTION

Cash at bank

	$		$
Capital	10,000	Purchases	200
Sales	250	Rent	150
		Electricity	75
		Balance c/f	9,825
	———		———
	10,250		10,250
	———		———
Balance b/f	9,825		

ACTIVITY 3

Here is a ledger account from the general ledger of a business.

Cash at bank

	$		$
Capital	10,000	Purchases	1,000
Sales	300	Rent	2,500
		Electricity	750
		New van	15,000

Required:

(a)   What is the balance brought down on this ledger account?

(b)   Is it a debit or a credit balance brought down?

For a suggested answer, see the 'Answers' section at the end of the book.

ACTIVITY 4

Here is a cash at cash at bank general ledger account at 30 June.

Cash at bank

		$			$
1 June	Balance b/d	4,200	3 June	Purchases	1,600
3 June	Sales	3,700	8 June	Telephone expenses	850
10 June	Sales	6,100	15 June	Equipment	2,000
15 June	Sales	4,900	28 June	Purchases	3,700
26 June	Sales	8,800	29 June	Salaries payable	14,200

Required:

(a)   Balance-off the account at 30 June.

(b)   What would a credit balance on the Bank T-account signify?

For a suggested answer, see the 'Answers' section at the end of the book.

Although this will be covered in more detail later in this publication, it is worth noting how the general ledger account balances from the trial balance will be used.

6.2   INCOME AND EXPENSE LEDGER ACCOUNTS

At the end of an accounting period, all income and expense account balances are closed-off and used to prepare the statement of profit or loss.

Do not show a balance c/f or balance b/f but instead put the balancing figure on the smallest side and label it 'profit or loss'.

The general ledger account balance will then be nil and it is then ready to use again in the next accounting period.

6.3 ASSET, LIABILITY AND CAPITAL LEDGER ACCOUNTS

At the end of an accounting period, all asset, liability and capital account balances will be carried forward as the opening balances at the start of the next accounting period.

Those balances will also be classified and arranged to prepare the statement of financial position.

Assets/liabilities at the end of a period = Assets/liabilities at start of the next period, e.g. the cash at bank ledger account balance at the end of one day will be the cash at bank ledger account balance at the start of the following day.

7 TRADE AND SETTLEMENT DISCOUNTS

7.1 TRADE DISCOUNT

A **trade discount** is a discount given to customers ordering in large quantities or as an incentive for to encourage regular customers to place more orders. Trade discounts are simply a reduction in the selling price of goods at the point of sale.

Trade discounts are given to customers for a variety of reasons. The main reason a trade discount is offered is to encourage customers to either purchase more goods over a period of time and/or to encourage customers to place larger individual orders.

For example, trade discount may be offered to customers as a reward for loyalty over a period of time. Alternatively, trade discount could be offered on any individual order to purchase, say, 100 units or more in a single transaction.

It is normal policy to show the percentage of trade discount on the face of a sales invoice. For example if the list price of goods is $100 and a 10% trade discount given then this is shown on the invoice as:

	$
List price	100.00
Less: 10% trade discount	10.00
	———
Net price	90.00
	———

The customer pays the net price. If sales tax is charged, it should be added to the net price, and the customer is required to pay the net price plus sales tax. Different percentages of trade discount may be applied to different products, in which case the relevant percentage discount is normally shown against each product on the invoice before sales tax is calculated, as in the following presentation:

Product	Description	Quantity	Item price $	Discount	Total $
HS336	Table	1	100.00	10%	90.00
HS472	Chair	6	90.00	5%	513.00
					———
					603.00
Sales tax @ 20%					120.60
					———
					723.60
					———

Once again, trade discount is excluded from the general ledger of both the customer and the seller and both parties will account for this transaction at the value of $723.60.

Therefore, the transaction is recorded by the seller at the trade-discounted price and will be accounted for by the customer using the same monetary value. Therefore, trade discounts are not included in the accounting records of either the seller or the customer.

7.2 SETTLEMENT DISCOUNT – SELLER PERSPECTIVE

A **settlement discount** ('early settlement discount' or 'prompt payment discount') is a discount offered by the seller to the buyer for early payment of a debt i.e. within a specified period of time before the normal due date.

Typically, an invoice from a seller will state that payment is due 30 days from the invoice date. However, to persuade the customer to settle early, a percentage discount will be offered if payment is made before the due date. This discount is known as a settlement discount.

A settlement discount is therefore different in nature to a trade discount. A trade discount is a definite reduction in price that is **given** by the seller to the buyer. A settlement discount is a reduction in the overall invoice price that is **offered** to the customer. It is for the customer to decide whether to accept the early settlement terms offered and pay the reduced amount within the required timescale, or to pay the full invoice amount at a later date.

A **typical wording of a settlement discount** may be '4% cash discount for payment within 14 days otherwise net 30 days'. This may be abbreviated to: '4/14, net 30'.

This means that if the customer decides to pay the invoice within 14 days of the invoice date then the customer can deduct 4% from the invoice total and only pay the reduced amount. However, if the customer decides not to accept the settlement discount the full invoice amount should still be paid within 30 calendar days.

In practical terms if a seller offers settlement discount to a credit customer, there is no way of knowing, at the point when the invoice is prepared by the seller, whether the customer will take advantage of the settlement discount terms offered and pay the reduced amount. This is known as **'variable consideration'** as the seller does not know at the time the sale is recorded is recorded whether it will receive only the reduced (discounted) amount or the full amount.

A seller could therefore adopt one of the following approaches to deal with this situation:

- prepare the sale invoice for the full amount and, if the customer does pay early and claim the settlement discount, issue a credit note to reduce the sale and receivable recorded previously to acknowledge the discount allowed to the customer. If the customer does not pay early, the full amount is due as normal.

- prepare the sale invoice for the reduced amount (after applying the settlement discount) on the expectation that the customer will pay early and be entitled to the settlement discount.
Subsequently, if the customer does not pay early and is no longer entitled to the discount, the full amount is due and the additional amount received would be treated as if it was a cash sale.

Therefore, **in examination questions**, it will be stated whether a credit customer is expected to take advantage of settlement discount terms or not for the purpose of calculating amounts due from customers or to calculate and account for cash receipts from customers.

For example, a question may include be wording such as '...a business sold goods to a customer on credit. At the point of sale, the customer was (or was not) expected to take advantage of the early settlement discount terms offered.....'

If the customer **is not expected to take advantage** of the early settlement discount terms, the invoice prepared by the seller would consist of the following amounts:

	$
List price	200
Less: 3% settlement discount	Nil
Amount due from customer	200

The accounting entries recorded by the seller in the general ledger would be as follows:

Debit: Receivables $200

Credit: Sales $200

If, as expected, the customer does not take advantage of the settlement discount available, the full amount of $200.00 should be paid by the customer. When the cash is received, the accounting entries to record this would be as follows:

Debit   Cash $200

Credit   Receivables $200

If' however, the customer does take advantage of the settlement discount terms, they will pay $194.00. The total receivable of $200.00 must be cleared, even though only $194.00 has been received. This would be accounted for by making an adjustment to revenue as follows:

Debit   Cash $194 (97% of $200)

Debit   Revenue $6

Credit   Receivables $200

If the customer **is expected to take advantage** of the early settlement discount terms, the invoice prepared by the seller would consist of the following amounts:

	$
List price	200
Less: 3% settlement discount	(6)
Amount due from customer	194

In this situation, settlement discount allowed is excluded from the accounting records in the same way as trade discount is excluded from the accounting records. The accounting entries initially recorded by the seller would be as follows:

Debit   Receivables $194.00

Credit   Revenue $194.00

Subsequently if, as expected, the customer pays within ten days to take advantage of the early settlement terms, the receipt of cash will be accounted for as follows:

Debit   Cash $194.00

Credit   Receivables $194.00

If the customer does not take advantage of the early settlement terms, the full amount of $200.00 is due. When it is received, the additional receipt of $6 is accounted for as if it were an additional cash sale as follows:

Debit   Cash $200.00

Credit   Receivables $194.00

Credit   Revenue $6.00

ACTIVITY 5

Goods were sold to a credit customer at a list price of $1,250, subject to a trade discount of 20%. The customer has also been offered 2.5% discount for early settlement of the invoice. Show the relevant entries in the receivables and revenue general ledger accounts to record the initial transaction, and then record the subsequent receipt of cash in the receivables and the cash at bank account **if the customer is not expected** to take advantage of the settlement discount terms offered and subsequently pays outside of the discount period.

For a suggested answer, see the 'Answers' section at the end of the book.

ACTIVITY 6

Goods were sold to a credit customer at a list price of $1,250, subject to a trade discount of 20%. The customer has also been offered 2.5% discount for early settlement of the invoice. Show the relevant entries in the receivables and revenue general ledger accounts to record the initial transaction, and then record the subsequent receipt of cash in the receivables and the cash at bank account **if the customer is expected** to take advantage of the settlement discount terms offered, and subsequently pays within the discount period.

For a suggested answer, see the 'Answers' section at the end of the book.

ACTIVITY 7

Goods were sold to a credit customer at a list price of $1,250, subject to a trade discount of 20%. The customer has also been offered 2.5% discount for early settlement of the invoice. Show the relevant entries in the receivables and revenue general ledger accounts to record the initial transaction, and then record the subsequent receipt of cash in the receivables and the cash at bank account **if the customer is expected** to take advantage of the settlement discount terms offered, and subsequently pays after the discount period has expired.

For a suggested answer, see the 'Answers' section at the end of the book.

ACTIVITY 8

Goods were sold to a credit customer at a list price of $1,250, subject to a trade discount of 20%. The customer has also been offered 2.5% discount for early settlement of the invoice. Show the relevant entries in the receivables and revenue general ledger accounts to record the initial transaction, and then record the subsequent receipt of cash in the receivables and the cash at bank account **if the customer is not expected** to take advantage of the settlement discount terms offered but who subsequently pays promptly within the early settlement period.

For a suggested answer, see the 'Answers' section at the end of the book.

7.3 SETTLEMENT DISCOUNTS – CUSTOMER PERSPECTIVE

Discounts received arises when a settlement discount is taken by a business paying a supplier. The business will pay a reduced amount to the supplier in full settlement of the amount due.

The remainder of the debt is then transferred to the statement of profit or loss as a discount received (credit entry) increasing profit. This does need to be accounted for as the business will decide for itself whether to take advantage of the discount terms offered by the supplier.

When making the payment to the seller, the accounting entries will be as follows:

Accounting entries:

Debit	Payables	full debt
Credit	Cash at bank	reduced amount paid
Credit	Discount received	amount of discount

ACTIVITY 9

A purchase invoice with a value of $500 offering a 2% discount for early settlement is paid before the normal payment date by the business. Show the relevant entries in the payables and discounts received general ledger accounts of the customer.

For a suggested answer, see the 'Answers' section at the end of the book.

8 ACCOUNTING FOR SALES TAX

8.1 THE SYSTEM

Many developed economies operate a sales tax system. A business must pay sales tax on the goods and services it buys if those goods and services are supplied by a business registered to account for sales tax. This tax is collected by the seller, who then must pay the amounts collected to the tax authorities. In the UK this tax is known as Value Added Tax (VAT), but for the rest of this chapter it will be referred to as sales tax. Prices in shops normally include sales tax, but business-to-business transactions are often quoted excluding sales tax.

Only a business registered to account for sales tax is required to charge tax on its sales. A tax-registered business acts as a tax collector for the government. It pays over the tax levied on its own sales, but it can reclaim the sales tax suffered on its purchases.

A business must register for sales tax when its sales revenue or turnover reaches a specific limit or threshold, or it may be allowed to register voluntarily in some circumstances.

A sales tax registered business collects sales tax on goods sold and pays it to the tax authorities and can reclaim sales tax paid on its own purchases of goods, expenses and non-current assets. Therefore, in most cases, the business usually makes a net payment to the tax authorities.

Taxable supplies are goods and services sold subject to sales tax.

Input tax is sales tax paid to suppliers which is suffered and paid on purchases by a business.

Output tax is sales tax charged on sales by a business and collected on behalf of the tax authority.

Taxable supplies may be chargeable at different rates of sales tax, depending upon their nature. As an example, rates changed in the UK have varied between 5% and 20%. There is normally a **'standard rate'** along with a **'reduced rate'** for specified products or services such as domestic fuel charges. These vary by country and may change from time to time.

The supply or sale of some products or services may be **'zero-rated'** which means that a zero rate of sales tax is applied to the transaction, perhaps on clothing for children. In practical terms, this means that the business can reclaim sales tax suffered and paid on purchases, whilst collecting no sales tax on sales made. It will therefore normally receive refunds of sales tax suffered on purchases.

Exempt activities are those outside the scope of sales tax for, perhaps, banking transaction services and exports. Entities carrying on tax-exempt activities cannot charge sales tax on the sale or supply of goods and services and services supplied and nor can they reclaim sales tax on purchases made.

8.2 CALCULATING SALES TAX

There may be a need to calculate sales tax from either the gross figure (including tax), or the net figure (excluding tax). Prices quoted in by retailers to domestic customers are normally stated gross, but business-to-business prices are often quoted on a net basis.

All the following examples assume that the rate of sales tax is 20%.

EXAMPLE – net price to gross price

The net figure is provided and sales tax is added to this. The tax is calculated at 20% of the net amount. Therefore the gross amount is built up as follows.

Assume that the net selling price is $200.

	%	$
Net amount	100	200
Add tax @ 20%	20	40
Gross amount	120	240

EXAMPLE – gross price to net price

The gross figure is given, and the sales tax element within that price must be calculated. Using the structure above, we can see that the tax will be $\frac{20}{120}$ of the gross amount. This will be deducted to find the net amount, as shown below.

Assume that the gross selling price is $750. The tax will be $\frac{20}{120}$ of this, which is $125.

	%	$
Gross amount	120	750
Less tax @ $\frac{20}{120}$	(20)	(125)
Net amount	100	625

ACTIVITY 10

Calculate the sales tax element on the following supplies assuming a sales tax rate of 20%:

(a) $120 gross

(b) $480 gross

(c) $200 net

(d) $1,272 gross

(e) $17,484 gross

For a suggested answer, see the 'Answers' section at the end of the book.

Be aware that the ACCA FA1 syllabus and exam may apply any rate of sales tax, so ensure that you are able to calculate sales tax, based upon net and gross values for different rates using the approach noted above.

8.3   ACCOUNTING FOR SALES TAX

The business must record:

* The gross amount receivable from customers – trade receivables are presented gross in the statement of financial position.

* The gross amount payable to suppliers – trade payables are presented gross in the statement of financial position.

* Income and expenses are presented net of sales tax in the statement of profit or loss.

* The sales tax collected and owed to the tax authorities is offset against the sales tax suffered on purchases (and therefore recoverable) from the tax authorities. The net amount included in the statement of financial position. For many businesses, this will be a liability in the statement of financial position. If the net position is that more input tax has been suffered, there will be a receivable in the statement of financial position to reflect a refund due.

Most businesses account quarterly for sales tax and are usually required to settle amounts due within a specified time period.

EXAMPLE – sales tax and cash transactions

Consider a retailer who sells to domestic customers and states selling prices inclusive of sales tax. The gross price must therefore be split between the revenue due to the retailer and the sales tax collected on behalf of the tax authority. The example is based on the sale of goods with a gross price of $720 and a sales tax rate of 20%. The total invoice price will comprise:

	$	Double-entry	
Net	600	Credit Sales	This is the net sales value to the business. The statement of profit or loss will record a sale of $600.
Tax @ 20%	120	Credit Sales tax liability	This will be collected from the customer by the business, and then paid over to the authorities.
Gross	720	Debit Cash at bank	This is the cash received at the point of sale from the customer.

For a business that makes a cash purchase at a sales tax-inclusive price of $480, the following are the accounting entries required to record the transaction:

	$	Double-entry	
Net	400	Debit Purchases	This is the net cost to the business. The SPL will record a purchase of $400.
Tax @ 20%	80	Debit Sales tax recoverable	This tax will be paid over to the supplier, but then recovered from the tax authorities.
Gross	480	Credit Cash at bank	This is the cash paid at the point of sale by the business to the supplier.

EXAMPLE – sales tax on a credit sale

The example is based on the sale of goods with a net price of $6,000 and a sales tax rate of 20%. The total invoice price will comprise:

	$	Double-entry	
Net	6,000	Credit Sales (SPL)	This is the net sales value to the business. The statement of profit or loss will record a sale of $6,000.
Tax @ 20%	1,200	Credit Sales tax liability (SFP)	This will be collected from the customer by the business, and then paid over to the authorities.
Gross	7,200	Debit Trade receivables (SFP)	This is the trade receivable, the total amount receivable from the customer.

The steps to accounting for tax on this transaction are:

1   The net sale is credited to the sales account, the tax is credited to a sales tax account and finally the total is debited to trade receivables.

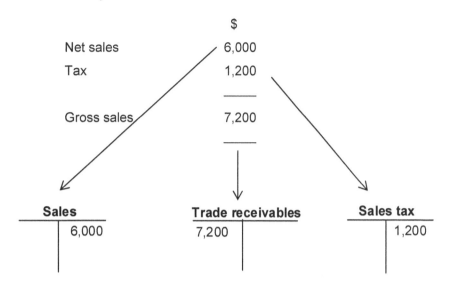

2   The customer pays the gross amount, clearing the debt.

Note that tax is not accounted for when the money is received from the customer. The tax has already been accounted for when the sale was made.

Sales	Trade receivable		Sales tax	Cash at bank	
6,000	7,200	7,200	1,200	7,200	
(1)	(1)	(2)	(1)	(2)	

EXAMPLE – sales tax on a credit purchase

The example is based upon the purchase of goods with a net cost of $4,000 and a sales tax rate of 20%. The total invoice cost will comprise:

	$	Double-entry	
Net	4,000	Debit Purchases (SPL)	This is the net cost to the business. The SPL will record a purchase of $4,000.
Tax @ 20%	800	Debit Sales tax recoverable (SFP)	This tax will be paid over to the supplier, but then recovered from the tax authorities.
Gross	4,800	Credit Trade payables (SFP)	This is the trade payable, the total amount payable to the supplier.

SOLUTION

The steps to accounting for sales tax on this transaction are:

1   The net purchase is debited to the purchases account as normal. Sales tax is debited to the sales tax account. Finally the total is credited to the trade payables account.

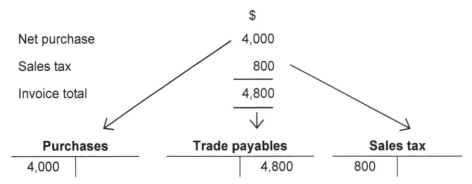

Purchases	Trade payables	Sales tax
4,000	4,800	800

2   When the business pays the debt to the supplier the total invoice amount is paid from the bank account and the amount showing as owing in payables is eliminated.

Purchases	Sales tax	Trade payables		Cash at bank
4,000	800	4,800	4,800	4,800
(1)	(1)	(2)	(1)	(2)

As before, sales tax is accounted for when the invoices are recorded, not when the invoices are paid.

8.4   SALES TAX ADMINISTRATION AND DOCUMENTATION

If a business is registered to account for sales tax there are documents and records that must be maintained and administration rules to be followed. Depending upon the size and nature of a business, it may need to make quarterly or monthly returns to account for sales tax suffered on (inputs) purchases, which, in principle, can normally be reclaimed or offset against sales tax on (outputs). Also, businesses may be required to account for sales tax on an accruals basis, with many smaller businesses able to account for sales tax on a cash basis. Some very small entities are able to account for sales tax on an annual basis. Most entities now complete their sales tax returns online and make any payment due (or receive refunds) by automated bank transfer.

Records must be kept of all sales and purchases. A sales tax invoice must be created for each sale and retained, with a copy given to the customer.

A business registered for sales tax must have a valid tax invoice from its supplier to be able to reclaim sales tax on purchases made and expenses incurred.

A tax invoice must show:

- Seller's name and address

- Seller's sales tax registration number

- Invoice date

- Description of the goods supplied to the customer, price charged together with the rate of sales tax and total sales tax charged.

8.5 PAYMENT OF SALES TAX

Payments must be made to the relevant tax authorities with a return (completed form) outlining the output tax charged on sales and input tax suffered on purchases. Payments are usually made quarterly but may be made more regularly to spread payments.

The following summary of a sales tax account identifies the source of the documentation and information used to account for sales tax. It should be noted that sales tax information is compiled from a range of sources.

Sales tax

	$		$
Sales tax re credit purchases	X	Balance b/f	X
Sales tax re cash purchases	X	Sales tax re cash sales	X
Sales tax per petty cash expenses	X	Sales tax re credit sales	X
Cash paid to tax authorities	X	Cash received from tax authorities	
Balance c/f	X		
	X		X
		Balance b/f	X

When making a return to account for sales tax, the following information is normally required:

- the business name making the return

- the sales tax registration number of the business to account for and administer sales tax

- the period covered by the return e.g. which quarter or month it relates to

- total value of sales (outputs) and output tax charged to customers by the business (boxes 1 and 6 on the following specimen sales tax return)

- total value of purchases (inputs) and input tax charged by suppliers (boxes 4 and 7 on the following specimen sales tax return)

- adjustments for errors in earlier returns

- the net amount due to (or from) the tax authorities for the return period – usually any payment due from the business accompanies the return submitted to the tax authorities (box 5 on the following specimen sales tax return).

In effect, the business is acting as a tax administrator and collector on behalf of the tax authorities when it accounts for sales tax. It must maintain detailed accounting records to support entries made on the sales tax return. The consequence of this is that, where a business charges more output tax on sales than it suffers input tax on purchases, it will make regular payments of sales tax to the tax authorities. If it suffers more input tax on purchases than output tax levied on sales, it will receive regular refunds from the tax authorities.

Specimen sales tax return (including hypothetical values)

		$
VAT due in the period on **sales** and other outputs	**Box 1**	41,593.60
VAT due in the period on **acquisitions** from other **EU Member States**	**Box 2**	3,078.00
Total VAT due (**the sum of boxes 1 and 2**)	**Box 3**	44,671.60
VAT reclaimed in the period on **purchases** and other inputs, including acquisitions from the EU	**Box 4**	23,215.53
Net VAT to be paid to HM Revenue & Customs or reclaimed (**Difference between boxes 3 and 4**)	**Box 5**	21,456.07
Total value of **sales** and all other outputs excluding any VAT. **Include your box 8 figure**	**Box 6**	268,199
Total value of purchases and all other inputs excluding any VAT. **Include your box 9 figure**	**Box 7**	111,811
Total value of all **supplies** of goods and related costs, excluding any VAT, to other **EU Member States**	**Box 8**	43,789
Total value of all **acquisitions** of goods and related costs, excluding any VAT, from other **EU Member States**	**Box 9**	15,390

If a **sales tax return and/or payment is submitted late** the tax authorities, it is possible that the business will be charged a penalty or surcharge. This may be a percentage of the outstanding tax to be paid.

The business may also be charged a penalty or surcharge if there are errors on the return so it is important to retain documentation and to take care to ensure that the information filed is complete and accurate and that it is submitted on time.

If an **error or omission** is discovered on a tax return which has already been submitted, the tax authorities must be contacted as soon as possible. If the tax authorities discover an error that the business did not make them aware of, the penalties may be significantly higher. The standard sales tax return form usually includes space available to make and explain any corrections required.

If there is a **change in the sales tax rate, the scope of the tax or documentation** required, the business must be prepared in advance of the date of change. This may include making staff aware of the changes, updating software that produces sales invoices and also the accounting system that processes accounting transactions. This could require a significant degree of planning and application, depending upon the size and nature of the business.

CONCLUSION

This chapter defined and explained the elements to the financial statements. The accounting equation was then defined, explained and illustrated, before progressing on to explaining the financial statements of a business. Finally, the principles of double-entry bookkeeping were introduced, explained and illustrated, along with recording transactions in ledger accounts.

The chapter introduced, explained and illustrated how to account for trade and early settlement discounts and sales tax.

You are now ready to progress on to developing our knowledge and understanding of recording broad range of transactions and events in the general ledger.

KEY TERMS

Asset – a present economic resource controlled by the business as a result of past events.

Gross profit – revenue from sales less the cost of sales in the accounting period.

Capital – the residual interest that the owner has in the assets of the business after all liabilities have been settled.

Expense – a decrease in assets or increase in liabilities which result in a reduction of capital due to the owner.

General ledger – the complete set of ledger accounts used by a business to record transactions. It may also be referred to as a 'nominal ledger' or 'chart of accounts'.

Journal – a record of accounting entries made to record non-routine transactions and to correct errors. Many journal entries relate to the preparation of the annual financial statements.

Income – consists of increases in assets or decreases in liabilities that result in an increase in capital due to the owner. correct errors.

Input tax – is sales tax paid to suppliers which is suffered and paid on purchases by a business.

The journal – is a record of accounting an accounting transaction recorded in the general ledger. The journal may be maintained in book form, a log or register in hard or soft copy.

Ledger account – a record of transactions assigned to a specific asset, liability, source of income or expense, along with a capital account for a sole proprietor. It will identify increases and decreases in that item during an accounting period.

Liability – a present obligation of the business to transfer an economic resource as a result of past events.

Net profit – gross profit less expenses incurred during the accounting period.

Output tax – is sales tax charged on sales by a business and collected on behalf of the tax authority.

Settlement discount – ('early settlement discount' or 'prompt payment discount') is a discount offered by the seller to the buyer for early payment of a debt i.e. within a specified period of time before the normal due date.

Statement of financial position – a statement of a business's assets, liabilities and capital at a specific point in time.

Statement of profit or loss – a statement of financial performance that shows the profit or loss earned by a business for an accounting period.

Taxable supplies – are goods and services sold subject to sales tax.

Trade discount – is a discount given to customers ordering in large quantities or as an incentive for to encourage regular customers to place more orders.

SELF TEST QUESTIONS

		Paragraph
1	Define and provide one example of a liability.	1.2
2	Define income and provide one example of income.	1.2
3	What is the accounting equation?	2.1
4	Define and provide one example of a non-current liability.	3.2
5	What is the general ledger?	4.1
6	When would a debit entry be required in a ledger account	4.2
7	When would a credit entry be required in a ledger account?	4.2
8	What is the journal?	5.1
9	What is trade discount?	7.1
10	What is settlement discount?	7.2
11	Define taxable supplies, input tax and output tax in relation to sales tax.	8.1

EXAM-STYLE QUESTIONS

1   Which of the following statements best defines a non-current asset?

    A   A non-current asset is any asset excluding cash at bank and inventories

    B   A non-current asset is an obligation due for payment after more than one year from the accounting year end

    C   A non-current asset is an asset acquired for use in the business on a continuing basis over a number of years to generate revenues and profits

    D   A non-current asset is an asset which will be converted into cash within the normal operating activities of the business, typically within twelve months

2   Which of the following statements best defines the journal?

    A   The journal is a record of year-end accounting adjustments

    B   The journal is a record of non-routine accounting transactions entered in the general ledger

    C   The journal is a record of all accounting transactions recorded in the general ledger

    D   The journal is a record of all corrections of errors made in the general ledger

3   A business sells goods to a customer. There are two alternative terms on offer, EITHER pay $2,000 taking 60 days' credit, OR pay within 7 days of the invoice date and receive a discount of 5%. At the point of sale, the customer is expected to take up the discount offer, and subsequently pays the correct amount immediately. How should seller record the sale in the accounting records?

    A   Debit Cash at bank $1,900   Credit Revenue $1,900

    B   Debit Cash at bank $1,900   Credit Revenue $2,000
          Debit Discount received $100

    C   Debit Receivables $1,900,   Credit Revenue $1,900

    D   Debit Bank $2,000   Credit Discount received $100
                                Credit Revenue $1,900

4   On 1 May, a business sold goods to a customer for $1,000 on one month's credit, with the offer of a discount of 2% for payment within 7 days of the invoice date. At the point of sale, the customer was expected to take up the discount offered. On 28 May, the customer sent payment by cheque for the appropriate amount. How should the payment from the customer be recorded in the accounting records?

    A   Debit Cash at bank $1,000   Credit Revenue $20
                                          Credit Receivables $980

    B   Debit Cash at bank $980   Credit Receivables $980

    C   Debit Receivables $980   Credit Revenue $1,000
          Debit Discount received $20

    D   Debit Cash at bank $1,000   Credit Discounts received $20
                                          Credit Receivables $980

PRACTICE QUESTION 1

ELEMENTS OF THE FINANCIAL STATEMENTS

State and explain the five elements of the financial statements.

For a suggested answer, see the 'Answers' section at the end of the book.

PRACTICE QUESTION 2

COMPONENTS OF THE FINANCIAL STATEMENTS

State and explain the components of a set of financial statements.

For a suggested answer, see the 'Answers' section at the end of the book.

Chapter 5

BANK SYSTEM AND TRANSACTIONS

This chapter describes the main methods of paying for goods and services. You may already be familiar with much of the content of this chapter, from having a bank account and a debit or credit card of your own. This chapter covers the central bank clearing system, banks and banking institutions, along with the processing and security features for a range of receipts and payment methods.

This chapter covers syllabus areas C1.

CONTENTS

1   Customer/bank relationship

2   Central bank clearing system

3   Types of receipt/payment

4   Preparing a cheque prior to despatch

5   Credit cards, debit cards and contactless payments

6   Automated bank payments

7   Unusual features of receipts and payments media and documentation

8   Banking monies received

9   Handling, storage and security of money

10   Banks and banking institutions

LEARNING OUTCOMES

At the end of this chapter, you should be able to:

- describe the relationship between a bank and its customer

- outline the working of a central bank clearing system

- recognise the obligation owed by a bank to its clients

- understand the content and format of a cheque

- prepare a cheque prior to despatch

- describe the procedure and documentation relating to the use of credit and debit cards

- describe other services offered by banks

- explain the correct procedure to cope with unusual situations associated with payments and receipts

- describe general procedures for dealing with cash, cheques, credit and debit card receipts and payments

- outline the purpose and format of paying-in documents

- understand procedures for banking cash receipts

- describe the key procedures for ensuring safety, security and, where appropriate, confidentiality over the handling of cash and cheques.

1 CUSTOMER/BANK RELATIONSHIP

1.1 RECEIVABLE AND PAYABLE

If a business pays $2,000 into a bank account then the bank owes that money back to the business. The bank is therefore a receivable of the business. Equally, the business is a payable from the bank's point of view.

Alternatively if the bank allows the business an overdraft then the bank is a payable of the business and the business is a receivable in the bank's eyes. The situation in one set of accounting records is a mirror image of the other.

The importance of this relationship is that the bank can use the business's $2,000 in order to invest and hopefully make a profit. This profit does not have to be repaid to the business. This is for the bank to retain. The bank must however repay the $2,000 as and when requested.

Banks provide a number of services to customers and often charge interest and commission. There are pure banking services such as operating current and business accounts which permit the use of direct debits and standing orders, overdrafts and loans. There are also other services such as the provision of insurance, tax advice and travel facilities.

1.2 BANKERS' OBLIGATIONS

Although a bank does not have to account to its customers for any profit that it makes with the money deposited, it does have a number of obligations to its customers:

- The banker must repay the amount of the deposit on demand or pay it to a third party when requested to by the drawing of a cheque or other authorised instruction, perhaps a direct debit or standing order. The bank does not have to pay a cheque in part. For example if a customer has only $100 in their bank account but draws a cheque for $160 then the bank is under no obligation to pay only $100. It should either pay in full or refuse to make payment altogether.

- The banker has a duty to honour a customer's cheques up to the amount of the bank balance or agreed overdraft if the cheque has been properly prepared.

- The banker must provide the amount of the balance on the account at any time on the request of the customer.

- The banker must provide a statement showing the transactions on the account for an agreed period within a reasonable time of the end of that period. The customer is not obliged to check the statement and therefore any errors made by the bank will usually be binding on the bank.

- The banker has a contractual duty not to disclose any information regarding the banking details or personal information of the customer unless instructed by the customer or compelled by law to do so.

- In more general terms the banker is expected to use a professional level of care and skill when dealing with the customer and their account.

1.3 CUSTOMERS' OBLIGATIONS

The main duty of the customer is to ensure that reasonable care is exercised when preparing cheques and other form of instruction to make payments. For example, cheques should be prepared so as to not mislead the bank and not to facilitate forgery.

2 CENTRAL BANK CLEARING SYSTEM

2.1 CLEARING BANKS

Major high street banks are known as clearing banks, for example, HSBC and Barclays Bank in the UK. These clearing banks settle the amount of cheques drawn on them and payable into their accounts through what is known as the clearing system.

2.2 THE CLEARING SYSTEM

As an example, a bank clearing system, the UK operates in the following manner:

- All cheques paid into, say, Lloyds Bank branches in a day are sent to Lloyds head office. They are sorted into groups according to the bank that the cheques are drawn on, for example all cheques drawn on HSBC Bank are grouped together.

- This process will take place in each of the clearing bank head offices' clearing departments.

- The end result may be that for that particular day Lloyds requires $18m from HSBC to cover the cheques paid into Lloyds branches that are drawn on HSBC Bank accounts. HSBC in turn requires $24m from Lloyds for cheques paid into HSBC branches drawn on Lloyds' accounts. This is settled by Lloyds paying the difference of $6m to HSBC through the accounts that each of the clearing banks hold at the Bank of England, the central bank for the UK.

- Each individual cheque is then sent to the branch on which it has been drawn. If the cheque is valid and the account has sufficient funds then the account will be debited with the amount of the cheque and the payee's account credited.

- Cheques drawn on other banks or other financial institutions are dealt with in the same system with one of the clearing banks acting as their agent.

- Cheques do not leave the branch if both the drawer (account holder) and the payee (person to whom the cheque is made out) have an account at that branch. Cheques are dealt with at head offices if the drawer and payee have accounts at different branches of the same bank.

Clearing systems may operate differently in countries outside the UK but the principles will be similar. The geographical size of a country or accessibility from one city to another may, for example, affect the speed of clearing receipts and payments.

2.3 TIMING OF THE CLEARING SYSTEM

The time taken to process the clearing of cheques has reduced in recent years. In some cases, such as when the drawer and payee of the cheque have accounts at the same branch of a bank, this may occur within one working day.

2.4 DISHONOURED CHEQUES

The paying bank may not necessarily pay all cheques. For example, if the cheque is incorrectly prepared or the drawer does not have sufficient funds in the bank account then the drawer's bank will not pay on the cheque. The cheque will be dishonoured. When a customer's cheque is dishonoured this means that the goods or services supplied have not yet been paid for. The business will seek an alternative form of payment from the customer.

3 TYPES OF RECEIPT/PAYMENT

3.1 CASH

Transactions may be paid for by notes and coins. A $10 or $50 note legally belongs to the person who possesses it and that person may spend it as they wish.

The fact that cash is portable and belongs to the person in possession of it is also a disadvantage. It can be lost, destroyed or stolen. In quantity, it is also quite bulky.

In terms of security and convenience, bank payments are preferred in business.

3.2 CHEQUES

Cheques are used for many receipts and payments, although they are declining in importance as electronic and digital forms of transaction grow in importance. If you have your own bank account, you may be familiar with cheques from your personal experience.

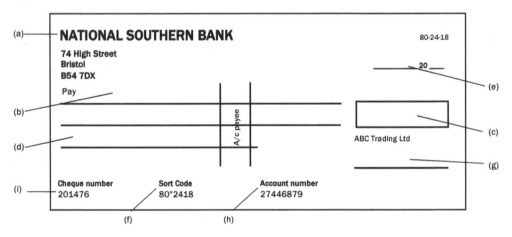

(a)   **Bank name and branch** – The cheque identifies the bank and branch of the bank where the payer has the account.

(b)   **Payee** – The person the cheque is payable to is called the payee. The payee's name is written on the top line of the cheque, after 'Pay'.

(c)/(d) **Amount** – The amount to be paid is written in both words and numbers. Amounts in pence are not written in words, but shown as figures.

(e) **Date** – The cheque must show a date. If the cheque has not been presented to the bank within six months of this date, the bank will treat it as out-of-date and refuse to honour it. Cheques are sometimes post-dated (dated in advance of the time they were prepared). Banks receiving post-dated cheques would refuse to accept them before the actual date on the cheque. The post-dating of cheques is not recommended by banks.

(f) **Bank sort code** – Every branch of every bank has a unique identifying number, known as a sort code, which is printed on the cheque. In the UK, it will have six digits.

(g) **The name of the account holder and signature of an authorised person (the 'drawer')** – This is the person making the payment by cheque. Cheques written by individuals are signed by the account holder (or one of the account holders, if there is more than one). With business cheques, the name of the individual signing the cheque and the name of the business (the account holder) may be different. For example, cheques written by ABC Co may be signed by any one of the managing director, chief executive officer, the chief accountant or the deputy chief accountant. The bank will keep a record of the signatures of the individuals who are authorised to sign a cheque on behalf of the business ('authorised signatories').

(h) **Account number** – The account number of the account holder is pre-printed on the cheque and is unique to each individual bank account.

(i) **Cheque number** – Each cheque is sequentially numbered. The cheque number is pre-printed on the cheque.

3.3 CROSSED CHEQUES

A cheque is crossed by drawing (or printing) two parallel vertical lines across it. When a cheque is crossed, the payment must be made into a bank account, it cannot be paid out in cash. This is a useful security procedure as it prevents cash payments being made to unauthorised persons should the cheque be lost or stolen.

Most cheques are now printed as a crossed cheque and with 'A/c payee' printed between the vertical lines. This is shown below.

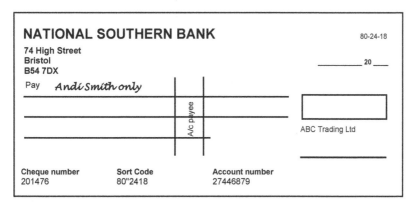

'A/c payee' stands for 'Account payee'. When a cheque is crossed with A/c payee:

- it must be paid into a bank account, because it is a crossed cheque, and

- it must be paid into the bank account of the person named as the payee on the cheque.

In other words, a cheque crossed A/c payee cannot be endorsed or signed over to another bank account holder. Endorsement is described in the next section. Most cheques are crossed A/c payee because it reduces the risk of loss as a result of theft or fraud.

3.4 ENDORSING A CHEQUE

A cheque may be endorsed by the payee unless it is an 'A/c payee' cheque.

Suppose, for example, that B Brown has written a cheque, payable to G F Dunn, for $500. It can be endorsed by the payee, G F Dunn writing their signature on the back of the cheque. The cheque can then be passed to another person to pay it into their own bank account. The wide use of 'A/c payee' cheques has significantly reduced the use of cheque endorsements.

ACTIVITY 1

1   Customers have obligations to their bank. Which of the following is a customer's obligation?

    A   To repay the amount of their deposits on demand

    B   Not to disclose any information regarding the affairs of the bank

    C   To use a professional level of care and skill in dealing with their accounts

    D   Not to draw up cheques in a way to facilitate forgery

2   When may a bank return a cheque to the payee?

    (i)   When it is more than six month out of date

    (ii)   When it is unsigned

    (iii)   When the account holder has insufficient funds to cover the cheque

    (iv)   When the cheque is crossed 'A/c payee' and it is presented by the named payee

    A   (i), (ii) and (iii)

    B   (i), (ii) and (iv)

    C   (i), (iii) and (iv)

    D   (ii), (iii) and (iv)

3   What is the effect of endorsing a cheque 'account payee'?

    A   It need not go through the clearing system.

    B   It cannot be transferred to another person for them to pay the cheque into their bank account.

    C   It can be transferred to another person for them to pay the cheque into their bank account.

    D   It enables someone other than the account holder to sign a cheque.

For a suggested answer, see the 'Answers' section at the end of the book.

3.5   STANDING ORDERS

Whilst many payments are made by cheque, there are other methods of making payments. For example, it is possible to instruct a bank to make regular payments for a fixed amount to a third party by means of a standing order.

A standing order is a written instruction to the bank by the payer to pay a certain amount on a regular basis (usually monthly) to a third party. This removes the need for anyone within the business to remember to make the payment and to write a cheque. The types of regular payments that are made by standing order are items such as insurance premiums or regular donations to charity. The standing order can only be amended or cancelled by the authorised signatory of the bank account who originated the payment.

3.6   DIRECT DEBITS

A bank can also pay a third party on behalf of a customer by a direct debit. This is very similar to a standing order, the main difference being that it is the receiving business that initiates the direct debit and specifies the amount it wants to collect. Also, the amount and frequency of payment can vary with a direct debit.

The types of payments that a business might make using a direct debit include payments of regular bills such as telephone and electricity charges that vary month by month. For example, the electricity provider will instruct its bank to collect a specified amount from the bank account of their customer, perhaps after the electricity meter has been read so that usage for the previous month can be confirmed and the cost calculated. The direct debit will not be honoured id there are insufficient funds in the account-holders bank account.

3.7   CREDIT TRANSFER

A credit transfer is a further method of instructing a bank to make a payment to a third party. This is usually done by the customer completing a credit transfer form in favour of the third party. This form is typically attached to the bottom of a bill or invoice received by the customer and, when completed, is then handed into the bank and the funds are transferred from the payer's bank account to the payee's bank account.

This method of payment is suitable for one-off payments or irregular payments to suppliers. Credit transfer forms (Bank Giro Credit) may be attached to bills or invoices for items such as gas, electricity and telephone charges.

3.8   BANKER'S DRAFT

A banker's draft is a payment instrument prepared by a bank at the request of a customer. It can only be paid into an account maintained by the payee named in the draft. The bank will usually require notice from a customer if a banker's draft is required and they will normally charge a fee for its preparation. Upon preparation of the draft, the customer's bank account is immediately charged with the amount of the draft, plus any charges or fees applicable, even though the recipient of the draft ('the payee') may not receive and present it for payment for several days.

In effect, a banker's draft ids a cheque drawn directly upon a bank. The benefit of the banker's draft to the payee is that there is no risk of the draft being dishonoured due to lack of funds on the part of the customer. This form of payment is less popular than it used to be as more individuals and businesses operate bank accounts and there is now a broader range of methods of making receipts and payments between two parties.

3.9 DIRECT PAYMENTS

Many business and personal bank accounts now permit the account holder to make a direct payment to another bank account. The payer needs to have the bank account details of the intended recipient (bank sort code, account number and account name) and is then able to set up a payment authority. The payment authority normally allows the payer flexibility in terms of the amount to be paid and the date of payment.

Individuals may find this beneficial, for example, when paying a tradesperson for work done relating to their property, or as a more convenient alternative to using a cheque. Normally the payer's bank will instigate controls to verify with the payer that the payment authority is valid (i.e. requesting that the account name, bank sort code and account number correct). The risk of error is reduced by the bank using standard templates for completion for information required. Banks are now also able to check the bank account details of the recipient to check whether it appears to be a valid account.

In addition, following the completion of the payment authority, before a payment is made the bank will instigate further controls to ensure that, for any payment requested, the correct recipient has been selected, and that the date and amount of the payment is correct. Such payments may now appear in the bank account of the recipient within a matter of minutes or hours.

Typical controls used in this situation include the bank requesting confirmation from the payer of a confidential password or code number, which may be communicated via the payer's personal mobile phone. A more recent alternative method of verifying a payment is to use the bank app which may use face recognition technology to enable the account holder to authorise a payment. There is obviously a risk to the account holder if they set up the payment authority using incorrect details.

4 PREPARING A CHEQUE PRIOR TO DESPATCH

Once supporting documentation for a payment has been correctly authorised, it is ready for payment and the cheque must be drawn up.

- The cheque must be correctly dated with today's date. A post-dated cheque is not strictly valid. Equally, a cheque that is dated more than six months previously will be regarded as 'stale' by the bank and not valid.

- The cheque should be prepared in the name of the correct payee. This means that it should be prepared using the full business name of the recipient to be paid.

- When a cheque is prepared, not only must it be for the correct amount, but the monetary amount in numbers must agree with the amount stated in words.

- If a cheque payment is for a single invoice or cheque requisition then it is a straightforward matter of copying down the correct amount onto the cheque. However, if the cheque payment is for a number of invoices, and possibly including credit notes to offset the amount due, then they must be correctly totalled in order to arrive at the correct amount for the cheque.

4.1 EXAMPLE

A business, Smith & Co, is about to pay one of its suppliers, Manning & Sons. The **receivables** ledger record of the amounts owed to Manning & Sons is given below:

Date	Invoice number	Amount
		$
13 December	105345	382.94
18 December	105448	114.26
20 December	Credit Note 273	102.45
23 December	106293	449.11
12 January	106331	152.83
15 January	106934	119.02
28 January	107018	229.30

It is now 30 January 20X4 and Smith & Co's policy is to pay all invoices net of credit notes for the previous month.

Prepare the cheque that will be issued to Manning & Sons.

4.2 SOLUTION

Cheque amount

		$
13 December	105345	382.94
18 December	105448	114.26
20 December	Credit Note 273	(102.45)
23 December	106293	449.11
		————
		843.86
		————

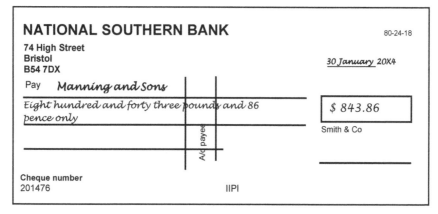

When a cheque has been written it will be removed from the cheque book, signed by the authorised signatory (or signatories) and then sent out to the payee. In order to keep a record of the amount of the cheque payment the counterfoil of the cheque should be completed. The counterfoil of the cheque is the small perforated section that remains in the cheque book when the cheque is removed.

The details to be included on the counterfoil are:

- the date of the cheque

- the payee of the cheque

- the amount of the cheque and

- the amount of any cash discounts taken (see later).

The counterfoil for the cheque payment to Manning & Sons would look like this:

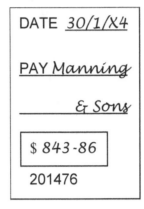

DATE *30/1/X4*

PAY *Manning*

& Sons

$ *843 -86*

201476

4.3 DESIGNATED SIGNATORIES

The individual who signs a cheque is effectively the final person to authorise that payment. The supporting documentation may be authorised and the cheque correctly prepared but it is the cheque signatory who finally signs the cheque and turns it into a valid form of payment. This highlights the importance of the cheque signatory who should be a suitably responsible person within the business. Many businesses require two designated signatories for a valid cheque.

The formalities to prepare a valid cheque, along with reliance upon designated signatories to ensure that payments are for valid business reasons help to ensure that cheque payments are secure methods of payment.

Clearly, cheque books should be retained in a secure environment unlit they are required, and signed blank cheques should ever be issued.

4.4 EXAMPLE

Each business will determine its own system of cheque signatories but a typical example may be as follows:

Amounts up to $5,000   One director

$5,001 to $10,000   Two directors

$10,001 to $20,000   One director plus the finance director

Over $20,000   Managing director/Chief executive officer plus the finance director

ACTIVITY 2

Suppose that the following cheques need to be signed as soon as possible:

	Cheque no.	Amount
		$
(a)	11723	5,379.20
(b)	11724	1,406.29
(c)	11725	293.50
(d)	11726	20,501.80

Given below are the authorised cheque signatories:

G Gammage	Finance Director
F Freud	Managing Director
P Palim	Marketing Director
T Timms	Finance Manager
S Simon	Production Manager

The cheque signatory limits are:

Amounts up to $1,000	One manager
$1,001 to $2,000	Two managers
$2,001 to $5,000	One director
$5,001 to $10,000	Two directors
$10,001 to $20,000	One director plus the finance director
Over $20,000	Managing director plus the finance director

Who can sign each of these cheques?

For a suggested answer, see the 'Answers' section at the end of the book.

5 CREDIT CARDS, DEBIT CARDS AND CONTACTLESS PAYMENTS

5.1 CREDIT CARDS

Credit cards are available in most countries and many are part of the VISA and MasterCard networks.

Credit cards may be used to purchase goods or services on credit. The customer receives a monthly statement detailing the purchases made and the amount due. If the full amount due is paid off within a specified time period there is no interest charge. However, if there is an outstanding amount remaining on the card, then interest will be charged by the credit card provider on this amount. There is sometimes also a yearly fee charged for the use of the credit card. A typical credit card is illustrated below.

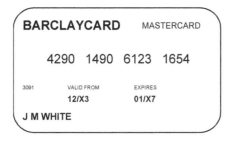
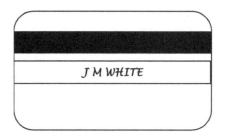

The key points to note on the front of the card are:

- the issuing company of the card (e.g. American Express, Morgan Stanley, etc.)

- the card has an individual number unique to that card

- the card will show the date from which it can be used, 'valid from' date, and the date until which it can be used, 'expiry date'. The card is not valid outside of these two dates, and

- the name of the card holder.

The reverse of the card has the following main details:

- a black magnetic strip which has encoded on it all of the details required for a computer to read the card, and

- the card holder's specimen signature.

Cards may also include additional security features such as a photograph of the account holder and holographic images. The UK has introduced a security system called 'chip and pin' under which cardholders may be asked to key in a personal four digit number when they pay with their card, rather than signing their name.

5.2 DEBIT CARDS

A debit card is a method of making a payment straight from an individual's bank account without writing a cheque.

If goods are purchased using a debit card (which looks similar to a credit card) then the card is processed in the same way as a credit card with a voucher being signed by the purchaser. The difference is that the purchaser's bank account is debited immediately with the amount of the purchase.

Depending upon the type of debit card that is used, the processing will take place either through the credit card system or through an EFTPOS (Electronic Funds Transfer at Point of Sale) system. EFTPOS enables the instant transfer of funds from the bank account of the purchaser to the account of the seller. This method of payment is very common for payments made by individuals, for example, when shopping or purchasing goods online.

5.3 CREDIT CARDS AND CHARGE CARDS

It is worth briefly distinguishing between a credit card and a charge card.

Credit cards are designed to give the holder choice as to whether to pay off all or only some of the outstanding balance on the card at the end of each month. If a balance remains at the end of the month then the holder will be charged interest on the outstanding amount.

A charge card however differs in this respect as the balance must be cleared in full at the end of each month. Popular examples of charge cards are American Express and Diners Club. The card provider may also charge an annual fee.

As far as the retailer is concerned the procedures for accepting payment by a credit card or a charge card will be very similar.

5.4   CONTACTLESS PAYMENTS

In recent years, many banks, retailers and other entities have developed and introduced contactless methods of payment. This may be part of the increased functionality offered by a debit or credit card, or may relate to other devices such as smartcards and smartphones.

When a debit card or credit card is capable of making contactless payments, the following symbol is normally visible on the card.

Similarly, retailers will display the symbol to indicate that contactless payment can be made by their customers.

One of the principal reasons why retailers introduced methods of contactless payment is to improve the speed of making transactions without customers having to sign a receipt or to use their pin number to authorise a transaction. A retailer needs to have a point-of-sale terminal that supports contactless payments. Most modern point-of-sale terminals used by retailers support both contactless payments and payments made using pin numbers. Consequently, contactless payments are often used for transactions of a relatively low value, such as the purchase of drinks and snacks in a coffee house, or to make payment for purchases in a supermarket.

In the UK, the limit for a contactless payment was initially set at £30, subsequently rising to £45 and is currently £100. The security feature that requires pin authorisation of a payment after regular use for contactless payments has also gradually increased over time.

Smartcards may be used for a wide range of activities, including the purchase and use of travel tickets. For example, Transport for London introduced the Oyster card which is a contactless smartcard that records the purchase and use of travel tickets, including season tickets. Examples of similar smartcards that record purchase and use of travel tickets include the PRESTO card in Toronto, the MetroCard in New York and the RioCard in Rio de Janeiro.

Apple Pay uses debit or credit card information linked with the card to make payments. Payments can be made by Apple Pay when using an iPhone, iPad, Apple Watch or Mac. Google introduced a similar system for android devices called Android Pay in the United States of America in 2015 which was introduced in the United Kingdom in the following year. Both payment methods now also include the facility to make payment for purchases within apps. It is possible to use Apple Pay or Android Pay for purchase transactions in excess of the contactless payment limit, in which case it is treated as a normal debit or credit card payment.

As with any payment system, it is essential that there are robust and reliable controls that minimise the risk of error or abuse resulting from loss or theft of any card or device which can be used for contactless payments. One key security feature is that the retailer does not have access to the customer credit or credit card number.

Controls that may be applied relating to the security of contactless payments include the following:

- customer choice whether or not to make contactless payments

- the customer has the right to request a receipt as evidence that the transaction that has taken place

- the customer has the right to challenge or query the legitimacy of a contactless payment that appears on their statement

- a maximum monetary limit placed on the value of a contactless payment – either by paying bank or by the retailer to limit their exposure to risk of loss resulting from misuse of lost or stolen cards

- a limit or restriction on the number of contactless payments that can be made before the bank or credit card company require authorisation of a transaction (e.g. by the customer using their 'chip-and-pin' number) to confirm that they are the valid user of the card

- data transmitted following authorisation of a transaction is encrypted and only the paying bank or card company will be able to match the transaction code with the account holder.

6 AUTOMATED BANK PAYMENTS

An automated bank payment is a transfer of money from one bank account to another, without the need for a paper 'transfer document' such as a cheque. Automated payments are often more convenient than paying by cheque. Standing orders and direct debits are common forms of automated payment. Another is BACS.

6.1 BACS PAYMENTS

BACS stands for Banks Automated Clearing System. It is a system for making payments between bank accounts of different banks that reduces the amount of paperwork and effort required.

BACS is used:

- for direct debit payments

- for standing order payments

- to make salary payments to employees

- to make payments to regular suppliers (whose banking details are known by the payer).

It is possible to instruct a bank to make BACS payments using a paper instruction, called a BACS payment listing. An example is shown overleaf.

NATIONAL SOUTHERN BANK

74 High Street, Bristol B54 7DX   Sort Code 80-24-18

BACS Payment Listing

Payment ref:	BACS
Name of customer:	ABC Trading Ltd Downland Road Twyford Berks
Account number:	27446879
Date:	

Authority is hereby given to National Southern Bank to make the following payments by BACS transfer from the account designated above.

Payee	Sort code	Account number	Amount $
		Total	

Please make these payments as soon as possible and debit our account with the total shown above

Authorised signature   Date

Most businesses send the instructions by computer disk to a BACS reception centre, or by electronic communication. This electronic data is then processed at a BACS processing centre, and the payments are then made 'automatically' through the banking system.

7 UNUSUAL FEATURES OF RECEIPTS AND PAYMENTS MEDIA AND DOCUMENTATION

In a perfect world, nothing goes wrong. Ideally, when payments are received from a customer, they should be processed without any difficulty or complication. From time to time, however, unusual situations might arise.

- A **cheque may be incorrectly completed** by the customer. When payments by cheque are received through the post, the accounts department should ensure that the cheque has been correctly prepared.

  If a cheque has been incorrectly completed, it should be returned to the customer. N such circumstances, there is usually an office procedure to follow to deal appropriately with the situation.

- **Out-of-date cheques.** A cheque that is more than six months out of date will not be processed by the bank. It would be unusual for any cheque to be more than just a few days old. However, there are occasions when a customer writes the wrong year on a cheque. This is often accidental, such as early in a new year. Sometimes, a customer may write in the wrong year deliberately, hoping to delay payment by completing the cheque incorrectly. Out-of-date cheques should be returned to the customer.

- **Credit card limits exceeded.** When a customer pays by credit card, the credit card company may refuse the payment because the customer's credit card limit has been exceeded. When a customer tries to pay by card in a shop, the payment will be rejected immediately by the automated checking system.

However, when a customer pays by post, for example by completing an order form which includes credit card details, the payment will not be rejected until later.

The credit card payment will be submitted to the bank, but will then be returned when the credit card company rejects it. On receiving notification of a rejected payment, the customer should be informed and asked to pay the amount due by a different method.

A supervisor should be informed of unusual situations with large payments because the customer could be deliberately delaying payment, or the attempt at payment may even be fraudulent – for example, a customer may try to pay with a stolen credit card.

7.1 PAYMENT DISAGREES WITH SUPPORTING DOCUMENTATION

Sometimes the amount of a payment may disagree with the supporting documentation. For example:

- A customer may pay an invoice, but send in a payment for the wrong amount. Checking the amount of the payment against the invoice or the customer's ledger account record will reveal this error.

- A customer may claim a settlement discount, but calculate the discount incorrectly, and so pay the wrong amount, for example, $90 instead of $95.

In situations where a credit customer is entitled to settlement discount in excess of what has already been accounted for, this will normally be resolved by issuing a credit note to the customer for the additional settlement discount they are entitled to.

Mistakes of this kind can be corrected by referring the problem back to the customer. A general rule ought to be, however, that a business should bank the payments it receives, and deal with any issues or discrepancies later. For example, suppose that a business receives a payment of $950 in settlement of an invoice but. on checking. it is discovered that the invoice is for $960. The procedure should be to bank the payment for $950 immediately, and contact the customer to request the remaining $10.

It would be **bad business practice** to:

- send the incorrect payment back and ask for the correct payment in full, or

- hold on to the payment received without banking it, until the error is corrected.

Occasionally, you may be asked to **check the money from a cash register** against the recorded sales from the till roll. The amount of cash collected may be less than the total sales recorded by the cash register. If this happened, some money – possibly notes and coins – have gone missing. It is possible that it may have been stolen. The appropriate course of action may seem obvious:

- carry out the check again, to make sure that you did not make a mistake when counting the money received.

- calculate the amount of money that seems to be missing.

- inform the supervisor.

7.2 REIMBURSEMENT OF EXPENSES TO EMPLOYEES

Problems may also arise in relation to claims made by employees for reimbursement of expenses. Such problems could fall into one of three categories as considered below.

- The claim for payment may not have been authorised in advance. For example, an employee may have purchased some stationery for the office and is now seeking reimbursement, without having formerly sought prior authorisation.

- There may be insufficient supporting evidence. For example, the employee may be claiming for reimbursement of a train fare incurred for attending a training course, but they have failed to produce a receipt or ticket.

- The claim exceeds the employee's authorised limits. For example, an employee may have been required to work away and was advised not to spend more than $40 per night on an evening meal. The employee subsequently produces an expense claim for $50 per night.

Procedures should be in place to ensure that any claim falling under the above headings is referred to a higher-level signatory to review and decide upon whether it should be paid, than the decided upon by the usual signatory. This means that a more senior employee than the person who usually approves of the expenses is required to authorise them. They must treat each claim on a case-by-case basis. This means that they must look at the circumstances surrounding the breach of rules before deciding whether reimbursement should be made.

For example, the employee buying stationery without prior authorisation may have needed, for example, a printer cartridge in order to print documents to meet a deadline. The employee may have attempted to contact a more senior employee for authorisation and been unable to contact an appropriate person. It would be unfair if such reimbursement was to be denied. Alternatively, the employee may have purchased unnecessary items that were not required, in which case reimbursement should be denied.

ACTIVITY 3

---

1   Which form of payment allows a purchaser to immediately transfer money from their bank account to the seller's bank account?

    A   Cheque payment

    B   Charge card

    C   Credit card

    D   Debit card

2   Which form of automated payment would be useful in paying wages to employees?

    A   BACS

    B   Credit transfer

    C   Direct debit

    D   Standing order

3 In which of the following instances would a different form of payment be requested for the purchase of goods costing $40?

A When a customer pays by cheque

B When a customer's credit card company states that the transaction would exceed the set credit limit

C When a customer pays by $1 and $2 coins

D When a customer is only able to pay by debit card

For a suggested answer, see the 'Answers' section at the end of the book.

8 BANKING MONIES RECEIVED

Payments from customers sometimes go straight into the bank account of the business. Money received through direct debit payments and standing orders, and money received in BACS payments go straight into the bank account. These receipts must be checked, and recorded in the accounting records of the business.

In a similar way, payments received by credit card through a website are handled automatically by the computer system that processes the payments. A printout is produced of the payments received, but the money goes automatically into the business bank account.

However, when payments are received in notes or coin, or by cheque, the money has to be banked.

8.1 PAYING-IN SLIPS

When money is paid into a bank account, the payments should be accompanied by a paying-in slip. A paying-in slip gives details of:

- the quantities of banknotes and coins paid in

- each cheque paid in

- the total amount paid in.

An **example of a bank paying-in slip** is shown on the following page. If you have your own bank account, you should have paying-in slips of your own, either at the back of your cheque book or in a separate booklet of paying-in slips from the bank. There are often blank paying-in slips available in most bank branches, although, increasingly, modern technology removes the need for a written record of amounts paid in, with receipts issued by email to the customer.

As illustrated on the following page, the front side of a paying-in slip gives details of the business bank account, together with a summary of the notes and coins being paid in and the total value of the cheques. The term 'silver' refers to small silver coins of 5c and 10c denomination, and 'bronze' refers to 1c and 2c coins.

Bank Giro Credit

Date:	29/4/X4										$50	50	00

Code No.	82 09 54								
Bank	National Western Bank								
Branch	Bristol								
Account in the name of	Smith & Co								
Account No.	1	2	3	4	5	6	8	2	1
Number of cheques	3								
Fee	Paid in by / Ref:								
	PLEASE DO NOT WRITE BELOW THIS LINE								

$50	50	00
$20	60	00
$10	30	00
$5	0	00
$2	0	00
$1	5	00
50c	1	50
20c	0	00
Silver	0	25
Bronze	0	05
Total cash	146	80
Cheques POs, etc.	416	90
$	563	70

The reverse side of the paying-in slip is used to itemise the individual cheques. Similar forms are used, with appropriate changes for relevant currency, in other countries.

Cheques, POs, etc			Brought forward			Brought forward		
30-14-16 Cheque 105326	129	00						
42-08-61 Cheque 215371	81	70						
04-26-35 Cheque 352714	206	20						
Total carried forward			Total carried forward					
						Carried over $	416	90

8.2 PAYING NOTES AND COINS AND CHEQUES INTO A BANK ACCOUNT

To pay notes and coins and cheques into a bank account, the procedures are therefore to:

- Count the notes and coins correctly, and enter the details on the paying-in slip. Many businesses put coins into special bags provided by the bank.

- Write cheque details on the back of the paying-in slip.

- Total the cheque payments and enter this amount on the front side of the paying-in slip, together with the grand total of the amount being banked.

- Take the cash and cheques to the bank and pay it in. When large amounts are involved, a business may hire a security firm to take money to the bank.

Example: paying in notes and coins

The contents of a till have been checked and counted at the end of a day. The numbers of each type of note and coin are as follows:

Note/coin	Number
$50	2
$20	43
$10	159
$5	147
$2	20
$1	53
50c	52
20c	226
10c	367
5c	158
2c	362
1c	273

The business will keep a cash float, to put in the till at the start of the next day. The cash float for the following day remains in the business's safe overnight. The remaining cash is paid into the bank, using the night deposit box at the local branch of the bank.

Task 1

Work out the total amount of cash from the till for that day.

Task 2

The cash float for the following day is to be made up of 10 × $5 notes, 5 × $2 coins, 10 × $1 coins, 10 × 50c coins, 50 × 20c coins, 100 × 10c coins, 100 × 5c coins, 100 × 2c coins and 100 × 1c coins.

Prepare the bank paying-in slip for the amounts of cash to be paid in to the night safe.

Solution

Task 1

Note/coin	Number	Amount
		$
$50	2	100.00
$20	43	860.00
$10	159	1,590.00
$5	147	735.00
$2	20	40.00
$1	53	53.00
50p	52	26.00
20p	226	45.20
10p	367	36.70
5p	158	7.90
2p	362	7.24
1p	273	2.73
		————
		3,503.77
		————

Task 2

Note/coin	Number in till	Number for cash float	Number to be paid in to bank	Amount $
$50	2	–	2	100.00
$20	43	–	43	860.00
$10	159	–	159	1,590.00
$5	147	10	137	685.00
$2	20	5	15	30.00
$1	53	10	43	43.00
50c	52	10	42	21.00
20c	226	50	176	35.20
10c	367	100	267	26.70
5c	158	100	58	2.90
2c	362	100	262	5.24
1c	273	100	173	1.73
				————
Total				3,400.77
				————

Workings

		$			$
Silver	10c	26.70	Bronze	2c	5.24
	5c	2.90		1c	1.73
		————			————
		29.60			6.97
		————			————

Bank Giro Credit

Date: _____

Code No.	82 09 54
Bank	National Western Bank
Branch	Bristol
Account in the name of	
Account No.	
Number of cheques	
Fee	Paid in by / Ref:

PLEASE DO NOT WRITE BELOW THIS LINE

C3 OD92157A   C77

$50	100	00
$20	860	00
$10	1,590	00
$5	685	00
$2	30	00
$1	43	00
50c	21	00
20c	35	20
Silver	29	60
Bronze	6	97
Total cash	3,400	77
Cheques POs, etc.		
$		

8.3 CHECKING PAYING-IN SLIPS AGAINST RELEVANT DOCUMENTATION

The paying-in slip documents the amount of cash, cheques, and credit card vouchers paid into the bank account. Any discrepancy between the amounts of cash, cheques, and credit card vouchers paid in and the documented amounts on the paying-in slip should be identified and queried by the bank. If any errors have been made on the paying-in slip then this will cause problems with the bank and could lead to a delay in processing the payment into the business bank account.

It is therefore important that the paying-in slip is correct. Once completed, the paying-in slip should be reconciled to appropriate supporting documentation for each method of payment.

- The total amount of notes and coins entered onto the paying-in slip should agree with the total of notes and coins counted from the cash register, less any cash float retained for the next day.

- The individual amounts and totals for **cheques** that are entered onto the paying-in slip should be checked either to the original cheques or to any cheque listing or remittance list drawn up. Any cheque listing or remittance list should have been checked against the original cheques when it was prepared.

- The amount entered as a total for **credit card vouchers** should be checked against the card summary for accuracy. The summary of vouchers should, in turn, have been checked against the credit card vouchers when it was prepared.

8.4 BANKING CREDIT CARD PAYMENTS

Credit card payments may also need to be paid into a bank account. For example, a shop needs to bank its credit card payments from customers. With credit card payments:

- A summary of the credit card voucher payments needs to be prepared for the credit card company. This is handed into the bank.

- In addition, the total amount of credit card payments is included in the paying-in slip, together with the list of cheques and the total for cheque payments.

A card summary is a document giving details of the credit card payments being banked. This is a typical illustration of a card summary.

```
┌──────────────────────────────────────────────────────────────────┐
│  ┌──────────────────────────────────┐                              │
│  │ HAVE YOU IMPRINTED THE SUMMARY   │                              │
│  │ WITH YOUR RETAILER'S CARD?       │                              │
│  └──────────────────────────────────┘                             │
│  Bank Processing (White)                                           │
│  copy of Summary with your           ┌─────────┬─────────┐         │
│  vouchers in correct order:          │ ITEMS   │ AMOUNT  │         │
│                            ┌─────────┼─────────┼─────────┤         │
│  1.  SUMMARY               │ SALES VOUCHERS    │         │         │
│  2.  SALES VOUCHERS        │ (LISTED OVERLEAF) │         │         │
│  3.  REFUND VOUCHERS       │         │         │         │         │
│  KEEP Retailer's copies    │ LESS REFUND       │         │         │
│  (Blue & Yellow)           │ VOUCHERS│         │         │         │
│  NO MORE THAN 200          │         │         │         │         │
│  Vouchers to each Summary. │ DATE    │ TOTAL $ │         │         │
│  DO NOT USE Staples, Pins  │         │         │         │         │
│  Paper Clips                                                       │
│  NORTH BANK                   BANKING                              │
│                               SUMMARY                             │
│                                      ─────────────────            │
│                                      RETAILER'S SIGNATURE         │
│  ┌──────────────────────────────────────────────────────────┐   │
│  │ Complete this summary for every deposit of sales vouchers │   │
│  │ and enter the total on you normal current account         │   │
│  │ paying-in slip.                                           │   │
│  └──────────────────────────────────────────────────────────┘   │
└──────────────────────────────────────────────────────────────────┘
                                          SUMMARY – RETAILER'S COPY
```

- The front of the document gives the total of payments, less refund vouchers. (A refund voucher is produced when a customer returns goods to a retailer. The original credit card sales voucher remains valid, but a refund voucher is issued to cancel out the sales voucher.) The 'Items' column is for entering the **number** of sales vouchers and refund vouchers.

- The reverse side of the summary lists the amounts of the credit card vouchers and (if any) the refund vouchers.

	$	c	
1			
2			
3			
4			
5			
6			
7			
8			
9			
10			
11			
12			DO NOT TICK OR MAKE ANY MARKS OUTSIDE THE LISTING AREA
13			
14			
15			
16			
17			
18			
19			
20			
Total			Carried overleaf

Most businesses accept payments from both Visa and MasterCard. If so, a **separate summary voucher is needed for each type of card**.

The summary voucher must also be imprinted with the retailer's own card details, such as the retailer's name and its account number with the credit card company.

After the card summary has been filled in, the total of the payments (less refunds) is copied onto the reverse side of the paying-in slip, and added to the total of payments by cheque etc.

The credit card vouchers, the card summary and the paying-in slip are then all handed in to the bank.

9 HANDLING, STORAGE AND SECURITY OF MONEY

9.1 WHEN TO PAY MONEY IN TO THE BANK

It is not always possible to bank money received on the same day. However, unless only small amounts are involved, the aim should be to bank payments received as soon as possible.

Money should be banked as soon as possible, for two reasons:

- If payments are not banked, there is a risk of theft or loss.

- Paying money into the bank as soon as possible helps to keep the bank overdraft lower, and so minimises interest and finance charges.

Many bank branches have a night safe system, which allows deposits to be put into the bank after the bank has been closed for the day. A business can therefore make payments into a bank by putting the cash, cheques, card vouchers, paying-in slip and card voucher summaries into the bank's night safe. The bank will find the items in the morning and process the payments.

Many businesses prefer to use a night safe rather than hold money in the office overnight, to reduce the risk of theft or loss.

9.2 SECURITY MEASURES

When cash is held on business premises, it is important to keep it secure. For example:

- If a significant amount of cash is held on the premises overnight, it should be kept in a safe, rather than a desk drawer.

- Notes and coins should never be left lying around on desktops or in unlocked drawers. Even small amounts could easily be lost or stolen.

- When an individual is given the task of taking cash to the bank to pay it in, the physical safety of that person should be considered. When very large amounts of cash are involved, the business may hire a security firm to handle payments into the bank. If an employee does the banking, a security measure may be for the employee to be accompanied by someone else. It is also sensible to use different routes to the bank and also different trusted employees. There are instances where long-trusted employees who are routinely employed in banking are influenced by disreputable individuals or, indeed, who suddenly disappear with funds.

It is just as important for a business to ensure safe custody of cheques and remittances received from customers so that they can be properly accounted for and banked. One procedure that a business may adopt to ensure that all monies (including cheques and remittances received) are properly accounted for is to implement a system of segregation of duties between members of staff who may have access to cash, cheques and remittances in order to fulfil their work responsibilities e.g. to update the cash and bank records.

For example, the post received each morning should be opened in the presence of two persons, and a list made of cheques and remittances received. A different individual should then be responsible for updating the cash and bank records. Ideally, the update of other accounting records, such as the general ledger and the individual receivables' ledger accounts should also be performed by different persons.

By allocating responsibility to different members of staff for recording different aspects of a transaction, the risk of error or omission (whether deliberate or unintentional) should be reduced. It is recognised that this may not be possible to achieve in smaller businesses, but elements of this process can normally be adopted in most businesses to minimise the risk of loss or theft or errors in the receipt and recording of cheques and remittances received from customers.

ACTIVITY 4

Here is a final comprehensive exercise relating to paying cash into the bank.

At the end of 16 July 20X5 the cash, cheques and card vouchers from the tills of Bensons Retailers were counted and checked. The total amounts are to be paid into the bank account and the paying-in slip must therefore be prepared.

The card summary for North Bank card vouchers has already been prepared and is also presented below.

The amount of cash to be paid into the bank is made up as follows

Note/coins	Number
$50	1
$20	2
$10	17
$5	51
$2	40
$1	89
50c	258
20c	391
10c	307
5c	219
2c	381
1c	245

The cheques paid into the till during the day have been listed as

Drawer	Amount $
Unifloss Ltd	279.30
A Amad	27.18
H Knight	55.19
P Dilip	104.72
N C Fisher	31.95
L Lister	82.82
Z Szolai	131.04

	$	c	
1	101	23	
2	78	19	
3	11	21	
4	41	30	
5	(11	29)	
6	5	97	
7	23	30	
8	10	00	
9			
10			DO NOT TICK OR MAKE ANY MARKS OUTSIDE THE LISTING AREA
11			
12			
13			
14			
15			
16			
17			
18			
19			
20			
Total	259	91	Carried overleaf

Benson Retailers banks with the Brighton branch of Aylesford bank (sort code 16 39 64) and its account number is 17234552.

Complete the paying-in slip given below for the banking for 16 July 20X5.

Cheques, POs, etc			Brought forward			Brought forward		
Total carried forward			Total carried forward					

Date ——————   Account ——————   Carried over $ ____

Bank Giro Credit

Date: _____

			$50	
Code No.	16 39 64		$20	
Bank	Aylesford Bank		$10	
Branch	Brighton		$5	
Account in the name of			$2	
			$1	
Account No.			50c	
Number of cheques			20c	
Fee	Paid in by / Ref:		Silver	
			Bronze	
			Total cash	
			Cheques POs, etc.	
	PLEASE DO NOT WRITE BELOW THIS LINE			
			$	

C3 0D92157A   C77

For a suggested answer, see the 'Answers' section at the end of the book.

10 BANKS AND BANKING INSTITUTIONS

10.1 SERVICES OFFERED BY BANKS

High street (or 'retail') banks are usually regarded as providers of a range of banking services to individuals and businesses. This includes operation of cheque or current account services, along with a range of savings and loan account services. Banks are normally subject to strict regulation by government, including authorisation to operate and regular monitoring and supervision to minimise the risk of bank failure or inappropriate conduct. In recent years, the distinction between the services offered by high street banks and other banking institutions has become less marked. However, it is still useful to consider the services traditionally offered by retails banks and other banking institutions.

The range of services provided by banks normally includes the following:

- current account operation, including cheque and payment clearing facilities

- provision of loan and overdraft facilities

- savings accounts and related products

- foreign exchange and currency services

- provision of safe custody or security facilities

- financial advice to individuals and businesses.

10.2 TELEPHONE AND INTERNET BANKING

Most banks now offer personal and business bank accounts that allow telephone and online banking, with some bank accounts based solely upon telephone and internet activity, rather than using the traditional bank branch network to transact business. Such accounts enable the account holder to make regular or ad hoc payments to others provided that they have the bank account details of the intended recipient. Similarly, third parties can make direct payments into another bank account without the need to write and post cheques or visit a bank branch.

Additionally, businesses are now more willing to disclose their bank account details to customers so that they can make direct payment into a nominated bank account following the supply of goods and services. Some businesses also have the facility to integrate the bank account with their accounting systems so that accounting records are automatically updated to reflect payments received from customers. Note that the ACCA FA1 syllabus and exam assumes that the bank account is not integrated with accounting systems.

Note that telephone and internet banking is simply another way for account holders to initiate or authorise a range of payments (such as direct payments and standing orders) or to access bank services (such as ordering foreign currency).

Confidentiality and security of data is clearly an important issue for the operation of such accounts. Typically, controls focus upon ensuring that only the account holder can gain access to the bank account details, including the ability to review transactions and statements and entering into new transactions. Although the detail of which controls are applied and operated by an individual bank may differ, they normally have common features.

For example, there may be a multiple-stage access process applying controls such as passwords, pin numbers, personal security questions and account history questions.

To minimise the risk of an account holder making an incorrect payment, there are usually standard template documents to complete to provide the account details of the intended recipient. As the documents are completed, there will normally be a 'logic checks' applied by the bank to ensure that the information appears to be complete, such as checking that the six-digit bank sort code has been provided and falls within accepted number ranges. The account holder is usually asked to check and confirm that the details submitted are correct and complete before the payment request is accepted by the bank. Finally, the bank may also contact the account holder, perhaps using their mobile phone, to send an automated voice or text message stating that a new payment authorisation has been set up and to contact the bank immediately if they have not initiated this account activity.

10.3 SERVICES OFFERED BY BANKING INSTITUTIONS

In addition to high street banks, there are other banking institutions involved in banking activities to a greater or lesser extent. These institutions often focus upon a specialised range of banking activity, rather than providing the broad range of services offered by high street banks. The range of services provided by banking institutions may include the following:

- accepting savings or deposits from customers

- lending money subject to specified criteria or within specified parameters

- providing mortgage facilities

- providing leasing and hire purchase facilities

- providing factoring and invoice discounting services

- providing letters of credit to businesses involved with importing or exporting

- merchant or investment banking activities to provide finance to businesses

- corporate finance advice to businesses.

CONCLUSION

Banks are very important to businesses, providing a convenient and secure place to keep funds and also a source of financing when a business is short of cash. In this chapter you have seen how cheques, standing orders and direct debits as well as debit cards are useful ways to pay for goods and services. In addition, credit and charge cards are convenient payment devices too.

Generally most transactions are completed correctly and the cash, cheques, credit card vouchers and so on can be paid into the business bank account using appropriate forms. However, an awareness of problems which can occur may help to identify and avoid potential problems at an early stage. For example, if a cheque is received from a customer, it should be reviewed to ensure that it is complete (e.g. properly prepared, signed and dated, with the amount in words and figures agreed) before it is processed and banked, to avoid having to deal with a cheque returned by the bank.

All transfers of cash, cheques and so on within a business and in transit to the bank need to be handled with care and with appropriate security to avoid loss, theft or destruction and to provide a transaction trail.

KEY TERMS

BACS – Automated payments by bank transfer. BACS is commonly used to pay salaries to employees and to pay regular suppliers.

Charge card – A charge card is similar to a credit card, however, the balance must be paid in full every month.

Credit card – A form of payment whereby the cardholder makes payment to a retailer from an agreed credit facility. The outstanding amount is settled by the cardholder to the credit card company.

Crossed cheque – A cheque is crossed by drawing two parallel vertical lines on it. A crossed cheque must be paid into a bank account.

Debit card – Payment medium allowing instant payment from a customer's bank account to a retailer electronically.

Designated signatory – Person authorised to sign a cheque in defined circumstances.

Direct debit – Order to a bank to make regular payments out of a bank account. The amounts to be paid are notified to the bank by the payee (the account holder having given written authority to the bank for the payee to do this).

Drawer of a cheque – Account holder of person/business writing a cheque.

Payee – The person being paid.

Standing order – An order to a bank to make regular payments out of a bank account. The amount to be paid is notified by the account holder.

SELF TEST QUESTIONS

		Paragraph
1	What is the relationship that exists between a bank and its customer?	1
2	State an obligation a bank has to its customers.	1
3	Explain how a central bank clearing system works.	2
4	Identify three separate items which appear on a cheque.	3
5	What does it mean when a cheque is crossed with 'A/c payee'?	3
6	What is meant by endorsing a cheque?	3
7	Give two examples of payments that may be made by direct debit and standing order.	3
8	What details appear on a cheque counterfoil?	4
9	What is meant by a designated signatory?	4
10	Distinguish between a credit card and a debit card.	5
11	What are BACS payments usually used for?	6
12	Explain what makes a cheque invalid.	7

13 Why is it important to reconcile a paying-in slip with its appropriate
supporting documentation?   8

14 Are credit card vouchers included on the normal paying-in slip when paying
in money at the bank?   8

15 Why should businesses try to pay monies received into their bank account
as promptly as possible?   9

16 State a procedure that would improve the security of taking cash to the bank.   9

EXAM-STYLE QUESTIONS

1   What is the bank clearing system?

A   Agreeing a loan or overdraft between bank and customer

B   The transfer of cheques between the payee's bank to payment at the drawer's
bank

C   The electronic transfer of funds enabling a supplier to be instantly paid by debit
card

D   Checking customer references before they are given a credit card

2   Which is unique to a bank customer?

A   Account number

B   Cheque number

C   Drawee

D   Sort code

3   A parent makes a regular monthly payment from their account to their child's bank
account to cover living expenses during their time at college or university.

What method of payment is the parent using?

A   'Account payee' crossed cheque

B   BACS

C   Direct debit

D   Standing order

4   A bank dishonours a cheque on a partnership account because there are insufficient
funds on the account. Who must now pay the outstanding amount?

A   The bank

B   The partnership

C   The payee of the cheque

D   The person who was the authorised signatory

5   When banking cash, general security procedures should be followed wherever possible. Which of the following is the most risky?

    A   Ensuring that the employee taking the cash to the bank or night safe is accompanied by another employee

    D   Going to the bank or the night safe at different times of day or by a different route

    C   Using the same responsible employee to take the cash to the bank

    D   Using a security firm to transport the cash to the bank if necessary

For suggested answers, see the 'Answers' section at the end of the book.

Chapter 6

PAYROLL

For many businesses, a major item of expense is the cost of its workforce, referred to as 'payroll costs'. This chapter explains how wages and salary payments are calculated and paid. It covers the syllabus area for payroll.

This chapter covers syllabus areas D1.

CONTENTS

1   Payroll system

2   Processing the payroll

3   Basic pay calculations

4   Overtime pay, bonuses and commission

5   Authorisation

6   Security and control

7   Accounting for payroll

LEARNING OUTCOMES

At the end of this chapter, you should be able to:

*   understand payroll systems

*   understand the duties of employers in relation to taxes, state benefit contributions and other deductions

*   record hours worked: timesheets, clock cards

*   calculate gross wages for employees paid by hour, by output (piecework) and salaried workers

*   define and calculate bonuses, overtime and commission, given the details of each scheme

*   describe the documentation required for recording the various elements of wages and salaries

*   recognise the need for payroll to be authorised and identify appropriate authorisation, security and control procedures

- make other deductions from wages – trade union subscriptions, payroll saving, pension contributions and payroll giving

- identify various methods for making payments to employees

- account for payroll costs and payroll deductions.

1 PAYROLL SYSTEM

The payroll is a list of the employees of the business and the money due to each.

A payroll list is produced each time that employees are paid.

- Wage earners are paid weekly.

- Salary earners are paid monthly.

Sometimes, employees earn a fixed amount every week or every month. Sometimes there are variations in the amount employees earn, due to overtime payments or bonuses or commissions which add to their pay.

1.1 GROSS PAY AND NET PAY: DEDUCTIONS

The total amount earned in a week or month by an employee is referred to as **gross pay**.

This is not the amount of money that the employee receives, because deductions are made from the gross pay, and the employee receives only the gross pay less deductions. This is known as the employee's **net pay**.

The deductions from pay are usually a combination of:

- statutory deductions, and

- non-statutory or voluntary deductions.

Statutory deductions are deductions from pay that are required to be made by law, for example: income tax and social security. These deductions from gross pay are made by the employer and paid to the relevant taxation authority. In this situation an employer acts as the agent of the taxation authority, both calculating and collecting taxation and social security amounts due from the employee.

For example; in the UK income tax for employees is deducted under the 'Pay As You Earn' scheme along with National Insurance and paid over to HM Revenue and Customs by employers.

Non-statutory deductions are voluntary deductions from pay that the employee chooses to make.

	$
Gross pay	A
Less:	
Statutory deductions	(B)
Non-statutory deductions	(C)
	———
Net pay or 'take-home' pay	A – B – C
	———

What this means is that when an employee is paid, only the net pay or take-home pay is received, and the employer pays the other amounts deducted to other businesses ('external agencies') such as the tax authority, trade union or pension management company as appropriate.

1.2 NON-STATUTORY DEDUCTIONS

The employee may authorise the employer to make other 'non-statutory' deductions from their earnings Examples are:

(a)   pension contributions

(b)   deductions under a payroll charitable donation scheme

(c)   deductions under a payroll savings scheme

(d)   trade union subscriptions

(e)   deductions under holiday pay schemes

(f)   certain other voluntary deductions agreed by the employer (for example, fees for use of the company sports club).

ACTIVITY 1

The following figures have been extracted from a trader's records in respect of wages and salaries for the month of July:

(i)   Wages and salaries (gross) $6,300

(ii)   Income tax $1,600

(iii)   Employees' pension contributions $600

(iv)   Employer's pension contributions $700

1   What is the total amount the trader will have to pay for wages and salaries for July?

   A $4,100

   B $4,800

   C $6,300

   D $7,000

2   What is the net pay received by employees?

   A $4,100

   B $4,200

   C $4,800

   D $5,600

For a suggested answer, see the 'Answers' section at the end of the book.

2 PROCESSING THE PAYROLL

To process the payroll, for each employee, an employer must:

- calculate the gross wage or salary for the period

- calculate the income tax payable out of these earnings

- calculate the employee's state benefit contributions that are deductible

- calculate any non-statutory deductions

- prepare a payslip showing the gross pay, deductions and net pay

- make the payment of net pay to the employee

- calculate the employer's state benefit contributions payable to the tax authority.

For all employees collectively, the employer must:

- make the payments of all the deductions from pay plus the employer's state benefit contributions to the appropriate businesses

- record the payroll costs in the accounting system.

2.1 PAYSLIPS

A payslip will accompany each payment of salary or wages to an employee. It shows how the amount paid has been arrived at and how much has been deducted in relation to statutory deductions for taxation and social security. Other, non-statutory, deductions will also be shown on the payslip.

An employee receiving a payslip means that, even if the employee receives wages or salary payments directly into a nominated bank account, the employee is notified of the payment and how much it is, upon receiving the payslip. Payslips may be distributed to employees at work, posted to their home address or available via the employer's secure website.

A payslip must show details of:

- gross pay

- deductions (itemised separately)

- net pay (net pay is sometimes called 'take-home pay').

However, there isn't a standard layout for a payslip and so payslips of different employers can look very different.

An example is shown below:

Dickson Engineering					
Employee:		T C a r d e w		**Employee no.**	
NI No:	TY 45 67 78 L	Tax code: 473L		Date: 11/01/X4	Tax period: Wk 40
PAY FOR WEEK ENDING: **11/01/X4**		**Hours**	**Rate** $	**AMOUNT** $	
Basic		40.0	7.50	300.00	
Overtime		5.0	15.00	75.00	
Shift allowance		2	10.00	20.00	
GROSS PAY				**395.00**	
Pension (Employer's pension contribution $25.00)				15.00	Year to date $
Trade union subscription				10.00	
TOTAL PAY				**370.00**	**16,605.00**
PAYE				57.92	2,711.32
Employees' social security (Employer's social security $36.71)				30.85	
NET PAY				**281.23**	

2.2   MAKING PAYMENTS TO EMPLOYEES

Most employers will have a set day on which employees are usually paid, and it is the payroll department's responsibility to ensure that wages are paid on the correct due days.

Weekly paid employees will be paid at least once a week, normally on the same day each week. Usually the pay day will be either Thursday or Friday.

Monthly paid employees will be paid once a month, and there will be a formula for determining the pay day. For example, this may be:

- the last day of the calendar month

- the last Thursday or Friday of the calendar month

- the same date each month, such as the 26th.

Employees may be paid their wages in several ways:

- in cash (but this is now less common)

- by cheque payable to the employee

- by bank giro transfer

- through the Banks Automated Clearing System (BACS).

Making payments by these methods has been described in an earlier chapter.

2.3 PAYMENTS TO OUTSIDE AGENCIES

Payments to outside agencies, such as the tax authority, pension management companies and trade unions are made regularly by employers on behalf of employees when statutory and non-statutory deductions have been made. The supporting documentation for these payments is the payroll itself. When these payments are made, they must be recorded in the bank general ledger account.

ACTIVITY 2

---

1   Which of the following does not appear on a payslip?

    A   Gross weekly wage for the employee

    B   Tax paid to date by the employee in the tax year

    C   Deductions paid by the employee

    D   Details of the employee's expected pension

2   Which is the most convenient way for a large employer to pay salaries electronically?

    A   BACS

    B   Bank giro transfer

    C   By cash

    D   By cheque

For a suggested answer, see the 'Answers' section at the end of the book.

3   BASIC PAY CALCULATIONS

3.1 ELEMENTS OF GROSS PAY

The amount of pay to which an employee is entitled may be earned in a variety of different ways, including:

(a)   Basic pay, such as:

    (i)   wages paid according to the number of hours worked

    (ii)   salaries (usually a fixed amount and paid monthly)

    (iii)   wages paid according to the output of the employee.

(b)   Other pay, such as:

    (i)   overtime pay, for extra hours worked by the employee

    (ii)   shift pay, to compensate for unsocial hours.

(c)   Bonuses and commission, such as:

    (i)   bonuses paid under bonus schemes, based on productivity, or profitability

    (ii)   commission paid, normally based on sales.

3.2 BASIC PAY FOR HOURLY PAID EMPLOYEES

Some employees are paid on the basis of a set amount for every hour that they work. This may be so even if they have agreed to work a certain number of hours per week. If hours in excess of the agreed amount have been worked, or hours are worked outside set times, they may be paid at a different rate, as overtime. Overtime is discussed more fully later.

Workers paid on the basis of an hourly rate normally receive their pay weekly.

3.3 RECORDING HOURS

If an employee is paid according to the number of hours worked, there must be a method of recording the hours worked.

The exact method will vary according to the type and size of the employer, but some examples are described below.

(a) **Clock cards**

Each employee has an individual card which is inserted into a machine at the start of the working day, and again at the end of the working day. The machine records on the card the times of arriving and leaving work.

An example of the format of a clock card is given below. In this example the employee has 'clocked on' at 08.49 on Monday morning by inserting the clock card into a machine which stamps the time on the card. When the employee next places the card in the machine – breaking for lunch at 12.12 on Monday – the card slips further down into the machine and therefore the time stamp appears above the previous one. The employee returns to work at 12.55 on Monday and 'clocks off' at 16.42. Tuesday shows a similar pattern.

The example contains space for the payroll department to analyse the time between basic hours and overtime hours. It may also contain space to record the basic pay and overtime pay, along with deductions.

Week no . . . . Name		Ending	
Time	Day	Basic	Overtime
16.22	Tu		
13.07	Tu		
12.01	Tu		
08.29	Tu		
16.42	Mo		
12.55	Mo		
12.12	Mo		
08.49	Mo		

(b)   **'Smart' cards**

Clock cards may be replaced by smart cards. These cards record the same information, but it is recorded on a magnetic strip on the card. Smart cards may also be used for other purposes not related to the payroll.

(c)   **Timesheets**

Each employee is required to fill in a list of the hours worked on a standard form, known as a timesheet. The timesheet may require additional information, such as what tasks the employee carried out, and how long each task took. After completion, the timesheet is then, usually, authorised by the supervisor/manager.

Weekly, fortnightly or monthly timesheets may also be used. These are more common among professional salaried staff, such as solicitors or accountants, who are not paid on an hourly basis, but when the employer needs to know the time spent working on behalf of each client, so that the client can be charged accordingly. Normally the employee will need to keep daily records which are summarised, so that entries are not omitted.

A simple timesheet for an hourly paid worker may look like this:

Week no			Ending			
Name			Payroll No			
Job no	Start	Finish	Quant	Check	Hours	Cost
L12	M0830	1230				
	M1330	1700				
	T0830	1100	1,000	JK	10.00	

The timesheet should also record idle time. Idle time occurs when the employee is unable to complete a task because of something outside their control, for example waiting for a replacement part to be delivered. The cost of each job is completed later by the payroll department.

A weekly timesheet for a professional salaried employee may look like this:

Week no			Ending . . . .
Name			Staff no
Client number	Name		Hours
B088	Brown J		9.50
D301	Doe J		11.50
S111	Smith J		12.25
AA01	Administration		1.75
		Total	35.00

The weekly timesheet may contain space for daily totals, or they may be kept by the employee separately. If the employee is paid overtime, there will be space to record this on the timesheet.

In addition to calculating the amounts owed to employees, businesses need to keep track of the costs incurred in manufacturing, perhaps for cost control purposes or to arrive at a selling cost for a job or product.

One simple approach to keeping track of costs is to have a system of **job cards**. These cards may be used in circumstances where each job undertaken has the potential to be unique, such as work done on cars in garage workshops.

Each job is allocated an identifying number and the time and materials applied to it can then be recorded on the job card.

JOB COST RECORD			
Job no		Customer	
Date started		Date completed	
Materials			
Part no	Quantity used	Unit cost	Total cost
TOTAL			
Labour			
Employee no	Hours used	Hourly rate	Total cost
TOTAL			
Overhead			
TOTAL JOB COST			

Example

A garage repairing cars for customers has three employees. Whenever one of the employees is working on a car, they are required to complete a job card for that particular job. Upon completion of the job, the customer is then invoiced for the total on the job card. A typical job card for a recent repair is shown below.

JOB COST RECORD			
Job no 107/2007		Customer . . . .Bakewell	
Date started . . . . . 13/06/2007 . . .		Date completed . .13/06/2007	
Materials			
Part no	Quantity used	Unit cost	Total cost – $
QV3	4	$12.20	48.80
TT43	2	$52.40	104.80
TOTAL			153.60
Labour			
Employee no	Hours used	Hourly rate	Total cost
2	6	$28	168.00
TOTAL			168.00
Overhead			6.80
TOTAL JOB COST			$338.40

This form of record will enable the business to justify charging a customer a particular amount for work done on a vehicle, or to enable it to determine whether or not it made a profit or a loss on a job that was undertaken for a fixed cost.

An alternative form of record is better suited to manufacturing, particularly where there are complicated manufacturing processes that may be undertaken in different sequences or combined in different ways. These documents are called **route cards**.

ROUTE CARD			
Project	Product	Identification	
Manufacturing process/supplier		Batch ID/date	
Operation	Comments	Initial	Date

Example

Building a customised truck body may be tackled in a variety of different ways. Perhaps painting can be done before or after certain fabrication work has been completed, perhaps electrical work can be done at different stages in the process, and so on. A route card may be prepared in advance to give staff an indication of how a unit or a batch should be made. If staff are empowered to make such decisions themselves then the card should be completed in as the work progresses so that the approach being taken can be reviewed regularly and any lessons drawn for future reference. A simplified example of a completed route card for the manufacture of a customised truck is shown below:

ROUTE CARD			
Project: Alpha	**Product**: Big Tow	**Identification**: T0256	
Supplier		batch ID/date	
Metal Co		207960T	
Wheel Co		4XT346	
Electrical Co		43578	
Paint Co		3217TYH	
Operation	**Comments**	**Initial**	**Date**
Frame construction	None	TA	16/06/07
Wheel welding	None	BT	27/06/07
Electrical installation	Authorisation of GT received for overrun	FA	28/06/07
Painting	None	YH	03/07/07

3.4 CALCULATING BASIC PAY

To calculate basic pay for hourly paid workers (excluding overtime), the hourly rate is simply multiplied by the number of hours worked.

Example

An employee worked 35 hours during a particular week. How much was the employee be paid if their hourly rate is $4.50 per hour?

Solution

Their pay will be 35 hours @ $4.50 = $157.50

3.5 BASIC PAY FOR SALARIED STAFF

Some employees are paid a set amount on the basis that they work for a standard number of hours every week. The amount that they are paid is usually expressed as an annual sum.

For example, an employee may be paid $12,000 per annum, for working from 9.00am till 5.00pm Monday to Friday (with a one hour lunch break), and with an entitlement to 20 days of annual leave (in addition to public holidays).

Such employees are often referred to as salaried staff, and their earnings are referred to as salary. There is no difference in principle between the treatment of wages and salary on the payroll. Salaried staff usually receive their pay monthly.

When an employee is paid an agreed annual salary, the salary will be spread evenly over the year. The spreading disregards the periods over which holidays are taken, so that the employee knows precisely how much pay they will receive.

The way in which the salary is spread is:

(a)   Weekly paid   1/52 of the annual salary

(b)   Fortnightly paid   2/52 of the annual salary

(c)   4-weekly paid   4/52 of the annual salary

(d)   Monthly paid   1/12 of the annual salary

Some salaried staff may be entitled to overtime if they work in excess of the agreed hours. Others may not be entitled to overtime, or only after they have worked a certain number of extra hours.

Overtime is discussed more fully later.

3.6 BASIC PAY FOR EMPLOYEES PAID BY PIECEWORK

If an employee is paid by piecework, it means that payment is made according to the number of items produced by the employee. It usually applies where a high number of small items are produced. It would clearly be inequitable to apply piecework where an employee was expected to complete only a handful of items each week as pay would fluctuate too greatly.

Piecework is often used as an incentive for the workers to work more productively as they can see a direct correlation between their output and their pay.

Piecework can only be applied if an employee's output can be recorded. This is usually done using a job card. A card is prepared for every job, and records the time spent on that job by every employee.

The rate of pay for employees paid by piecework is expressed as a specified amount of pay for a given number of items. It may be an amount per item, per 100 items, or even per 10,000 items, depending on the level of expected output.

The formula is:

Basic pay = Number of units produced × Rate of pay per unit

Piecework schemes can also offer higher rates where more than a certain number of items is produced. For example, an employee may be paid $5 each for the first 100 boxes of components packed, and $6 for any extra boxes packed.

Sometimes the piecework system is backed up by a minimum wage. For example, an employee may be paid $6 for every 100 buttonholes, but not less than $80 per week.

In the simplest case, the employee's basic pay will be the number of items produced, multiplied by the rate per item. This will need to be modified where there are differential rates, by applying the appropriate rate to the appropriate number of items. If a minimum wage is guaranteed, the basic pay will need to be increased to this level if the pay calculated using piecework rates is lower.

Example

Employees A, B and C are each paid by piecework. The terms of their employment are as follows:

(a) Employee A is paid a flat rate of $1.33 for every box produced. In a given week, Employee A produced 121 boxes.

(b) Employee B is paid $0.99 for every box produced, with a guaranteed minimum wage of $80 per week. In a given week, Employee B produced 75 boxes.

(c) Employee C is paid $1.33 each for the first 125 boxes produced, and $1.47 for each subsequent box. In a given week, Employee C produced 145 boxes.

How much basic pay will each employee receive that week?

Solution

They will receive the following amounts of basic pay:

			$
(a)	Employee A:	121 boxes @ $1.33	160.93
			_____
(b)	Employee B:	75 boxes @ $0.99 =	74.25
	guaranteed minimum wage of		80.00
			_____
(c)	Employee C:	125 boxes @ $1.33	166.25
		20 boxes @ $1.47	29.40
		____	_____
		145	195.65
		____	_____

ACTIVITY 3

A business manufactures packing cases and employs a number of people on a piece rate scheme of $3.00 for each packing case made. If an employee produces more than 100 packing cases in a week, any extra packing cases produced over 100 are paid at a rate of $4.00 per packing case. All employees have a guaranteed minimum weekly wage of $300. In the last week an employee produced 109 packing cases.

What was the employee's gross pay for the last week?

A $300

B $327

C $336

D $436

For a suggested answer, see the 'Answers' section at the end of the book.

---

4 OVERTIME PAY, BONUSES AND COMMISSION

4.1 OVERTIME

Normally an employee is required to work for a set number of hours every week. There may however be occasions when the employer will ask the employee to work for longer hours. Overtime is the time worked over and above the employee's basic working week.

Overtime must not be confused with flexitime. In a flexitime system an employee is allowed to work extra hours earlier in the week or month, in return for which fewer hours need to be worked later on. The overall number of hours worked in a given time period (e.g. a month) remains constant.

4.2 HOURLY PAID WORKERS

Hourly paid workers may be paid overtime at various different rates. For example, the hourly rate of overtime may be the same as the basic rate of pay or higher than the basic rate of pay.

It may either be expressed as a higher monetary amount, or as a proportion of basic pay, such as 'time and a half'.

The hourly rate of overtime may vary according to when the overtime is worked. For example the evening rate may be 'time and a half', whereas the weekend overtime rate may be 'double time'.

The hourly rate may vary with the number of overtime hours worked. For example the first 5 hours may be paid at 'time and a half', and additional hours paid at 'double time'.

4.3 CALCULATING OVERTIME PAY – WEEKLY PAID WORKERS

Overtime pay is the number of hours of overtime worked, multiplied by the rate at which overtime is paid.

Example

An employee normally works a 35 hour week, and is paid $5 per hour. In one week the employee worked 12 hours of overtime, one hour each week day, plus 7 hours on Saturday.

How much is the overtime pay if:

(a)   the employee is paid time and a half for all overtime hours?

(b)   the employee is paid time and a half for evening overtime and double time for weekend overtime?

(c)   the employee is paid time and a half for the first 8 hours overtime and double time thereafter?

Solution

The employee's overtime pay is:

				$
(a)	Basic rate of pay	$5 per hour		
	Overtime rate of pay	$5 × 1½ = $7.50 per hour		
	Overtime pay	12 hours @ $7.50 per hour		90.00

				$
(b)	Basic rate of pay	$5 per hour		
	Overtime rate of pay – evenings $5 × 1½ = $7.50 per hour			
	Overtime rate of pay – weekends $5 × 2 = $10.00 per hour			
	Overtime pay	5 hours @ $7.50 per hour		37.50
		7 hours @ $10.00 per hour		70.00
		Total		107.50

(c)	Basic rate of pay	$5 per hour		
	Overtime rate of pay – first 8 hours $5 × 1½ = $7.50 per hour			
	Overtime rate of pay – excess hours $5 × 2 = $10.00 per hour			
	Overtime pay	8 hours @ $7.50 per hour		60.00
		4 hours @ $10.00 per hour		40.00
				100.00

4.4 SALARIED STAFF

Not all salaried staff are paid overtime for any additional hours worked. If they are, the rate at which overtime is paid may vary according to when the overtime is worked, in precisely the same way as for weekly paid employees.

The difference is that the pay of salaried staff is usually expressed as an annual rate, and this must be converted to an hourly rate before the overtime can be calculated.

This is done by dividing the annual salary by 52 to give the weekly salary, and further dividing this by the number of hours an employee is contracted to work for.

It should be noted that the contract of employment may override this calculation, setting a rate of overtime pay.

Example

Employee K works a 35-hour week for an annual salary of $18,200. Employee K is expected to work up to 5 hours of overtime for no extra pay, but thereafter will be paid overtime pay at the rate of time and a half. In a particular week, Employee K worked 8 hours of overtime. What is Employee K's overtime pay?

Solution

Employee K's basic hourly rate of pay is:

$18,200 × 1/52 × 1/35 = $10.00

The hourly rate of overtime pay, at time and a half, is:

$10.00 × 1½ = $15.00

Employee K will not be paid for the first 5 hours of overtime, so overtime pay is as follows:

(8 – 5) hours = 3 hours @ $15 = $45.00

4.5 BONUSES

Bonus schemes are schemes under which employees receive additional amounts of earnings, as a reward for good work, in addition to their normal pay.

The essence of a bonus scheme is that additional pay will be earned if targets are achieved or exceeded. The scheme should set out the exact details and the dates of payment.

Examples of bonuses which may be earned are:

(a)   If the department's output exceeds a set limit, a bonus may be paid for every extra unit.

(b)   If sales made exceed a target in any one month, a proportion of the excess is divided between the salesforce.

(c)   If the profits of the business exceed target, every employee may receive a bonus based on their basic pay.

(d)   If an employee achieves a certain quality of work, a bonus may be earned.

(e)   If a long-term contract is completed early, each employee may receive a bonus related to how early the contract is completed.

(f)   If the profits of the business increase by a set percentage, the senior managers receive a bonus related to their basic pay.

Example

Supersales operates various bonus schemes.

1   Normal output of the toy department is 1,000 dolls per week. For every doll produced in excess of 1,100 per week, each employee of the department receives an extra 5¢.

2   If the total sales in the retail outlets exceed $1 million in any one month, 2% of the excess is shared between the sales team.

3   If profits exceed $90 million, every employee receives a bonus of one week's pay.

4   If a junior employee receives a top grade assessment from their supervisor on four consecutive occasions, that employee receives a bonus of $10.

5   Supersales Co has several contracts spanning 9 months or more. Each employee involved in the contract receives a bonus of one day's pay for every week by which the contract is completed early.

6   If Supersales Co's annual profits increase by 5% or more per annum, the senior managers receive a bonus of 1% of their basic annual pay.

The following additional information is relevant:

(a) Employee T works in the toy department, and is paid $100 per week. In one week, 1,230 dolls were produced.

(b) Employee S is a member of the sales team, and is paid $150 per week. In April, sales were $1.7 million. Employee S's proportionate share of the bonus is 0.5%.

(c) Employee R is a junior employee paid $65 per week. Employee R received four consecutive top grade assessments. Employee R was employed on one of the long-term contracts, which was completed two weeks early.

(d) Employee P is a senior manager, and is paid $36,000 per annum.

Supersales Co's profits for the year have just been announced as $92 million, a 5.5% increase over the previous year.

What bonuses will each employee receive?

Solution

(a) **Employee T**

	$
Scheme 1. 130 extra dolls @ 5c	6.50
Scheme 3. Profits exceed $90m, one week's pay	100.00
Total bonus	106.50

(b) **Employee S**

	$
Scheme 2 Total bonuses 2% × $(1.7–1)m = $14,000	
Profit share of 0.5%	70.00
Scheme 3. Profits exceed $90m, one week's pay	150.00
	220.00

(c) **Employee R**

	$
Scheme 3. Profits exceed $90m, one week's pay	65.00
Scheme 4. 4 top grade assessments	10.00
Scheme 5. Contract completed 2 weeks early	
2 days pay 2/5 × $65	26.00
	101.00

(d) **Employee P**

	$
Scheme 3. Profits exceed $90m, one week's pay	
1/52 × $36,000	692.31
Scheme 6. Profits increased by 5.5%, 1% of basic pay	360.00
	1,052.31

ACTIVITY 4

Employee B and C work for Smash Co which operates the following bonus schemes:

1   A bonus of $10 for every complete $1m by which sales exceed $100 million in any one month.

2   A bonus of $5 for every 10 boxes of components produced by any one worker in one week in excess of 1,000 boxes.

3   A bonus of 10% of the week's pay for any week in which the department's output exceeds 10,000 boxes.

In one week Employee B produced 980 boxes, and Employee C produced 1,030 boxes. The department as a whole produced 10,500 boxes. The figures for the previous month showed that sales were $102.7 million. Employees B and C have basic weekly pay of $120 and $130 respectively.

What bonus will they each receive?

For a suggested answer, see the 'Answers' section at the end of the book.

4.6   COMMISSION

In some jobs, employees may be remunerated by a basic salary, plus an additional amount specifically related to that employee's performance.

Commission is an amount paid to an employee based on that employee's performance.

Commission is most commonly paid to salesperson, based on the volume or value of sales that they have achieved in a given period. In some cases they may have a very low basic salary, so that commission forms the largest part of their pay. In its simplest form, commission will usually be expressed as a percentage of sales achieved in the previous period e.g. 1% of sales.

Commission may also be paid at different scales, so that the higher the sales, the higher the rate and level of commission. For example, a salesperson may be paid 2% commission on the first $10,000 of sales, 2.5% on the next $10,000, and 3% on any additional sales.

This basis may be appropriate where an employee sells a large number of small value items. If the salesperson instead sells higher value contracts, the level of commission may vary with the value of the contract. For example, the rate of commission may be 2% for contracts with a value up to $10,000, 2.5% for contracts with a value up to $20,000, and 3% for larger contracts.

Since the incentive is for the employee to make a large volume of sales, it is important for the employer to ensure that the salesperson is rewarded only for good sales. The commission scheme may contain a condition that the commission will be paid only when the customer has paid, or when the customer's creditworthiness has been checked.

Example

A salesperson receives a commission of 2% on the value of all machinery sales, with an additional 0.5% for any item of machinery sold for more than $10,000. In addition the salesperson receives a further 0.5% on sales in excess of $100,000 per month.

During July the salesperson's total sales amounted to $110,000. Included in this were two expensive machines, one sold for $12,000, and the other for $17,000.

How much commission did the salesperson earn?

Solution

The salesperson earns commission of:

		$
Basic commission	$110,000 × 2%	2,200
Expensive machines	$(12,000 + 17,000) × 0.5%	145
Sales over $100,000	$(110,000 – 100,000) × 0.5%	50
		———
Total commission		2,395
		———

ACTIVITY 5

Employee K is paid commission of 5% on the first $20,000 of sales, and 7.5% on any sales in excess of that amount. However, Employee K is only paid the commission when either the customer has paid for the order, or has taken out a financing agreement.

In October Employee K made sales of $35,000. However, two customers declined to pay or take out a financing agreement. One had ordered goods costing $1,500, and the other goods costing $2,500.

How much commission will Employee K receive?

For a suggested answer, see the 'Answers' section at the end of the book.

5 AUTHORISATION

5.1 WHY IS AUTHORISATION REQUIRED?

When an employee is paid on the basis of hours worked, or work done, pay will vary from week to week. It is the payroll department's responsibility to calculate gross pay each payday. The payroll department can only calculate gross pay on the basis of documentation they receive recording the employee's hours of work or work done.

The employee often prepares this documentation. It should not be possible for an employee to overstate the hours worked, or work done, as this would result in them being overpaid. It is therefore important that any documentation prepared by the employee is reviewed and approved by a responsible person, such as a manager before it is paid. Any overtime worked must also be authorised.

5.2 HOW SHOULD THE DOCUMENTATION BE AUTHORISED?

The documentation completed by the employee should be authorised by the employee's supervisor, or other person in a managerial capacity. The records should be countersigned to indicate that they have been authorised.

The time at which the authorisation is required may vary, for example:

- hourly paid workers who complete timesheets may need to have them countersigned each time they complete a different job

- hourly paid workers who complete job cards may need to have them authorised when the job covered by the card is finished

- salaried staff completing weekly timesheets may have them authorised at the end of the week. This is particularly important when overtime is paid.

When a defined procedure for authorisation is not followed, the payroll department should refer the documentation back for authorisation before calculating the gross pay.

5.3 AUTHORISATION OF RATES OF PAY

The rate at which an employee is paid will be recorded on the payroll records. Only changes to the rates of pay which are authorised and notified through the personnel department should be recorded and used when calculating gross pay.

5.4 JOB AND DEPARTMENT CODES

Most of the documents used for recording an employee's hours worked also record the jobs on which the employee has worked. As well as being used to calculate the employee's pay, the documents are used to show the labour costs of the various jobs. The timesheets must contain the correct job codes so that the labour costs are allocated properly.

Along with job codes, the documentation may include department codes. This records not only the job that was done, but the department for which the work was carried out. This may be important when allocating the cost of idle time, or administration time.

5.5 AUTHORISATION OF THE PAYROLL

It is also normal for a responsible person within an business to review and approve the payroll before it is processed and payment made to employees. This is a final check of reasonableness to ensure that it is in line with expectations. The review and authorisation may be accompanied by a summary of employee joiners and leavers since the previous payroll to understand why employee numbers have changed. It may also be accompanied by a summary of factors to explain other changes from expectations, such as payment of bonus or overtime in excess of normal practice.

6   SECURITY AND CONTROL

6.1   INTRODUCTION

All information held on the payroll is highly confidential and must be kept secure.

The information is highly sensitive as most employees will not know what other employees are paid, or what the salary scales of more senior employees are.

Other information is personal to the employee, such as whether the employee has joined the staff pension scheme, or contributes to charities through the payroll giving scheme, along with personal data such as bank account details and home address.

6.2   PRESERVING CONFIDENTIALITY

The steps that should be taken to preserve confidentiality include:

- not discussing an employee's pay details with another employee

- not leaving documents containing personal data about an employee open and available for others to read, including open files on a computer

- not leaving computers unattended during processing of the payroll

- putting files, papers and discs away in locked cupboards, or in the payroll department to which unauthorised personnel do not have access

- not allowing or enabling access to payroll files to unauthorised personnel.

6.3   SECURITY

Processing the payroll results in significant sums of cash paid being to employees and outside agencies.

Where notes and coins is involved for wages paid in cash, it must be kept in a safe between the time it is collected from the bank, the time when wage packets are prepared, and the subsequent distribution of the wage packets. It is advisable for the wage packets to be prepared in a locked room if possible. Certainly, access to unauthorised personnel should be denied during this period. Payment of wages in cash is now less common than it used to be.

If payments of wages and salaries are made by bank transfer, or by cheque, the cheque book and transfer details must similarly be retained in a secure place.

6.4   THE ROLE OF THE PERSONNEL DEPARTMENT

The main responsibilities of the personnel department are:

(a)   the recruitment of new employees

(b)   preparing records of the employees' personal details

(c)   updating records of the employees' personal details

(d)　maintaining any other records relating to the employees, such as:

　　(i)　records of absences, and the reasons

　　(ii)　details of pay reviews

　　(iii)　notes of progress or appraisal meetings

　　(iv)　training records.

In some cases the personnel department will also be responsible for processing the payroll. In other words, the payroll function will be one part of the personnel department. More often, the two functions are separate, but there is a certain amount of overlap. For example, the personnel department will keep details of an employee's rate of pay and hours of work, and contributions (if any) to the company pension scheme. These details are also needed by the payroll department.

The separation between personnel and payroll is useful in maintaining controls over the payroll as it enables records to be compared:

- to ensure that employees who have left the business are no longer being paid

- to highlight whether 'dummy employees' have been invented by employees in payroll department as a way of committing fraud.

Controls applied within payroll aim to ensure that employees are correctly paid the right amount at the right time and with correct deductions. Proper authorisation and checking provides much of that control.

7   ACCOUNTING FOR PAYROLL

Payroll costs are a form of expenditure for an employer, and the expenditure must be recorded in the accounting system. Here is an example of a payroll record for a business with only two employees. It employs P Singh and M Chan.

Week 40

Employee	Gross pay	Pension	Income tax	Employee's state benefit	Net pay	Employer's pension	Employer's state benefit
	$	$	$	$	$	$	$
P Singh	395.00	15.00	57.92	30.85	291.23	15.00	36.71
M Chan	406.25	22.00	64.77	41.33	278.15	15.00	43.82
	801.25	37.00	122.69	72.18	569.38	30.00	80.53

A normal weekly payroll will look something like this, but with a longer list of employees. The payroll shows not just the gross pay, deductions for tax and net pay of the employees. It also shows the additional payroll costs of the employer, and in this example, these consist of:

- employer's state benefit contributions.

- employer's contributions to a pension scheme for employees. These contributions are in addition to gross pay, and are not deductions from the employees' wages.

The totals for each column in the payroll are posted using journal adjustments to the general ledger accounts.

7.1 POSTING PAYROLL DETAILS TO THE GENERAL LEDGER

Payroll costs are an expense for the employer, and the expense must be recorded in an expense account in the general ledger.

The net wages or salaries need to be paid to the employees. The various deductions from gross pay need to be paid to the appropriate outside agency to which they are payable, and the employer's state benefit contributions and pension contributions also need to be paid to outside agencies. These payments are likely to occur some days after the employees have been received their net pay so, for a short time, the amounts payable to the outside agencies are unpaid liabilities of the business. Until the money is paid to the agencies, the amounts due to the agencies are payables of the business.

In posting the payroll details to the general ledger:

- the payroll expense is recorded in an expense account. This may be called the wages and salaries expense account

- the amounts payable to the employees and to the various outside agencies (the liabilities of the business), are recorded in a separate general ledger account. This may be called the wages and salaries payable account.

Posting the payroll to the general ledger should be completed using the following steps:

Step 1   Gross pay – take the total for gross pay and:

Debit   Wages and salaries expense account

Credit   Wages and salaries payable account

Step 2   Additional contributions by the employer (state benefit and pension contributions) – take the total of each type of contribution by the employer to total payroll costs and:

Debit   Wages and salaries expense account

Credit   Wages and salaries payable account

Step 3   Take-home pay for employees

This is paid to the employees immediately, so by the time the payroll is recorded, the payment has already been made. Take the total of net pay (take-home pay) from the payroll, and:

Debit   Wages and salaries payable account

Credit   Bank account

Step 4   Amounts payable to outside agencies

When the payroll details are posted to the general ledger, these payments are unlikely to have been made yet, so the amounts are still payable, and the outside agencies are payables.

Take each column in the payroll that represents an amount owing to an outside agency. These are the columns for deductions from employees' pay and the columns for the employer's state benefit contributions and pension scheme contributions. For each of these totals:

Debit   Wages and salaries payable account

Credit   A payable account for the outside agency.

At the end of this process, the balance on the wages and salaries payable account should be nil.

These steps are shown in the following T accounts.

Wages and salaries payable account

	$		$
Bank (net wages and salaries paid)	X	Wages and salaries expense account:	
		Gross pay	X
		Employer's state benefit	X
Taxation authority	X	Employer's pension contribution	X
Pension scheme payable	X		
Payables for any other non-statutory deductions	X		
	X		X

The balance on the wages and salaries payable account should be nil.

Wages and salaries expense account

	$		$
Wages and salaries payable account:			
Gross wages and salaries	X		
Employer's state benefit	X		
Employer's pension contribution	X		

There is a debit balance on this account, because it is an expense account.

Taxation authority account

	$		$
		Wages and salaries payable account:	
		Income tax deductions	X
		Employees' state benefit	X
		Employer's state benefit	X

There is a credit balance on this account because it is a liability account, representing a payable of the business.

Pension payable (non-statutory deductions) account

	$			$
		Wages and salaries payable account:		
		Employees' contributions		X
		Employer's contributions		X

There is a credit balance on this account because it is a liability account, representing a payable of the business.

The example here does not have any other payables for non-statutory deductions, but if there are any such deductions, such as employee subscriptions to a trade union or donations by employees to a charity, they would be accounted for in a similar way. There would be a debit entry for the deduction in the wages and salaries payable account and a credit entry in the payable account for the external agency (trade union, charity, and so on).

Bank account

	$			$
		Wages and salaries payable account:		
		Net wages (take-home pay)		X

Payments from the bank account are recorded as credit entries.

ACTIVITY 6

Here are the totals from TTC's January payroll:

Total gross pay	$6,172.20
Total employer's state benefit	$488.20
Total income tax	$1,029.96
Total employees' state benefit	$445.20
Total net pay	$4,697.04

Task

Post the above to the relevant general ledger accounts.

For suggested answers, see the 'Answers' section at the end of the book.

ACTIVITY 7

Post the following payroll details to the appropriate general ledger accounts using T-accounts, and balance the wages and salaries payable account.

Week 40

Employee	Gross pay	Pension	Income tax	Employees' state benefit	Net pay	Employer's pension	Employer's state benefit
	$	$	$	$	$	$	$
P Singh	395.00	15.00	57.92	30.85	291.23	15.00	36.71
M Chan	406.25	22.00	64.77	41.33	278.15	15.00	43.82
	801.25	37.00	122.69	72.18	569.38	30.00	80.53

For suggested answers, see the 'Answers' section at the end of the book.

7.2 PAYMENT METHODS

Businesses may use a range of methods to pay their employees as follows:

- cash payment, with an employee receiving their individual pay packet containing their net pay in notes and coins plus payslip each week. This may be appropriate when there are relatively few employees and there is little handling of notes and coins to enable wage packets to be prepared each week, or perhaps if an employee does not have a bank account.

- cheque payment, with an employee receiving a cheque for their net pay plus payslip, each week or month as appropriate. This may be appropriate when there may be some variation in weekly or monthly pay (perhaps due to overtime or bonus payment) for each employee.

- direct or automated payment of the net pay into the individual bank account of an employee each week or month as appropriate, with payslip provided separately. This is appropriate for employers who have a significant number of employees and where a business operates automated and computerised systems and processes. This is becoming increasingly common.

CONCLUSION

Wages and salaries are often one of the largest items of expenditure for a business. Personnel department is the part of a business that deals with wages and salaries.

Wages and salaries are calculated as gross pay less various deductions statutory deductions such as income tax and non-statutory deductions such as donations to charity or contributions to savings schemes. Payments may be made by BACS, cash, cheque and so on.

Gross pay is calculated in a variety of ways based on hours worked, sometimes including overtime, on the amount of work completed or as a proportion of an annual salary. Bonuses and commissions are sometimes paid as incentives.

As the elements of wages and salaries may be quite detailed, it is important that they are correctly documented and authorised. Records as well as the actual pay need to be kept secure and carefully controlled.

Payroll is calculated and payment made by cash or some form of bank payment. Wages and salaries are, therefore, ultimately paid from the bank account and recorded in the general ledger.

KEY TERMS

Gross pay – Money due to an employee **before** deductions for income tax and NIC, etc.

Net pay – Money payable to an employee **after** deductions for income tax, NIC, etc.

Non-statutory deductions – deductions from employees' earnings authorised by the employee, rather than required by law, such as contributions to savings schemes and trade union subscriptions.

Payroll – List of employees and the wages or salaries due to each individual.

Payslip – Document given to each employee giving details of pay and deductions from pay.

State benefit contributions – Amount paid by employees (and possibly the employer) to the state for purposes of social security.

Statutory deductions – deductions made from employees' earnings required by law, such as deductions for income tax.

SELF TEST QUESTIONS

		Paragraph
1	Define a payroll system.	1
2	What is the difference between gross pay and net pay?	1
3	How is the total cost of wages and salaries to the employer calculated?	1
4	List four deductions from an employee's pay.	1
5	What must an employer do to process the payroll?	2
6	Give two ways of recording hours.	3
7	What is meant by 'piecework'?	3
8	What is the difference between overtime and flexitime?	4
9	Give two examples of when a bonus may be paid.	4
10	What is commission and who receives it?	4
11	How should payroll documentation be authorised?	5
12	Explain the steps to be taken when posting the payroll to the general ledger.	7

EXAM-STYLE QUESTIONS

1   An employee works as a fruit-packer and paid according to the number of boxes of fruit packed. By what method of remuneration is the employee paid?

　　A　Commission

　　B　Paid by the hour

　　C　Piecework

　　D　Salaried

2   An employee is paid a basic salary of $2,000 per month. Income tax on the salary is $350 and state benefit contributions amount to $180. The employer also pays state benefit contributions of $210.

　　In June the employee is also entitled to a bonus of $100 on which no tax or other deductions are payable.

　　How much was the employee's net 'take-home' pay for June?

　　A　$1,260

　　B　$1,360

　　C　$1,540

　　D　$1,570

3   An employee earns a basic wage rate of $5.00 per hour for a 35-hour week and at the rate of time-and-a-half for any additional hours worked. Last week the employee worked 43 hours.

　　What is the employee's gross pay for last week?

　　A　$175

　　B　$215

　　C　$235

　　D　$322.50

4   From which account are wages and salaries paid directly to employees?

　　A　Bank

　　B　Payroll

　　C　Wages and salaries payable

　　D　Wages and salaries expense

For suggested answers, see the 'Answers' section at the end of the book.

Chapter 7

CASH AND BANK

When payments are received from customers, whether from receiving a cheque or receiving an electronic or automated payment, it needs to be recorded in the accounting system. The procedure for banking receipts was explained in an earlier chapter. The same is also true for payments made by the business. This chapter explains how receipts and payments are recorded in the accounting records. It focuses on the syllabus area of recording transactions.

This chapter covers syllabus areas F1.

CONTENTS

1   Recording cash and credit transactions

2   Recording and analysing receipts

3   Recording and analysing payments

4   Posting receipts and payments from the cash records to the general ledger

5   Authorising and making payments

LEARNING OUTCOMES

At the end of this chapter, you should be able to:

- identify the documentation accompanying payments and receipts

- recognise the importance of accurately recording all payments and receipts

- identify the main ways to ensure that only authorised payments are made

- record payments and receipts in the cash records, general ledger and memorandum only payables and receivables ledger accounts.

1 RECORDING CASH AND CREDIT TRANSACTIONS

1.1 INTRODUCTION

Cash transactions are those where payment is made or received immediately (i.e. when payment is exchanged at the point of sale/purchase). Sales and purchases made by cheque or immediate bank transfer are therefore classed as cash transactions. The main reason for this is that, traditionally, such transactions would be processed using a cash register or cash till. The cheques and cash in the till would be counted at the end of the day and transferred to a bank account.

Credit transactions, on the other hand, occur when goods are sold or purchased and paid for at a later date and, increasingly, are more commonly paid for using electronic payments methods and are referred to as bank transactions.

For the sake of simplicity the content in this chapter refers to payments and receipts of cash being made out of the 'cash at bank' general ledger account, rather than distinguishing between 'bank ledger' and a 'cash ledger'.

1.2 CASH AND CREDIT TRANSACTIONS

When cash is received (i.e. increase in an asset) the entry in the cash at bank general ledger account is a debit. When cash is paid out (i.e. a reduction in an asset) the entry in the cash at bank general ledger account is a credit.

Businesses receive money from credit customers who are paying invoices and from customers who do not have a credit account. From an accounting perspective, there is an important difference between receipts from credit customers and receipts from customers without a credit account.

- **Receipts from credit customers** have to be recorded, not just in the general ledger, but also in the individual 'memorandum only' receivable ledger account of each credit customer. With computerised accounting systems, the memorandum-only information is updated simultaneously at the same time as the general ledger.

  The initial credit sale is recorded at the time that transaction was entered into as follows:

  Debit: Receivables   to record the amount owing to the business

  Credit: Sales   to record the income earned

  When a credit customer subsequently pays the amount due, the accounting records are updated to show that the customer has paid the money owed.

  In this situation, the accounting entries required in the general ledger will be:

  Debit: Cash at bank   to record the receipt of cash

  Credit: Receivables   to reduce or clear the amount owing to the business

- **Receipts from customers without a credit account** are treated as cash sales. These receipts may come from takings in a cash register or through orders by post, telephone or e-mail, where payment is by cheque, credit card or some form of immediate automated or electronic payment. Cash sales are only recorded as and when they occur.

  In this situation, the accounting entries required in the general ledger will be:

  Debit: Cash at bank   to record the receipt of cash

  Credit: Sales   to record the income earned

1.3 CHECKING RECEIPTS AGAINST RELEVANT SUPPORTING INFORMATION

When a business has receipts from cash sales, the amount received must be checked to ensure that all the receipts are complete. The total value of receipts in notes and coins, cheques, and credit and debit card vouchers should be calculated separately, to obtain three separate totals. The total value of receipts by cheque and by credit and debit cards is found by going through the cheques and credit/debit card vouchers one by one and adding up their total value. Some calculators produce a printed list of the individual cheque or credit/debit card voucher amounts.

When the total value of receipts has been calculated in this way, it may be possible to the compare this total with a till roll (for cash received recorded by a cash register) or a printout of credit card receipts (for receipts taken and recorded through a credit card machine). The two totals should be equal.

1.4 REMITTANCE LIST

When money is received from credit customers, it is important to ensure that each receipt is properly recorded. A common method of doing this is to start by preparing a remittance list or cash received list. A remittance list is simply a list of each receipt, with details of who the money has come from and the amount of the receipt.

The following is a typical remittance list:

Customer name	Account number	Amount received $
A C Bryan	1037	265.40
Flowers Limited	1002	319.64
E Patel	1053	396.61
P Taylor	1025	236.98
F Willis	1129	326.89
Young Fashions	1042	115.79
Perry & Co	1079	163.26
L Connor Limited	1023	115.37
O McGovern	1152	327.36
J Shepard	1116	372.45
Cole and Porter	1014	325.67
P Smith	1046	235.89
D Iqbal	1103	117.80

The account number here is the customer's account number, which is the account number in the memorandum only receivables ledger. This number may be obtainable from the remittance advice from the customer, if there is one, or from the copy of the invoice held by the accounts office.

A remittance list may also be prepared by a small business that does not have a cash register but receives money from customers during the course of each day. In this case, all receipts from customers would be recorded immediately on the remittance list.

Example

H Chan works for Bradshaw Electrical Repairs. H Chan carries out repairs to household appliances and is called out to repair washing machines, fridges and other household items. For each call out, a fee is charged that is paid either in cash or by cheque.

When H Chan finishes each job, a receipt is completed and handed to the customer, giving details of the amount charged and acknowledging that the customer has paid. H Chan keeps a carbon copy of each receipt, and from these carbon copies a remittance list of all of the receipts from customers during the day can be prepared.

A remittance list might look something like this:

Date	Customer	Work done	Amount $
12 June	F Bond	Washing machine repair	62.30
12 June	V Assam	Fridge repair	41.78
12 June	T Poll	Freezer repair	56.02
			———
			160.10
			———

The remittance list is a document for recording receipts from customers. Each day or week, the details from the remittance list should be used to update the general ledger. When a business receives a large number of receipts, it is often a good idea to split them into manageable batches of transactions, and to process each batch separately.

1.5 CHECKING RECEIPTS FROM CREDIT CUSTOMERS AGAINST THE INVOICE

When money is received from a credit customer, the receipt should be matched against the invoice or invoices that the customer is paying.

2 RECORDING AND ANALYSING RECEIPTS

2.1 CONTEXT

Details of all receipts should be recorded in the accounting records.

The first step is to make a produce a cash record – this may even be transaction summary obtained from the bank of transactions which have been processed through the bank account.

Many businesses find it more convenient to maintain separate records of cash receipts and payments. The purpose of a cash receipts records is to record:

- receipts from credit customers settling invoices

- all other receipts, including those for cash sales.

Each receipt from a credit customer must be recorded individually. Receipts from cash sales can be recorded as a total. The cash receipts records should be updated regularly, perhaps every day in large businesses.

A cash receipts record will contain several columns, typically as follows:

FOLIO CR14

Date	Reference	Total	Receivables	Cash sales	Sales tax	Other
		$	$	$	$	$

2.2 ENTERING RECEIPTS IN THE CASH RECEIPTS RECORD

Details of receipts are entered in the cash receipts record as follows:

Date   This is the date the money is received.

Reference   This could be one column or several columns. It is needed to identify who the receipt is from or what it is for.

- It may show the name of the credit customer, the account number and possibly the number of the invoice being paid.

- For cash sales, it may simply state 'Cash sales'.

- For other items of income or receipts the analysis column headings may be used to indicate the nature of the receipt, such as 'bank interest received'.

The details in the reference column usually indicate the other part of the double entry to record the transaction in the accounting system. For example if the cash receipts are from sales the details should read 'sales'.

Total   The total amount of the receipt is entered in the total column.

The remaining columns are for further analysis and should be appropriate to the business.

Receivables If the receipt is from a credit customer, the total amount of the receipt should be entered in the receivables column. There is no need to split this amount between the net sale value and sales tax. The sales tax on a credit sale was recorded earlier when the sales invoice is raised and recorded in the accounting records.

Cash sales If the receipt is for cash sales, the total amount received is shown in the total column. If the business is registered to account for sales tax, the cash sales column is used to record the amount of the sales **excluding sales** tax as sales tax has not yet been accounted for on these transactions. If the business is not registered to account for sales tax, the total receipts relating to cash sales should be recorded in this column.

Sales tax This column is used to record any sales tax received for anything other than credit sales invoices. If the business is registered to account for sales tax, the cash sales column should show the amount of the sale excluding sales tax and the tax on the sale should be shown in the sales tax column. The amount in this column and the amount in the cash sales column agree to the amount in the total column.

The reason for recording the sales tax on receipts from cash sales (and on other sources of income, if any) is that sales tax is recorded for the first time in the accounting system at this point.

This is illustrated in the example below.

Other A business may occasionally receive money from other sources, such as interest on a bank deposit account, or receipt of cash from a bank loan. If other receipts are uncommon, a single column may be used to record them, and the Reference column will be used to explain the nature of the receipt.

On each row of the cash receipts record, the figure in the total column should agree to the sum of the amounts in the receivables, cash sales, sales tax and any other columns used.

Example

The following amounts were received on 19 October 20X6.

(a) Payment of invoice number 69 by BL Lorries (account number S239), total $4,700.

(b) Payment of invoice number 70 by MA Meters (account number S314), total $2,820.

(c) Payment of invoice number 78 by Tanktop Limited (account number S205), total $3,100.

(d) A cash sale of $1,200 including sales tax at 20%.

Task

Write up the cash receipts record and total each of the columns.

Solution

Cash receipts record   FOLIO CR14

Date	Reference	Total $	Rec'bles $	Cash sales $	Sales tax $
19.10.X6					
	BL Lorries, a/c S239	4,700	4,700		
	MA Meters, a/c S314	2,820	2,820		
	Tanktop Ltd, a/c S205	3,100	3,100		
	Cash sale	1,200		1,000	200
		11,820	10,620	1,000	200
		G/L ref	G?L ref	G/L ref	G/L ref

Notes

1   In a manual accounting system, each page in the cash receipts record is normally numbered sequentially, for reference purposes. In a computerised system, there is likely to be a similar sequential reference. The page number is referred to as its 'folio' number. Here, the page of the record has been given an imaginary folio number of CR14.

2   Cash sale. Sales tax = $1,200 × (20/120) = $200. The value of the cash sale to the business is $1,200 × (100/120) = $1,000. These are the figures entered in the sales tax and cash sales columns, and together they match the amount of $1,200 for that item in the total column.

3   Receipts entered in the cash receipts record should be banked intact in order to reduce the risk of fraud or error. If the business needs cash for petty cash payments then it should cash a cheque. Most receipts are likely to be in the form of cheques and electronic or automated receipts.

4   The cash receipts record should include general ledger account references to identify which general ledger accounts have been updated when the transactions have been processed. In addition, for receipts from credit customers, there will also be a receivables ledger reference to update the memorandum only individual receivables ledger accounts.

ACTIVITY 1

The following remittance list has been prepared showing receipts for 1 June:

Customer name	Account number	Amount received
		$
A C Bhatt	1037	265.40
Flowers Limited	1002	319.64
E Murphy	1053	396.61
P Taylor	1025	236.98
F Willis	1129	326.89
Young Fashions	1042	115.79
Perry & Co	1079	163.26
L Connor Limited	1023	115.37
O McGovern	1152	327.36
J Shepard	1116	372.45
Cole and Porter	1014	325.67
P Smith	1046	235.89
D Smith	1103	117.80

The summary information from the cash register printout for 1 June was as follows:

Totals	$
Cash	1,151.50
Cheques	513.71
Credit/debit card (agreed to end of day reconciliation)	815.74
	2,480.95

These details agree with the amount of cash, cheques and card vouchers in the till. Sales tax within cash register receipts amounts to $413.49.

Enter these amounts in the cash receipts record.

For a suggested answer, see the 'Answers' section at the end of the book.

KAPLAN PUBLISHING

ACTIVITY 2

The records for a business show the following for 20 April:

Cash register receipts	$
Cash	441.68
Cheques	227.44
Credit/debit cards	129.79
	———
	798.91
	———

The sales tax in the cash receipts amounts to $133.15.

Cheques received in the post from credit customers were as follows:

Value of cheque from D Middleton, account 5469   884.84

Record this information in the cash receipts record and then post the totals to the relevant accounts.

For a suggested answer, see the 'Answers' section at the end of the book.

2.3   CASH PAID DIRECTLY INTO THE BANK ACCOUNT

Many businesses receive cash directly into their bank accounts, by means of

- BACS payments

- standing order receipts and direct debit receipts

- automated or electronic receipts.

In such cases, the business may not know about the receipt until it receives a bank statement or a listing of receipts from the bank, although the customer is likely to send a notification of payment when paying by BACS.

If the bank statement contains previously unidentified receipts, the procedures are much the same as described already for receipts by cheque.

- Check that the correct amount has been paid. The bank statement should give some information to help with identifying who the money has come from.

- Enter the amounts received in the cash receipts record on the date you are aware of the items.

- Post the totals from the cash receipts record to the relevant accounts in the general ledger.

3 RECORDING AND ANALYSING PAYMENTS

3.1 CONTEXT

Details of all payments made should be recorded in the accounting records. The first step is to make a produce a cash payments record – this may even be transaction summary obtained from the bank of transactions which have been processed through the bank account.

The records of receipts and payments are often maintained separately. The purpose of a cash payments records is to record:

- payments made to credit suppliers settling invoices outstanding

- all other payments, including those for cash purchases.

Each payment to a credit supplier must be recorded individually. Payments relating to cash purchases can be recorded as a total. The cash payments records should be updated regularly, perhaps every day in large businesses. There are likely to be more analysis columns for payments and the example below gives an impression of what it may look like.

Date	Cheque number	Payee/ supplier account number	Total	Payables	Sales tax	Insur- ance	Wages and salaries	Petty cash	Other	Discount received
			$	$	$	$	$	$	$	$
		Totals								
			G/L ref	G/L ref	G/L ref	G/L ref	G/L ref	G/L ref	G/L ref	G/L ref

Completing the cash payments record

1   Date. This is the date of the payment.

2   Cheque number. When payment is by cheque, the cheque number should be shown. Cheques should be used and recorded in sequential number order. If they are not, there may be a security problem with a missing cheque. If payment is by another method, such as BACS, the payment method should be shown here.

3   Payee, supplier account number. This column is for entering the identity of the payee. If the payment is to a trade payable, the payable's account number in the payables ledger should be shown too.

4   Total. This column is for showing the total amount of the payment. It is the total paid out of the business bank account.

5   Payables. If the payment is to a credit supplier, the purchase was recorded at the time the purchase was made, including accounting for any sales tax on the transaction if appropriate. Here, the focus is upon the subsequent payment to clear the total amount due to the supplier. The total amount of the payment should also be entered in this column.

6   Other analysis columns. The other analysis columns are for providing an analysis of payments other than payments to credit suppliers. They should be used for payments to suppliers who do not provide credit facilities (where the payment is supported by a cheque requisition), for payments of expenses, for

payments of wages and salaries and for withdrawals of money from the bank for petty cash. Where there is an amount for sales tax in the payment, the sales tax element should be shown separately in the sales tax column, and the analysis columns for the expense should show the amount excluding sales tax. Each column should represent an account in the general ledger (such as an expense account or the sales tax account).

7   The cash payments record should include general ledger account references to identify which general ledger accounts have been updated when the transactions have been processed.

In addition, for payments to credit suppliers, there will also be a payables ledger reference to update the memorandum only individual payables ledger accounts.

8   There may also be an additional memorandum column to show any early settlement discount received.

ACTIVITY 3

FFP makes the following payments in respect of various credit invoices and other items.

*   Payment of $4,230 on 23/7/X4 to N Hudson. A settlement discount of $130 was taken. This was paid by cheque (cheque number 1003). The payables ledger reference code is P4153.

*   On 24/7/X4, $2,350 to G Fazaal in respect of an outstanding invoice, by cheque (cheque number 1004). The payables ledger reference code is P4778.

*   On 28/7/X4, purchase of inventory, **not on credit**, of $960 including sales tax of $160 (cheque number 1005).

*   On 30/7/X4, payment of a salary by cheque of $2,500, using cheque number 1006. (There is no sales tax on wages and salaries).

Enter these transactions into the cash payments record.

For a suggested answer, see the 'Answers' section at the end of the book.

3.2   TOTALLING THE CASH PAYMENTS RECORD

The columns of the cash payments record should be totalled and arithmetic accuracy should be checked by adding up the totals of all the analysis columns (but not the total in the discounts received column) to agree to the total payments made.

ACTIVITY 4

Following on from the previous activity, total each of the columns of the cash payments record and check that the totals agree.

For a suggested answer, see the 'Answers' section at the end of the book.

ACTIVITY 5

On 22 June 20X3 Viking Paper made three cheque payments. The original documents for these transactions are given below.

Task

Write up the relevant details of these documents in the cash payments record, and total all relevant columns.

Payables ledger references are the following:

Computer Supplies   PL 32
Step Wholesale Supplies   PL 56

Viking Paper always takes advantage of any settlement discounts offered from suppliers.

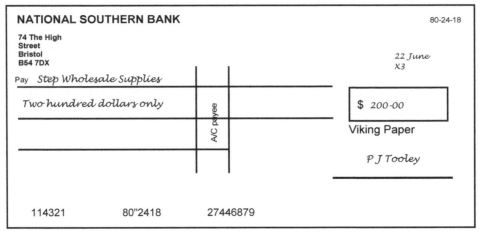

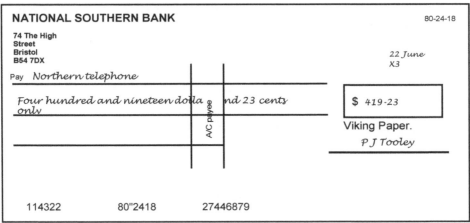

Note: Payment of the telephone bill, which includes Sales tax at 20%

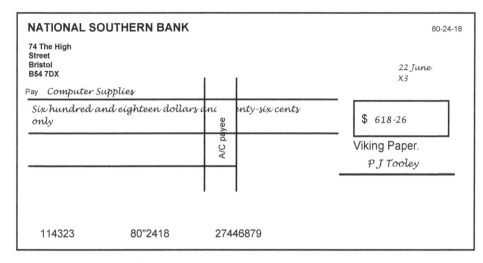

NATIONAL SOUTHERN BANK 80-24-18

74 The High
Street
Bristol
B54 7DX

22 June
X3

Pay *Computer Supplies*

Six hundred and eighteen dollars and [t]wenty-six cents only

A/C payee

$ *618-26*

Viking Paper.

P J Tooley

114323   80"2418   27446879

Note: A discount of $32.54 was taken on this payment to Computer Supplies.

For a suggested answer, see the 'Answers' section at the end of the book.

4 POSTING RECEIPTS AND PAYMENTS FROM THE CASH RECORDS TO THE GENERAL LEDGER

4.1 POSTING TRANSACTIONS FROM THE CASH RECEIPTS RECORDS TO THE GENERAL LEDGER

Having listed (or obtained a bank listing) of receipts, which have been suitably analysed and referenced, it is now possible to post the transactions into the general ledger using the principles of double-entry bookkeeping.

The accounting entries in the general ledger are as follows:

Debit:	Cash at bank	$ with the total of receipts
Credit:	Sales Tax	$ with the total of sales tax on cash sales
	Receivables	$ with the total receipts from credit customers
	Cash sales	$ total of the net amount of cash sales
	Other	$ of any other receipts e.g. bank interest received

Remember that, in a computerised system the update of the memorandum only receivables ledger accounts will happen simultaneously with the update of the general ledger. It is not a separate activity as it would be in a manual accounting system.

Example

The following entries have been made in the cash receipts record for 19 October.

Date	Reference	Total $	Rec'bles $	Cash sales $	Sales tax $	Other $
19.10.X6						
	BL Lorries, a/c S239	4,700	4,700			
	MA Meters, a/c S314	2,820	2,820			
	Tanktop Ltd, a/c S205	3,100	3,100			
	Cash sale	1,200		1,000	200	
	Totals	**11,820**	**10,620**	**1,000**	**200**	

Task

Post these entries into the general ledger and the memorandum only receivables ledger accounts for individual credit customers.

Solution

The totals should be posted to the ledger accounts as follows.

General ledger:

Bank

Date	Details	Folio	$	Date	Details	Folio	$
19.10.X6	Sundry receivables	CR14	10,620				
19.10.X6	Sales	CR14	1,000				
19.10.X6	Sales tax	CR14	200				

Sales

Date	Details	Folio	$	Date	Details	Folio	$
				19.10.X6	Bank	CR14	1,000

Sales tax

Date	Details	Folio	$	Date	Details	Folio	$
				19.10.X6	Bank	CR14	200

Receivables

Date	Details	Folio	$	Date	Details	Folio	$
				19.10.X6	Bank	CR14	10,620

Receivables ledger:

BL Lorries

Date	Details	Folio	$	Date	Details	Folio	$
				19.10.X6	Bank	CR14	4,700

MA Meters

Date	Details	Folio	$	Date	Details	Folio	$
				19.10.X6	Bank	CR14	2,820

Tanktop Ltd

Date	Details	Folio	$	Date	Details	Folio	$
				19.10.X6	Bank	CR14	3,100

4.2 POSTING TRANSACTIONS FROM THE CASH PAYMENTS RECORDS TO THE GENERAL LEDGER

Having listed (or obtained a bank listing) of payments, which have been suitably analysed and referenced, it is now possible to post the transactions into the general ledger using the principles of double-entry bookkeeping.

The accounting entries in the general ledger are as follows:

Debit	Sales Tax	$ with the total of sales tax on cash purchases
	Payables	$ with the total payments to credit suppliers
	Cash sales	$ total of the net amount of cash purchases
	Other	$ of any other payments e.g. bank interest paid
Credit:	Cash at bank	$ with the total of payments

Each column in the cash payments book represents an account in the general ledger.

- The total column is for the cash at bank account.

- The sales tax column is for tax payable to the tax authorities.

- The payables column is for the payables account.

- Each of the other columns represents an expense account in the general ledger (or possibly an asset account).

It is likely that there will be more analysis columns for payments than for receipts.

There may also be memorandum only discount received information annotated within the cash payments records. This will be a discount received for early settlement ('prompt payment') of an amount before the due date. If this is the case, the accounting entries required in the general ledger will be:

Debit	Payables	$
Credit	Discount received	$

Remember that, in a computerised system the update of the memorandum only payables ledger accounts will happen simultaneously with the update of the general ledger, including any discount received for early settlement of amounts due. It is not a separate activity as it would be in a manual accounting system.

Example

The following entries have been made in the cash payments record for 19 October.

Date	Reference	Total $	Payables $	Cash purchases $	Sales tax $	Wages $	Discount rec'd $
19.10.X6							
	LS Shah, a/c P340	2,300	2,300				
	BA Chan, a/c P720	5,200	5,200				
	OS Mosis, a/c P234	1,870	1,870				30
	Cash purchases	3,000		2,500	500		
	Wages	5,300				5,300	
	Totals	**17,670**	**9,370**	**2,500**	**500**	**5,300**	**30**

Task

Post these entries into the general ledger and the memorandum only payables ledger accounts for individual credit suppliers.

Solution

The totals should be posted to the ledger accounts as follows.

General ledger:

Bank

Date	Details	Folio	$	Date	Details	Folio	$
				19.10.X6	Payables	CP14	9,370
				19.10.X6	Purchases	CP14	2,500
				19.10.X6	Sales tax	CP14	500
				19.10.X6	Wages	CP14	5,300

Payables

Date	Details	Folio	$	Date	Details	Folio	$
19.10.X6	Bank	CP14	9,370				
19.10.X6	Disc rec'd	CP14	30				

Purchases

Date	Details	Folio	$	Date	Details	Folio	$
19.10.X6	Bank	CP14	2,500				

Wages

Date	Details	Folio	$	Date	Details	Folio	$
19.10.X6	Bank	CP14	5,300				

Discount received

Date	Details	Folio	$	Date	Details	Folio	$
				19.10.X6	Payables – Osmosis	CP14	30

Payables ledger:

LS Shah

Date	Details	Folio	$	Date	Details	Folio	$
19.10.X6	Bank	CR14	2,300				

BA Chan

Date	Details	Folio	$	Date	Details	Folio	$
19.10.X6	Bank	CR14	5,200				

OS Mosis

Date	Details	Folio	$	Date	Details	Folio	$
19.10.X6	Bank	CR14	1,870				
19.10.X6	Disc rec'd	CR14	30				

ACTIVITY 6

1   A sole trader introduced $1,000 into the business by cheque. What is the double entry to record this transaction?

A   Debit Petty cash   Credit Capital

B   Debit Bank   Credit Capital

C   Debit Capital   Credit Petty cash

D   Debit Capital   Credit Bank

2   Jang purchased goods from a credit supplier. The cost of the goods was $250 on which the supplier added sales tax which was charged at 20%. Jang is registered to account for sales tax. How should this transaction be recorded in Jang's accounting records?

A   Debit Purchases $250, Credit Payables $250

B   Debit Purchases $250, Credit Payables $300
Debit Sales tax $50

C   Debit Purchases $250, Credit Bank $250

D   Debit Purchases $250, Credit Bank $300
Debit Sales tax $50

For suggested answers, see the 'Answers' section at the end of the book.

Remember that, whether a business uses computerised or manual accounting records, it needs to record and retain the same information. Users of computerised records therefore need to be familiar with how information is presented so that they understand the information they are using. For example, debits may be presented as positive (plus) items and credits may be presented as negative (minus) items in a computerised document that lists transactions, rather than presenting transactions in ledger account format.

5   AUTHORISING AND MAKING PAYMENTS

It is important that payments are only made for goods, services and expenses ordered and received by the business. Therefore if a payment is required, there must be sufficient evidence of that the goods, services or expenses have been received so that the payment is for a legitimate reason.

Computerised accounting systems may also generate payments in the form of automated direct payments and electronically-produced cheque payments to suppliers and others owed money by a business.

In these situations, it is vital that a suitably responsible person (a senior member of staff not directly involved in the process to raise and authorise payments) regularly reviews and approves payment transactions. It is also important that any payments made, in whatever form they may take, are subject to appropriate checks and controls to confirm that they are valid payments for goods and services received. No payments should be made without appropriate authorisation.

CONCLUSION

The management and control of cash and bank transactions is of fundamental importance to any business. In an earlier chapter we looked at the procedures for dealing with cash receipts and payments, ensuring that all receipts and payments are properly recorded and accounted for. We also noted the importance of checking monies received and paid to any supporting documentation, checking the calculation of any entitlement to discounts and issuing written receipts.

In this chapter you saw how receipts and payments are recorded in the cash and bank records of the business. Remember:

- a receipt of cash is recorded as a debit in the cash at bank ledger account

- a payment is credited to the cash at bank ledger account

- sales tax is recorded when the sales tax liability occurs which is when a cash sale or purchase takes place or the date when an invoice was created in respect of credit transactions

- sales tax and discounts received columns in cash and bank records are memorandum items. They must still be recorded in the general ledger.

KEY TERMS

Remittance list – A list of cheques received from customers.

Settlement discount – Discount for early payment of an invoice. Recorded in the general ledger as discounts received.

Trade discounts – A discount on the price of goods or services, agreed in advance (and often granted to regular customers or for bulk purchases).

SELF TEST QUESTIONS

		Paragraph
1	Where do receipts from credit customers have to be recorded?	1.2
2	What is a remittance list?	1.4

EXAM-STYLE QUESTIONS

1   Which of the following are the accounting entries required to record a cash purchase of $600 from Georgio Caterers?

   A   Dr Purchases $600; Cr Georgio Caterers $600

   B   Dr Georgio Caterers $600; Cr Purchases $600

   C   Dr Purchases $600; Cr Cash $600

   D   Dr Cash $600: Cr Purchases $600

2   The total of the discounts in the cash payments record for April 20X7 is $80. One part of the double-entry required to reflect this will be recorded in the trade payables account.

   What is the other accounting entry required to properly record this transaction in the general ledger?

   A   Dr Revenue

   B   Cr Revenue

   C   Dr Discount received

   D   Cr Discount received

3   Sales tax is recorded in the cash records:

   A   When a sale is made on credit

   B   When a cheque is received from a credit customer

   C   When a cash sale takes place

   D   When discounts are received

For suggested answers, see the 'Answers' section at the end of the book

Chapter 8

MAINTAINING PETTY CASH RECORDS

Most business expenditure is paid out of the business bank account, by cheque, BACS transfer, direct debit, or other payment methods. Occasionally, however, small items of expense need to be paid for in cash. Cash may be needed to pay for small items of incidental or occasional expense, such as office refreshments or cleaning materials. Cash expenditure needs to be controlled carefully, to prevent theft, and to ensure that it is properly recorded.

This chapter explains the nature of petty cash, how petty cash systems are organised and operated and how expense items are recorded in the accounting system. It covers the syllabus area of maintaining petty cash records.

This chapter covers syllabus areas F2.

CONTENTS

1   Operation of petty cash

2   Documentation

3   Authorisation

4   Security of cash

5   Queries and problems

6   Manual petty cash records

7   Imprest and non-imprest methods

8   Petty cash reconciliation

LEARNING OUTCOMES

At the end of this chapter, you should be able to:

•   recognise the types of transaction likely to be paid out of petty cash

•   account for petty cash using imprest and non-imprest methods

•   exercise control over petty cash and recognise how control can be maintained

•   record petty cash claims

•   reconcile the petty cash to cash in hand.

1 OPERATION OF PETTY CASH

1.1 HOW PETTY CASH WORKS

The petty cash system of a business usually operates as follows:

Step 1 An employee pays personally for a business expense, such as refreshments the office or a train fare to attend a meeting, and obtains a receipt for the payment.

Step 2 The employee then reclaims the expense from the business through the petty cash system, by completing and signing a petty cash voucher and handing over the receipt for the money spent.

Step 3 The expense is then recorded as a business expense in the general ledger. This process is explained later.

2 DOCUMENTATION

To ensure that the petty cash system is not abused and that payments are made to meet only valid business expenses, there must be a system of authorisation for petty cash claims.

In addition, for accounting purposes, all payments out of petty cash must be properly documented.

2.1 PETTY CASH VOUCHERS

The initial record of any petty cash claim is a petty cash voucher. Blank petty cash vouchers are obtainable from stationery suppliers in pads, and each voucher is torn off the pad as and when it is used. An example of a blank voucher is shown below:

Petty Cash Voucher No. _____		
Date _____		
For what required	AMOUNT $	¢
Signature _____		
Authorised _____		

Notes on completing a petty cash voucher

- Petty cash vouchers have a unique identification number. For control purposes, they should be numbered sequentially by the person in charge of petty cash.

- Each voucher should be dated when it is prepared and authorised.

- The details of the expenditure and the amount should be included in the voucher. If there is a receipt, this should be attached.

- The person claiming the petty cash should sign the voucher.

- The person authorising the claim should also sign the voucher.

3 AUTHORISATION

Authorisation of petty cash claims is an important issue. Each business should have a policy regarding who is permitted to authorise petty cash claims. The following alternative approaches may be considered:

The person responsible for the petty cash, the petty cashier, may be given responsibility for authorisation of all petty cash claims.

A senior employee, other than the petty cashier, such as the chief accountant, may be required to authorise all petty cash claims.

The petty cashier may authorise all claims up to a specified amount, whilst another appropriate person authorises claims above this amount.

3.1 AUTHORISATION PROCEDURE

The person authorising the petty cash claim must make two checks.

- The claim should be supported by adequate documentation proving the expense is for valid business purposes, such as a receipt.

- The claim should not exceed the petty cash limits of the business. Claims above a certain amount should be made as an expenses claim for payment by cheque or BACS, and not as a petty cash claim for payment in cash.

The petty cashier should refuse to make a petty cash payment unless the claim has been properly authorised, as evidenced by the signature on the petty cash voucher.

3.2 SUPPORTING DOCUMENTATION

To ensure that a petty cash claim is a valid business expense, each claim must be supported by documentation demonstrating that the expense is genuine. Before the petty cash claim is authorised, this supporting documentation must be checked.

Most types of petty cash claim are for straightforward office expenses such as the purchase of refreshments, cleaning materials or small travel expenses for staff to attend meetings etc. In these situations, a simple receipt or till roll receipt is sufficient evidence of the payment for the expense. For bus, train or taxi fares, the ticket itself is probably sufficient evidence.

However, if the payment includes sales tax that can be reclaimed from the tax authorities, a proper sales tax receipt showing the supplier's name and sales tax registration number is required. Most till roll receipts do show this information.

In each case the supporting documentation should be attached to the petty cash claim.

Sales tax as part of the expense

Provided there is a valid tax receipt (i.e. a written receipt containing the supplier's sales tax registration number), the sales tax included in a cash payment can be claimed back from the tax authorities. To record the sales tax properly, the amount of the tax should be shown in the petty cash voucher. The voucher will therefore show the expense exclusive of tax, the sales tax and the total expense inclusive of tax. The sales tax should be itemised on the tax receipt.

ACTIVITY 1

Below is a till receipt. Sales tax is set at 20%:

Price's Stationers	
15 Reams A 4 paper	$17.80
200 Envelopes	$5.00
Total	$22.80
Received with thanks 30/5/X7	
Sales tax registration: 72 38 237 840	

Task

Complete the petty cash voucher.

Petty Cash Voucher No. _____		
Date _____		
	AMOUNT	
For what required	$	¢
Supporting documentation		
Signature _____		
Authorised _____		

For a suggested answer, see the 'Answers' section at the end of the book.

3.3 NO SUPPORTING DOCUMENTATION

Some expense claims may not have a supporting receipt. For example, the employee may have lost the receipt, or an employee may have paid for a train fare to a meeting, and the ticket was collected upon leaving the train.

In such circumstances, most businesses have a policy that the claim can still be authorised if it is deemed to be reasonable. This may involve authorisation by the manager responsible for the claimant's work, as this manager is most likely to be able to judge whether, say, a journey, did take place and was for a valid business reason.

3.4 PAYMENTS IN ADVANCE

In some instances, an employee may not have enough cash to purchase the item from their own money and then reclaim it from petty cash later. The employee will therefore ask the petty cashier for cash in advance to pay for the item or the expense. Any such advance payment must be authorised by an appropriate person.

When the expenditure has been incurred, the employee will normally be required to provide appropriate documentation of the actual expense (typically, a receipt) and return any surplus cash to the petty cashier.

In such cases, a petty cash voucher is initially completed for the amount of cash taken, and when the surplus cash is returned, the voucher is then amended to show the actual correct amount of the expense.

Example

The managing director's assistant is required to buy some light refreshments for a board meeting but does not have enough personal cash on hand to do so.

The assistant makes a claim from petty cash for $10, the estimated price of the items required. The actual expense is $8.47, which includes sales tax at 20%.

How would this be dealt with?

Solution

Step 1   The petty cashier must obtain authorisation for the cash payment from an appropriate person, such as the managing director or chief accountant. Therefore a petty cash voucher is completed for $10 and suitably authorised.

Petty Cash Voucher	No. 698		
Date *3 April 20X9*			
For what required		AMOUNT $	¢
Refreshments including sales tax @20%		10	00
Signature *MD's Assistant*			
Authorised *Chief accountant*			

Step 2   The managing director's assistant buys the goods which actually cost $8.47 including sales tax. The assistant returns the surplus cash of $1.53 to the petty cashier together plus a receipt for $8.47.

Step 3   The receipt is attached to the petty cash voucher and the voucher is altered to show the actual cost of the goods purchased. The net amount is sales tax is $8.47 × (100/120) = $7.06. The sales tax element is $8.47 − $7.06 = $1.41.

Petty Cash Voucher	No.	698	
Date *3 April 20X9*			
For what required		AMOUNT $	¢
Refreshments		7 ~~10~~	06 ~~00~~
VAT		1	41
Total		8	47
Signature *MD's Assistant*			
Authorised *Chief accountant*			

4   SECURITY OF CASH

Petty cash is usually kept in a metal tin or box with a lock and key. The notes and coins held to meet petty cash claims is usually referred to as the 'float'. Inside the petty cash tin, there will be the float of notes and coins (and a pad of petty cash vouchers) plus receipts for payments of petty cash expenses made from the float. Every so often the petty cash float is topped up by withdrawing more cash from the bank account.

Clearly, there is a security problem with petty cash, and it is important that:

- the petty cash float plus vouchers are kept in a secure place, such as a locked desk drawer, to avoid loss and deter theft

- only designated responsible individuals should be permitted to make petty cash payments.

To reduce the risk of loss, a business should maintain a cash float only as much as it considers reasonably necessary, so that if the cash float is lost or stolen, the amount of the loss is minimised.

5 QUERIES AND PROBLEMS

Occasionally, when petty cash claims are being processed, a query may arise. Possible reasons for this include:

- a petty cash voucher may not have been signed by an authorised person

- the petty cash voucher may be incomplete in some way, perhaps a receipt is not attached.

The person making the claim should be advised that petty cash claims cannot be paid if they are incomplete or without proper authorisation. The claimant should be asked why authorisation has not been obtained and to complete the claim properly.

There could be a perfectly understandable reason for this. For example, there may be only two persons permitted to authorise claims, and they may both be absent. There should be established procedures for dealing with such circumstances. Usually, the query should be referred to someone more senior for a decision.

Alternately, the claimant may simply not have tried to obtain the necessary authorisation. If this is the case, the claimant should be asked to do so.

- There may be insufficient supporting documentation as evidence of the expense. For example, the claimant may have forgotten to obtain a receipt, or the claim may be for a local bus fare and there is no receipt. Unless there are established procedures for dealing with such situations, the query should be referred to a more senior person for a decision.

- If the petty cash claim exceeds the limit for payments from the petty cash float, the claimant should be asked to make an expenses claim in line with the business's normal procedures.

6 MANUAL PETTY CASH RECORDS

Although petty cash payments are usually quite small, they must be properly accounted for. A petty cash record may be maintained using a book, log or similar document. This record will be used as the basis for recording petty cash transactions in the general ledger.

Most of the petty cash transactions are payments for expenses. However, money withdrawn from the bank account to top up petty cash should also be recorded. Top-ups of the petty cash float are recorded in the petty cash record as cash received and in the bank records as a cash payment.

Recording petty cash transactions is similar to recording bank transactions. However, as receipts into petty cash will be withdrawals of cash from the bank account, there is no need for any further analysis of the petty cash receipts.

Petty cash payments could be for a range of different expenses, so there will be a need for analysis of the payments made. This analysis will normally be consistent with the general ledger expense account headings.

The petty cash payments records should therefore enable the following to be recorded:

- the petty cash voucher number

- brief details of the expense

- the total amount of the expense

- analysis columns, including a column for sales tax.

6.1 RECORDING PETTY CASH PAYMENTS

The source documents for recording petty cash payments in the petty cash book or log are the petty cash vouchers. At regular intervals, perhaps weekly or every time the petty cash float is topped up, these petty cash vouchers should be recorded in the petty cash book or log.

- Each voucher represents one petty cash transaction, and should be entered on one line of the book or log.

- The vouchers should be recorded in sequential number order (according to their identifying number).

The payments are analysed in the petty cash book or log so that the expenses can be posted to the relevant accounts in the general ledger. There should be an analysis column in the petty cash book or log for each expense account in the general ledger for which petty cash expenses may be incurred.

When an expense includes sales tax, the amount of the expense in the Total column should be for the total spending, including the sales tax. In the analysis columns, however, the sales tax is shown separately, and the other analysis columns record the net expense i.e. excluding sales tax.

Example

Given below are a number of petty cash vouchers.

Task

Write up the petty cash book or log to record these transactions.

Petty Cash Voucher	No. 340		Petty Cash Voucher	No. 341	
Date 22/3/X3			Date 22/3/X3		
	AMOUNT			AMOUNT	
For what required	$	¢	For what required	$	¢
Postage stamps	7	10	Stationery (inclusive of 20% VAT)	28	00
Signature P Nelson			Signature V Bacon		
Authorised J Falk			Authorised J Falk		

Petty Cash Voucher	No. *342*
Date *22/3/X3*	

For what required	AMOUNT $	¢
Rail fare	6	40

Signature   *R Andrew*

Authorised   *J Falk*

Petty Cash Voucher	No. *343*
Date *26/3/X3*	

For what required	AMOUNT $	¢
Tea, coffee	3	49

Signature   *M Baston*

Authorised   *J Falk*

Petty Cash Voucher	No. *344*
Date *26/3/X3*	

For what required	AMOUNT $	¢
Taxi (no VAT invoice)	2	40

Signature   *M Johnson*

Authorised   *J Falk*

Petty Cash Voucher	No. *345*
Date *26/3/X3*	

For what required	AMOUNT $	¢
Rail fare	11	40

Signature   *R Andrew*

Authorised   *J Falk*

Solution

Petty cash book or log

Date	Receipts $	Voucher/ Ref no	Details	Total payment $		Sales tax $		Travel expenses $		Office expenses $		Postage $		Stationery $		Sundry $	
22/3		340	Stamps	7	10							7	10				
22/3		341	Stationery	28	00	4	66							23	34		
22/3		342	Rail fare	6	40			6	40								
26/3		343	Refreshments	3	49					3	49						
26/3		344	Taxi	2	40			2	40								
26/3		345	Rail fare	11	40			11	40								

7 IMPREST AND NON-IMPREST METHODS

7.1 IMPREST SYSTEM FOR PETTY CASH

Petty cash payments are regularly made by most businesses. From time to time the cash balance is topped up so that it does not run out. There are several systems for topping up the petty cash float. The most common system used is the imprest system.

A petty cash box or tin is set up with a specified amount of cash. This amount of cash is known as the **imprest amount.** This should be enough cash to cover foreseeable petty cash expenses for, say, two to four weeks. The aim is to avoid having to top up petty cash too often, but at the same time avoid having too much cash in the petty cash float, where it could be at risk of loss or theft.

Completed petty cash vouchers are stored in the petty cash tin whenever cash is paid out. Periodically, the amount of cash in the tin is topped up to the original imprest amount. When this happens, the petty cash vouchers in the tin should be taken out, and filed away safely. (Before they are filed away, they should be used to record the transactions in the petty cash book or log. This is explained later.)

The amount of cash required to top up the petty cash float is therefore the amount of money taken out since the last time it was topped up. This should be the total value of the vouchers in the petty cash tin.

A check can therefore be made, when petty cash is topped up, that the amount required to top up the petty cash float is the total value of the vouchers in the tin. This is a useful security check, to deter the theft of cash. Indeed, the petty cash tin can be checked at any time and the total of the cash on hand plus the value of the petty cash vouchers should equal the imprest total.

The petty cash float is topped up with cash obtained by a payment from the bank account.

ACTIVITY 2

The petty cash system of HHG is operated on an imprest system, and the imprest amount is $100. The petty cash float is topped up every week.

At the end of one particular week, there are petty cash vouchers in the tin for $4.67, $12.90, $2.99, $5.06 and $16.25.

How much cash should be withdrawn from the bank to restore the petty cash float to $100?

For a suggested answer, see the 'Answers' section at the end of the book.

7.2 NON-IMPREST SYSTEM

Most petty cash systems operate with an imprest system, because there is an in-built check to make sure that cash is not lost or stolen. However, it is also possible to set up a system that is not an imprest system, and to simply top-up the cash float every so often.

For example, suppose a business estimates that the weekly petty cash expenditure is approximately $50, and it wants to top up the petty cash float every two weeks. Withdrawals from petty cash are made using the procedures already described.

A petty cash float could be set up with an initial amount of $100. Every two weeks, a further $100 would be withdrawn from the bank account to supplement the petty cash float.

This system could work well if petty cash expenditure each week is, in fact, below $50. However, problems may be encountered if expense claims are higher than expected in any two-week period, so that the petty cash float may be insufficient to meet all valid claims. Equally if expenditure was significantly less than $50 each week, then a large surplus float would develop, possibly increasing the risk of loss or theft of cash.

As the imprest system is more common, the remainder of the chapter is based on this system.

7.3 RECORDING PETTY CASH RECEIPTS

When cash is received to top-up the petty cash float it is normally being topped up to the imprest amount (or any other amount in a non-imprest system). Therefore, the cash that is increasing the petty cash float is from the bank account.

The petty cash log or book will simply show the receipt of cash from the bank and the date of the receipt.

Example

A petty cash system has an imprest amount of $50. On 26 March there is a cash float remaining of $1.21 plus vouchers showing claims of $48.79.

Task

Calculate the amount of cash required to top-up the petty cash float to restore the imprest amount ox on 26 March 20X3 and record this amount in the petty cash log or book.

Solution

The amount required to restore the petty cash imprest amount is $48.79. This covers the claims made during the period and tops up the cash float to the imprest amount of $50.

The entry in the petty cash log or book would be shown as follows:

Date	Receipts	Payments			
		Voucher number	Details	Total payment	Sales tax
	$			$	$
26/3	48.79		Bank		

Petty cash log or book entry

The cash paid to restore the petty cash float is cash withdrawn from the bank account. Therefore the bank ledger account will show a payment on the same date for the amount of cash required, in the example above $48.79.

7.4 TOTALLING THE PETTY CASH LOG OR BOOK

When all petty cash receipts and payments have been made during a period, they must be recorded in the petty cash log or book. The analysis of payments must be totalled in preparation for them to be recorded in the general ledger. This may be done, either at the time the cash float is topped-up or at fixed intervals, for example at the month-end.

ACTIVITY 3

On 1 May 20X3 a business established a $100 float (the imprest amount) for the first time. During the week ended 8 May the following petty cash vouchers were stored with the petty cash log or book when the claims were paid:

Petty Cash Voucher	No. 832		
Date 1 May X3			
For what required	AMOUNT	$	¢
Printing letterheads (including 20% VAT)		31	50
Signature B Gordon			
Authorised P Cash			

Petty Cash Voucher	No. 833		
Date 1 May X3			
For what required	AMOUNT	$	¢
Taxi (no VAT invoice)		7	40
Signature A McDougall			
Authorised J Falk			

Petty Cash Voucher	No. 834		
Date 3 May X3			
For what required	AMOUNT	$	¢
Tea, coffee		8	23
Signature S P Oak			
Authorised P Cash			

Petty Cash Voucher	No. 835		
Date 4 May X3			
For what required	AMOUNT	$	¢
Stationery (including 20% VAT)		12	49
Signature J Wilson			
Authorised P Cash			

Petty Cash Voucher	No.	836		Petty Cash Voucher	No.	837	

Date 5 May X3			Date 5 May X3		

For what required	AMOUNT $	¢	For what required	AMOUNT $	¢
Taxi (VAT invoice attached) Tax @ 20%	11	30	Train fare	6	50

Signature B Phipps	Signature J Wilson
Authorised P Cash	Authorised P Cash

On 8 May the amount of cash required to restore the petty cash float to $100 was withdrawn from the bank.

Task

Write up all of these entries in the petty cash log or book. Ensure that the payments side is totalled and that all of the totals cross-cast.

For a suggested answer, see the 'Answers' section at the end of the book.

7.5   POSTING PETTY TRANSACTIONS INTO THE GENERAL LEDGER

When the petty cash log or book has been totalled, the total amounts are then posted to the relevant accounts in the general ledger, as follows:

For cash paid into the petty cash float from the bank account:

- Debit   Petty cash
- Credit   Bank

For expense payments out of the petty cash:

- Credit   Petty cash account with the total of payments
- Debit   Sales tax account with the total in the sales tax analysis column
- Debit   Expense accounts with the total for each expense analysis column

ACTIVITY 4

Record the following transactions in the petty cash log or book and post the month end totals into the general ledger. The balance brought down on the petty cash account on 1 September 20X4 is the imprest amount of $50.

Date

2nd	Coffee purchased for $1.89 (no sales tax)
4th	Repair to light switch $12.00 ($2.00 sales tax)
10th	Taxi fare $5 (no sales tax)
15th	Pay cleaner $15 (no sales tax)
25th	Repairs $5.88 ($0.98 sales tax)

The imprest float was restored on 30 September.

For a suggested answer, see the 'Answers' section at the end of the book.

8 PETTY CASH RECONCILIATION

Each time the petty cashier pays out a sum of money from the petty cash float then this payment must be supported by a valid, authorised petty cash voucher. Each petty cash voucher is, in turn, retained until the petty cash float is due to be topped up to the imprest amount.

8.1 CASH AND VOUCHERS

At any point in time the cash notes and coins in the petty cash float plus the vouchers for amounts reimbursed should be equal to the initial amount in the petty cash box, the imprest amount. For control purposes it is important that this is checked at regular intervals.

ACTIVITY 5

A petty cash system is operated with an imprest amount of $200. Each Friday, just before the petty cash float is topped up to $200, the amount of cash is counted and the vouchers supporting payments made in the week are totalled. On this particular Friday the cash in the petty cash float consisted of the following:

Quantity

4	$20 notes
2	$10 notes
2	$5 notes
5	$1 coins
3	50c coins
7	20c coins
15	10c coins
6	5c coins
4	2c coins
9	1c coins

The petty cash vouchers for payments made paid during the week were as follows:

Petty Cash Voucher	No. 731

Date 19/6/X5

For what required	AMOUNT $	¢
Rail fare	11	30
Taxi	4	60
	15	90

Signature   S Pilau

Authorised   J Morris

Petty Cash Voucher	No. 732

Date 19/6/X5

For what required	AMOUNT $	¢
Tea biscuits	6	73

Signature   P Peers

Authorised   J Morris

Petty Cash Voucher	No. 733

Date 20/6/X5

For what required	AMOUNT $	¢
Milkman	21	90

Signature   P Peers

Authorised   J Morris

Petty Cash Voucher	No. 734

Date 19/6/X5

For what required	AMOUNT $	¢
Rail fare	27	00
Taxi x 2	8	60
	35	60

Signature   F T Winter

Authorised   J Morris

Task

Reconcile the imprest amount of $200 consisting of notes and coins on hand plus vouchers for payments made.

For a suggested answer, see the 'Answers' section at the end of the book.

8.2   DIFFERENCES ARISING

In Activity 5, the reconciliation of cash and vouchers showed that there were no differences arising. The notes and coins plus the vouchers totalled the imprest amount.

However, in some instances, when the reconciliation is carried out there may be differences. Whenever a difference arises this must be investigated immediately. Possible reasons for differences may be:

(a)   petty cash vouchers prepared for an incorrect amount, but the correct amount being paid out in cash

(b)   an incorrect amount being paid out in cash, and

(c)   notes and coins lost or stolen from the petty cash float.

ACTIVITY 6

On Monday 3 January 20X2, just before the petty float was due to be topped up to the imprest amount of $50, the cash and vouchers at that time were counted.

The note and coins in the float were as follows:

$1 \times$ $5 note

$2 \times$ $1 coins

$6 \times$ 50¢ coins

$5 \times$ 20¢ coins

$3 \times$ 10¢ coins

$2 \times$ 5¢ coins

24¢ in small denomination coins

The following vouchers were with the float as evidence of recent payments made:

Petty Cash Voucher	No. *1142*	
Date *29/12/X1*		
For what required	AMOUNT $	¢
Stamps	6	50
Signature *G Jones*		
Authorised *P Smith*		

Petty Cash Voucher	No. *1143*	
Date *30/12/X1*		
For what required	AMOUNT $	¢
Taxi	7	00
Signature *P*		
Authorised *P Smith*		

Petty Cash Voucher	No. *1144*	
Date *30/12/X1*		
For what required	AMOUNT $	¢
Windowcleaner	21	00
Signature *G Jones*		
Authorised *P Smith*		

Petty Cash Voucher	No. *1145*	
Date *30/12/X1*		
For what required	AMOUNT $	¢
Bus fare	1	20
Signature *S Cameron*		
Authorised *P Smith*		

Petty Cash Voucher	No. *1146*		
Date *30/12/X1*			
		AMOUNT	
For what required		$	¢
Photocopying		1	66
Signature *G Jones*			
Authorised *P Smith*			

Task

Reconcile the cash and vouchers in the petty cash box to the imprest amount. Give possible reasons for any difference that is discovered.

For a suggested answer, see the 'Answers' section at the end of the book.

CONCLUSION

We have now looked at how most payments are made by a business and recorded in the accounting system. Even the smallest amounts must be justifiable, be properly evidenced and authorised. The expenditure must then be recorded correctly in the petty cash log or book, and then in the general ledger.

The petty cash book may be kept on the imprest or non-imprest system.

Float plus the vouchers for recent payments should be reconciled regularly to identify and resolve any issue identified.

KEY TERMS

Imprest system – System commonly used to account for petty cash, whereby the total amount of cash in the petty cash float is periodically topped up to a given limit. At all times, the petty cash vouchers plus the notes and coins in the float should be equal to this limit.

Petty cash float – The value of notes and coins held at any point in order to make petty cash payments. It should be held in a secure location and under the control of a responsible person.

Petty cash voucher – Document kept in the petty cash giving details of money paid out and the reasons for the expense.

SELF TEST QUESTIONS

		Paragraph
1	How should petty cash vouchers be numbered?	2
2	What two checks must the person authorising a petty cash claim make?	3
3	What document should ideally support a petty cash claim?	3
4	Could petty cash claims be paid with no supporting documentation?	3
5	Explain how petty cash is kept secure.	4
6	What is meant by the imprest system?	7
7	How are top-ups of petty cash recorded?	7
8	State three reasons why the total of cash and vouchers in a petty cash box might not equal the imprest amount.	8

EXAM-STYLE QUESTIONS

1   Petty cash can be checked and reconciled at any time, even if the petty cash log or book is not up to date. Which of the following formulae is used for reconciling petty cash?

A   Petty cash vouchers – Cash held = Imprest

B   Imprest + Petty cash vouchers = Cash held

C   Imprest + Cash held = Petty cash vouchers

D   Petty cash vouchers + Cash held = Imprest

2   The following petty cash payments include sales tax at 20%.

- $1.18
- $2.31
- $4.60
- $5.00
- $2.87
- $3.91
- $6.21
- $1.85
- $2.33
- $4.96

What is the total of sale tax relating to these payments in the petty cash log or book?

A $5.87

B $7.04

C $35.22

D $29.35

3   A petty cash system operates with an imprest amount of $200. Each Friday just before
     the petty cash is topped up to $200 the amount of cash is counted and the vouchers in
     the petty cash box are totalled. On one particular Friday, the petty cash float
     amounted to $97.80 and the petty cash vouchers totalled $102.20. How much is
     needed to restore it to its imprest amount of $200?

     A $102.20

     B $97.80

     C $4.40

     D $200.00

For suggested answers, see the 'Answers' section at the end of the book.

Chapter 9

SALES AND SALES RECORDS

This chapter explains the procedures for recording income from credit sales, from the preparation of an invoice to recording the income in the accounting records. It covers the syllabus area of sales and sales returns.

This chapter covers syllabus areas G1.

CONTENTS

1   Source documents for sales and sales returns

2   Types of discount – a reminder

3   General principles of sales taxes – a reminder

4   Preparing a sales invoice and credit note

5   Methods of coding data

LEARNING OUTCOMES

At the end of this chapter, you should be able to:

*   identify and recognise source sales documents

*   calculate and account for trade and settlement discounts

*   calculate and account for sales tax on transactions

*   complete sales invoices and process credit notes

*   code sales and customer records and data.

1 SOURCE DOCUMENTS FOR SALES AND SALES RETURNS

1.1 THE PURPOSE OF SALES INVOICES

When a credit sale is made, the cash from the sale is not received immediately. Instead, the customer receives the goods or services and will then pay at a later date. It is therefore necessary to have a record, and a reminder, of the fact that the customer owes the money for the goods or services sold. This evidence is created in the form of a sales invoice.

- One copy is sent to the customer as a reminder to pay.

- One or more copies are retained by the seller.

From **the seller's point of view**, the sales invoice serves a number of purposes.

- It is a record of the amount owed by the customer and the date by which the payment is due.

- It provides a record of the sale, and this can be used as a source document to enter the details of the sale into the accounting records.

From **the customer's point of view**, the invoice also has a number of purposes (to the customer, it is a purchase invoice).

- It is a reminder of the goods or services that were purchased, the amount payable to the supplier and when the payment is due.

- It provides a record of the purchase, and this can be used as a source document to enter the details of the purchase into the accounting records.

A sales invoice is also an official document for external bodies, such as the tax authority (HM Revenue and Customs in the UK). There are certain legal requirements that a sales invoice must comply with, particularly with regard to sales tax.

1.2 COPIES OF SALES INVOICES

When a sales invoice is prepared, it is usually produced in multiple copies. The top copy or main copy is sent to the customer. The remaining copies remain with the seller. The seller can use these copies for a variety of purposes:

- to update the accounting records (accounts department)

- to file for reference, for example in the event of a query or complaint by the customer (sales department or customer services department)

- to maintain good business and accounting records.

Records are not only essential for tax purposes, but also other governing bodies and local authorities may require a business to maintain certain records. In the UK, businesses need to keep all invoices (as well as quotations, order forms, credit notes, delivery notes, till rolls, banking records and other documents) for six years in case they are requested. Outside the UK, the details of which records must be retained, and for how long, may differ.

1.3 WHEN ARE SALES INVOICES PRODUCED?

In some cases, the sales invoice will be sent out to the customer with the goods or with the person providing the service, so that the customer receives the invoice with the goods or immediately the service is provided. However, it is more usual for goods to be sent to a customer with a delivery note (that the customer may be asked to sign as confirmation of receipt) and for the sales invoice to be sent out separately. This will always be the case if the goods are delivered to the customer's warehouse, and for the invoice to be sent to the accounts or buying department, which may be in different locations.

When an invoice is for provision of a service, the invoice is usually sent to the customer after the service has been provided. For example, if an accountant sends an invoice to a client for the time spent preparing monthly accounts, this invoice cannot be issued until the work is complete and the time charges are known.

In some cases, an invoice may be issued before the goods or services are provided. For example, in most forms of rental agreement, such as the hire of a car, an invoice is sent to the customer either in advance or at the start of the rental or hire period.

One important point is to determine the contract price to be invoiced in exchange for goods or services provided. This could be based upon, for example, a price list, or previous dealings with the customer or normal business practice. Part of this process includes assessing whether a customer will take up the offer of early settlement discount. Consequently, the income receivable will be variable, depending upon whether the customer takes up the early settlement discount offer (a lower amount is receivable) or does not pay promptly (the full amount is receivable). This issue was considered in Chapter 4 and will be revisited in this chapter.

1.4 CONTENTS OF A SALES INVOICE

Most of the essential contents of a sales invoice were covered in Chapter 2. However, there are also some further specific contents that an invoice must contain if the business is registered for sales tax or is a registered company.

Refer to the specimen sales invoice which follows explanation of the key invoice details as follows:

(a) **Customer name and address**

This is the name and address to which the invoice should be sent (the 'invoice address').

(b) **Name of the seller's business, business address and telephone number**

This shows the customer who the invoice is from, and contact details in the event of having any queries. The invoice may include some pre-printed payment instructions on the back. In the absence of any other such instructions, this information also shows the customer who to make the payment to and where to send it.

(c) **Invoice number**

Every invoice is given a number. The invoice number must be unique to the invoice so that the invoice can be specifically identified. When sales invoices are produced, they are numbered sequentially. This means that, when preparing sales invoices, and aware that the most recent invoice was numbered 47733, the next sales invoice will be numbered 47734, and so on.

(d)   **Invoice date**

The invoice date is important for accounting purposes, because it indicates the accounting period in which the sale has occurred. The date is also useful as a reference point for when the invoice should be paid.

The invoice date is often the same date as the delivery date, particularly when the delivery note and invoice are both generated by computer at the same time.

(e)   **Customer account number or reference**

The customer account number or reference is used internally by the business. Each credit customer (or 'account customer') has a unique account number or reference, in the form of a code. Customer account code numbers are used to update the receivables' ledger accounts of each credit customer.

(f)   **Details of the goods or services supplied**

This information allows both the business and its customers to see details of what is being sold and the price to be paid. Sometimes, this part of the invoice gives a general description of the goods or service. Sometimes, as in the example following, the goods or services are itemised in detail, and may show the inventory item code number and description, the quantity sold and the price per unit. The total amount payable for each item, if they are priced separately, is also shown. (If there is no discount to calculate, the total payable for an item is simply the quantity supplied in units multiplied by the price per unit.)

(g)   **Trade discounts**

Trade discounts are not always shown on an invoice. Discounts were discussed in chapter 4 and will be revisited in this chapter.

(h), (l) and (m)

Final total value

The total invoice value must be shown because this is the amount the customer is being asked to pay. When sales tax is included in the invoice, it is essential to show separately:

- the total payable excluding sales tax

- the sales tax payable

- the total payable including sales tax.

(i)   **Settlement terms**

The settlement terms state when the invoice should be paid. These terms are usually agreed when the customer makes an order, but it is certainly worth repeating the terms on the invoice as well. Sometimes, a percentage discount (known as a settlement discount) is given if the invoice is paid earlier than when payment would normally be due.

(j)   **Sales tax registration number**

When a business is registered for sales tax, it is given a unique registration number (by HM Revenue and Customs in the UK). This number must be shown on the invoice.

(k)   **Tax point**

The tax point on an invoice is the date when a transaction is deemed to have taken place for sales tax purposes. It enables the tax on the transaction to be recorded in the correct accounting period. Normally, the tax point is the invoice date.

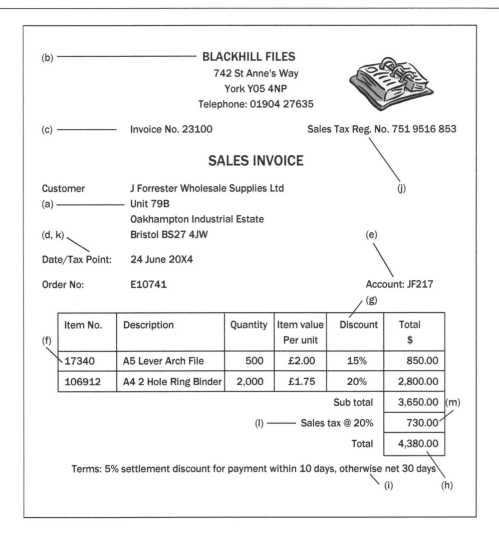

1.5 SETTLEMENT TERMS: TERMS SOMETIMES USED

Some specific words may be used in the settlement terms at the foot of a sales invoice and it may be useful to know the meaning of the following three terms.

- If settlement is stated as '**net 30 days**' this means that, in the absence of an offer of any settlement discount, the invoice should be paid within 30 days of the invoice date. Similarly, 'net 60 days' means that the invoice should be paid within 60 days of the invoice date. It is normal business practice to use '30 days', '60 days' or '90 days' as meaning '1 month' '2 months' or '3 months' respectively.

- The term '**E & OE**', appears on an invoice, it refers to 'errors and omissions excepted'. This means that the seller reserves the right to amend any error that is subsequently identified on the invoice.

- A sales invoice may include the term '**ex works**'. This means that the price quoted does not include the cost of delivery of the goods. The customer will therefore have to pay for the delivery of the goods separately, perhaps to a haulage firm that makes the delivery.

1.6 PURPOSE OF A CREDIT NOTE

A **credit note** is effectively the opposite of a sales invoice. It is a document issued to a customer stating that they no longer owe money for certain items.

A credit note will be required in the following circumstances when **an invoice has already been sent out** to the customer:

- a customer has returned some or all of the goods because they are damaged or faulty.

- a customer has returned some or all of the goods because they are not the goods that were ordered.

- a customer never received the goods although an invoice was issued.

- an error was made on the original invoice which is corrected using a credit note.

In each case is necessary to issue a credit note to the customer to reverse or correct the relevant part of the original invoice. This is done instead of cancelling the original invoice and issuing a replacement.

From the **seller's point of view**, the credit note serves the following purposes:

- it indicates that the amount shown on the credit note is no longer due from the customer.

- the details on the credit note are used for entering the information into the accounting records.

From the **customer's point of view**, the credit note serves similar purposes:

- it is evidence that the amount shown is no longer due to the seller.

- it can be used to update the customer's accounting records.

To the seller, the credit note is a credit note issued for 'sales returns'. To the customer, the credit note is a credit note received for 'purchases returns'.

1.7 COPIES OF CREDIT NOTES

It is usual practice to send out the top copy of the credit note to the customer and to use any remaining copies for filing, accounting, and control and reference purposes.

1.8 WHEN ARE CREDIT NOTES PRODUCED?

If a customer is issued with a credit note, it may be reasonable to suppose that the customer is dissatisfied in some way. In order to regain the customer's goodwill, it is important to issue the credit note as soon as possible, to show that the matter has been dealt with promptly.

1.9 CONTENTS OF A CREDIT NOTE

The information required on a credit note is very similar to the information on a sales invoice, although there are some differences. An example of a credit note is given below.

LEWIS.PAPER

47/49 Mill Lane
Manchester M23 6AZ
Telephone: 0161 872 3641

(a) ———————————————— **CREDIT NOTE**

(b) ——————— Credit Note No. 23100   Sales Tax Reg. No. 486 4598 220

Customer   J Forrester Wholesale Supplies Ltd
                Unit 79B
                Oakhampton Industrial Estate
                Bristol BS27 4JW

Date/Tax Point: 24 June 20X4

Original Invoice No: 21391 ——————— (c)   Account: 216340

Item No.	Description	Quantity	Item value	Discount	Total $
ST095	A4 Copier Paper Green	20 reams	£5.40 per ream	10%	97.20

	Sub total	97.20
Reason for credit note	Sales tax at 20%	19.44
Goods returned as damaged in transit —— (d)	Credit note total	£116.64

From this, it can be seen that the key differences between a sales invoice and credit note are as follows.

(a)   The words '**credit note**' are displayed prominently on the document, to avoid confusion with an invoice.

(b)   Instead of an invoice number, there is a unique credit note number. Like sales invoices, credit notes issued are numbered sequentially.

(c)   A reference should be provided to the original invoice number to which the credit note relates.

(d)   A reason for the credit note being sent out should be included.

Otherwise, credit notes and sales invoices have a similar appearance. To avoid confusion between the two, credit notes may be printed on different coloured paper from sales invoices.

2   TYPES OF DISCOUNT – A REMINDER

2.1   TRADE DISCOUNTS

Trade discounts are given to customers for a variety of reasons. The main reason a trade discount is offered is to encourage customers to either purchase more goods over a period of time and/or to encourage them to place larger individual orders.

It is normal policy to show the percentage of trade discount on the face of a sales invoice. The customer pays the net price. If sales tax is charged, it should be added to the net price, and the customer is required to pay the net price plus sales tax. Different percentages of trade discount may be applied to different products, in which case the relevant percentage discount is normally shown against each product on the invoice before sales tax is calculated, as in the following layout:

Product	Description	Quantity	Item price $	Discount	Total $
HS336	Table	1	100.00	10%	90.00
HS472	Chair	6	90.00	5%	513.00
					────
					603.00
Sales tax @ 20%					120.60
					────
					723.60
					────

Remember that trade discount is not recorded in the accounting records by either the seller or the customer.

2.2 SETTLEMENT DISCOUNT

A settlement (or prompt payment) discount is a discount that is offered to a customer if the invoice is paid by a specified date, prior to the end of the normal credit period.

Typically, an invoice will state that payment is due 30 days from the invoice date. However, to persuade the customer to pay early, a percentage discount will be offered if payment is made before the due date. This discount is known as a **settlement discount or prompt payment discount**.

A settlement discount is therefore different in nature to a trade discount. A trade discount is a definite reduction in price that is **given** to the customer. A settlement discount is a reduction in the overall invoice price that is **offered** to the customer. It is for the customer to decide whether to accept this discount and pay the reduced amount within the required timescale, or whether to pay the full invoice amount at some later date.

In practical terms if a settlement discount is offered to a credit customer, there is no way of knowing, at the point when the invoice is prepared, whether the customer will take advantage of the discount terms offered and pay the reduced amount. This is known as **'variable consideration'** as the seller does not know at the time sales revenue is recorded whether they will receive only the discounted amount or the full amount. A business could therefore adopt one of the following approaches to deal with this situation:

- prepare the sales invoice for the full amount and, if the customer should pay early to claim the settlement discount, issue a credit note for the discount allowed to the customer. If the customer does not pay early, the full amount is due as normal.

- prepare the invoice for the reduced amount (after applying the settlement discount) on the expectation that the customer will pay early and be entitled to the settlement discount. Subsequently, if the customer does not pay early and is no longer entitled to the discount, the full amount is due and the additional amount received would be treated as if it were a cash sale.

Therefore, **in examination questions**, it will be stated whether a credit customer is expected to take advantage of settlement discount terms or not for the purpose of calculating amounts due from customers, or to calculate and account for amounts received from customers.

For example, consider the situation of a business which sold goods to a customer at a price of $200, and the customer is offered 3% settlement discount for settlement within ten days of the invoice date.

If the customer **is expected to take advantage** of the early settlement discount terms, the invoice would consist of the following amounts:

	$
List price	200.00
Less: 3% settlement discount	(6.00)
	———
Amount due from customer	194.00
	———

In this situation, settlement discount allowed is excluded from the accounting records in the same way as trade discount is excluded from the accounting records. The accounting entries initially recorded by the seller would be as follows:

Debit   Receivables $194.00

Credit   Revenue $194.00

Subsequently if, as expected, the customer pays within ten days to take advantage of the early settlement terms, the receipt of cash will be accounted for as follows:

Debit   Cash $194.00

Credit   Receivables $194.00

If the customer does not take advantage of the early settlement terms, the full amount of $200.00 is due. When it is received, the additional variable consideration received is accounted for as if it were an additional cash sale as follows:

Debit   Cash $200.00

Credit   Receivables $194.00

Credit   Revenue $6.00

If necessary, refer back to chapter 4 which provides further detail and explanation of trade and settlement discounts.

ACTIVITY 1

1   What may appear on an invoice to indicate that delivery is not included?

    A   E & OE

    B   Ex works

    C   30 days net

    D   Settlement discount

2 Why are sales invoices prepared in multiple copies?

(i) To update the accounting records

(ii) To file for reference in case of customer query

(iii) For record keeping purposes in the business

(iv) For sending to the customer

A (i), (ii) and (iii)

B (i), (iii) and (iv)

C (ii), (iii) and (iv)

D All the above

3 How does a customer know to which transaction a credit note relates?

A By reference to the credit note number

B By reference to the amount of the credit note

C By the reason given for the issue of the credit note

D By reference to the quoted invoice number on the credit note

4 Three office chairs costing $77 each with an agreed trade discount of 10% have been delivered to a customer. What is the total of the invoice for the three chairs?

A $7.70

B $69.30

C $207.90

D $210.00

5 A sale was made to a credit customer at a price of $500, less trade discount of 5%. The customer is expected to take advantage of the early settlement discount terms and receive 4% discount for payment within ten days. What is the total of the sales invoice?

A $456.00

B $475.00

C $480.00

D $495.00

6 A sale was made to a customer at a price of $750. The customer is entitled to 6% trade discount. Early settlement discount of 2% has been offered to the customer for payment within ten days, but the customer is not expected to take advantage of this offer. What is the total of the sales invoice?

A $690.90

B $705.00

C $735.00

D $750.00

7   A sale was made to a customer at a price of $1,500. The customer is entitled to 6% trade discount. Early settlement discount of 3% was offered to the customer for payment within ten days, and the customer was expected to take advantage of this offer. Subsequently, the customer did not take advantage of the early settlement discount and paid after 30 days. What accounting entries are required to record the subsequent receipt of cash?

A   Debit Cash $1,410.00   Credit Receivables $1,410.00

B   Debit Cash $1,367.70   Credit Receivables $1,367.70

C   Debit Cash $1,410.00   Credit Receivables $1,367.70
                                       Credit Revenue $42.30

D   Debit Cash $1,367.70   Credit Revenue $1,367.70

8   Abacus made a sale to a credit customer at a price of $600, less trade discount of 10%. The customer is expected to take advantage of the early settlement discount terms and receive 4% discount for payment within ten days. What accounting entries should Abacus make to record this sale?

A   Debit Receivables $540.00   Credit Sales $540.00

B   Debit Receivables $518.40   Credit Sales $518.40

C   Debit Receivables $576.00   Credit Sales $576.00

D   Debit Receivables $516.00   Credit Sales $516

9   Aardvark made a sale to a customer at a price of $1,500. The customer is entitled to 6% trade discount. Early settlement discount of 2% has been offered to the customer for payment within ten days, but the customer is not expected to take advantage of this offer. What accounting entries should Aardvark make to record this sale?

A   Debit Receivables $1,380   Credit Sales $1,380

B   Debit Receivables $1,410   Credit Sales $1,410

C   Debit Receivables $1,500   Credit Sales $1,500

D   Debit Receivables $1,470   Credit Sales $1,470

For a suggested answer, see the 'Answers' section at the end of the book.

3   GENERAL PRINCIPLES OF SALES TAXES – A REMINDER

3.1   INTRODUCTION

Sales tax applies to most business transactions involving a transfer of goods or services. It is often referred to as a tax on consumption as it is the final consumer of the goods and services that usually incurs tax burden.

The basic principle is that businesses operate as the agent of the tax authority collecting the tax on their behalf and paying it over to them on a regular basis.

The rates of sales tax around the world vary, and therefore the percentage sales tax used in the exam may vary as well. However, it is not the amount of the tax that is important for the exam, but a keen understanding of the principles involved in accounting for that tax, whatever the rate may be.

3.2 BASIC CALCULATION OF SALES TAX

Whenever a business registered to account for sales tax makes a taxable supply of goods or services, it must charge its customers sales tax on all goods or services to which the tax applies. The basic calculation is to take a percentage of the invoice total (after deducting any trade discounts) and to round this amount down to the nearest cent or penny.

Therefore, for goods with a list price of $50.00 on which a 10% trade discount is allowed, and settlement discount of 3% (which was expected to be taken up by the customer) the net amount would be $43.65 (shown below) on which sales tax at the appropriate rate calculated and added.

List price	$50.00
Less: trade discount	$5.00
Less: settlement discount	$1.35 (i.e. 3% × $45.00)
	———
Net	$43.65

3.3 SALES TAX REQUIREMENTS

If a business is registered to account for sales tax, it must charge sales tax on its sales and must issue a sales tax invoice. To be a valid sales tax invoice, certain information must be included on the invoice.

(a) **Registration number**

All sales tax registered businesses will have a unique registration number. The requirement to include this number on the invoice enables the tax authorities to determine whether the invoice was raised by a valid registered business.

(b) **Tax point**

The tax point on an invoice is the date when a transaction is deemed to have taken place for sales tax purposes.

(c) **Rate of sales tax**

The rate of sales tax on an invoice must be shown. Rates vary from country to country and some countries may have more than one rate. The rate you need to apply in the exam will normally be given to you. Note that the FA 1 syllabus does not include accounting for sales tax on a reduced amount where settlement discount (i.e. prompt payment discount) has been offered. Therefore, sales tax should be calculated on the net amount using the appropriate rate of sales tax.

ACTIVITY 2

Complete the following sales invoice details:

4 widgets at $100 each	$400.00
1 grommit at $43 each	$43.00
	———
Sub-total	$443.00
Sales tax at 20%	
Amount payable	

Terms Net 30 days.

For a suggested answer, see the 'Answers' section at the end of the book.

4 PREPARING A SALES INVOICE AND CREDIT NOTE

You need to understand the administrative procedures that must be carried out before an invoice and credit note are raised and issued to the customer, along with how to prepare them. Although an integrated accounting system will generate invoices and credit notes as transactions occur, it is important to understand at what point they are raised and their content.

4.1 AUTHORISING THE PREPARATION OF AN INVOICE

A business should not send out an invoice to a customer until the appropriate time. Usually, this is after the goods have been delivered or the service has been provided. A person in authority should confirm that the goods or services have been provided, and that an invoice should now be prepared and issued.

The person who gives authorisation for an invoice to be prepared is likely to be an office manager, but arrangements will differ between different businesses. The purpose of authorising an invoice, however, is to avoid issuing invoices to a customer for goods or services that have not been delivered.

Credit notes, which reduce the amount owing by the customer, should only be issued when necessary, for example after confirming that goods were damaged in transit to the customer, or the wrong items were delivered, and should be properly authorised.

4.2 INFORMATION REQUIRED FOR A SALES INVOICE

When authorisation has been given for a sales invoice to be raised, the task will usually be the responsibility of an individual in the accounts department. This could be prepared manually or, as is increasingly the case, could be produced by a computerised system. Much of the information required would come from standing data files of product and price lists, along with the contact name and address of the customer.

The information for preparing the invoice could come from several different sources, such as:

- a customer purchase order

- a price list for items sold by the organisation

- a sales order

- a copy of a price quotation sent to the customer.

Customer details

In many instances businesses deal with the same credit customers (or account customers) regularly over a period of time. If so, it would be usual to maintain a file of customer details. The customer details needed to produce sales invoice are likely to be:

- customer name

- customer delivery address

- customer invoice address

- customer telephone number, fax number and e-mail details

- customer account number/code (for internal purposes)

- the agreed discount terms both for trade and settlement discounts.

If goods are supplied to a new customer then there will be no existing customer details and the ordering process should ensure that the relevant invoicing details for the customer are recorded when the order is placed.

Details of goods or services provided

The information requirements are:

- the quantity of goods or services to be invoiced

- the description and/or product coding of the goods

- the price of the goods or services

- the date of the invoice (usually the despatch date).

The quantity, description, code and price of the goods may be available from the customer's purchase order. However, if the business is unable to fulfil all of the customer's quantity requirements then the quantity to be invoiced may have to be identified from the despatch note or delivery note, so that the customer is invoiced only for goods delivered.

The code and price of the goods may be available from the customer's purchase order or a sales order form. Alternatively it may be necessary to look them up from the current price list.

Supply of services

If an invoice is to be raised for the provision of a service rather than the supply of goods then the information required is likely to come from different sources. The supply of services will usually involve the customer being charged with the time of the person supplying the service.

The actual time spent on the customer's job can normally be obtained from timesheets or job sheets and the hourly charge-out rate of the employee from the appropriate accounting records.

In many service situations, such as car repairs or machinery repairs, spare parts will also form part of the cost to the customer and therefore part of the invoice. The retail price of such parts will normally be taken from a current price list.

4.3 CHECKING AND APPROVING A COMPLETED INVOICE

When an invoice has been prepared manually, it should be checked against the original documents (the purchase order, price list, and so on) to make sure that there are no errors in the invoice details. In addition, a check should be made that all the required information has been included. If an invoice has been prepared by a computerised system, it should still be checked to ensure that the details are correct.

Although procedures vary between businesses, the responsibility for checking invoices may be given to the accounts supervisor. After the invoice has been checked and approved, it should be issued to the customer.

ACTIVITY 3

Given below are three customer purchase orders, an extract from the current price list and the relevant customer details. The most recent sales invoice number was 33825.

Customer details

Name	Accounting code	Address	Discounts agreed	
			Trade	Settlement
DU Enterprises	D46	Finch Estate Dartmouth Devon EX55 99R	5%	Net 30 days
P J Freeman	F12	New Street Plymouth Devon PL4 7ZU	–	3% for payment within 10 days, net 30 days
Tab Design	T03	22 Fairmount Rd Tavistock Devon TA4 8BB	10%	4% for payment within 10 days, net 30 days

P J Freeman is expected to take advantage of the early settlement discount offered.

Tab Design is not expected to take up the early settlement discount offered.

Today's date is 22 June 20X4.

Price list extract

Code	Description	Price $
Y29DI	Plain self-seal envelopes	7.99 per 500
Y29WW	White window envelopes (A4)	8.80 per 500
Y13BP	Economy manila plain (A5)	6.20 per 1,000
Y14BW	Economy manila window (A5)	7.50 per 1,000
Y21BP	Economy manila plain (A4)	10.60 per 1,000
Y22BW	Economy manila window (A4)	11.30 per 1,000
W66MS	Whiteboard marker set (6)	4.90
W67MS	Whiteboard marker set (10)	8.30
W41OD	Document wallets (paper)	4.21 per 50
W42OK	Document wallets (plastic)	15.80 per 100
W55OP	Document zipper wallets (plastic)	8.60 per 10
A91FF	Accordion expanding file	3.40
A34SP	Suspension files (paper)	26.70 per 50
P52LK	Personal lockable file	28.30

From the information you are required to prepare sales invoices to be sent out with the orders for these goods.

PRINTING UNLIMITED

80 New High Street

Exeter

Devon EX4 2LP

Telephone 01233 464409

Tax Reg. No. 486 4598 220

SALES INVOICE

Invoice No:

Customer   PJ Freeman

New Street

Plymouth

Devon PL4 7ZU

Customer ref:

Date/Tax Point: 22 June 20X4

Order No: E10947

	$
10,000 A5 economy manila plain envelopes	
10,000 Window envelopes white A4	
Less; early settlement discount	
Sub total	
Sales tax at 20%	
Invoice total	

Terms:

PRINTING UNLIMITED

80 New High Street

Exeter

Devon EX4 2LP

Telephone 01233 464409

Tax Reg. No. 486 4598 220

SALES INVOICE

Invoice No:

Customer   DU Enterprises

Finch Estate

Dartmouth

EX55 99R

Customer ref:

Date/Tax Point: 22 June 20X4

Order No: E10948

	$
200 Suspension files	
500 Document wallets (paper)	
400 Document wallets (plastic)	
Total for goods before discount	
Less: trade discount of 5%	
Sub total	
Sales tax at 20%	
Invoice total	

Terms:

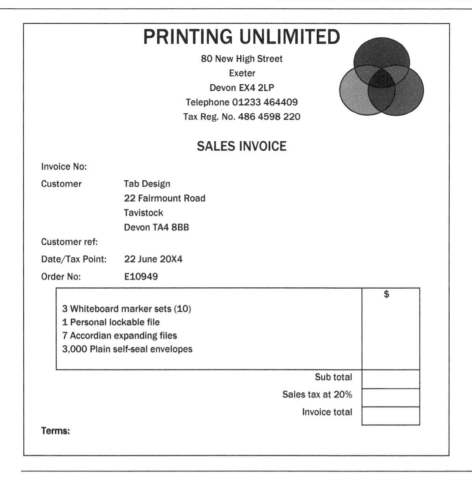

PRINTING UNLIMITED

80 New High Street
Exeter
Devon EX4 2LP
Telephone 01233 464409
Tax Reg. No. 486 4598 220

SALES INVOICE

Invoice No:

Customer   Tab Design
                  22 Fairmount Road
                  Tavistock
                  Devon TA4 8BB

Customer ref:

Date/Tax Point: 22 June 20X4

Order No: E10949

	$
3 Whiteboard marker sets (10)	
1 Personal lockable file	
7 Accordian expanding files	
3,000 Plain self-seal envelopes	
Sub total	
Sales tax at 20%	
Invoice total	

Terms:

For a suggested answer, see the 'Answers' section at the end of the book.

4.4 OBTAINING THE DETAILS FOR A CREDIT NOTE

The procedures and processes for authorising, preparing and checking and approving a credit note are very similar to those for a sales invoice. This is perhaps not surprising, since preparing a credit note is simply the reversal of all or part of an earlier sales invoice, or the correction of an earlier sales invoice. Remember that when credit notes are issued, they are numbered sequentially.

Customer details

The customer details can be obtained from the file of customer records or from a copy of the original invoice.

Details of goods returned

When a customer returns goods, there should be a check of the quantities returned and their condition. When the goods have been checked, some form of **goods returned note** should be completed. This will include details of the goods returned and usually the reasons for their return. If the reason for the credit note is not goods returned as such but a change in price or an allowance for poor work, then the source document may be a letter, a fax, an e-mail, or even a note on the original invoice.

This information is part of what is required for the credit note. However, as well as knowing the **quantity** of goods returned, we also need to know the price originally charged to the customer. The list price can be found from the price list that was in issue at the date of the original invoice and any trade discount allowed should be identified from the customer details file or a copy of the original invoice.

Correction of invoice errors

If a credit note is to be issued to correct an error on the original invoice rather than for the return of any goods from the customer, then the details for the credit note will normally be available from the original invoice together with any subsequent correspondence with the customer giving details of the amount and reason for the correction.

4.5 SALES TAX ON CREDIT NOTES

When a credit note is issued, the amount of sales tax payable is also reduced. The sales tax on the credit note should be calculated in the same way as on the invoice.

ACTIVITY 4

A credit note needs to be prepared for Tab Design, for sales returns. The amount of the credit note was $28.30 before sales tax at 20%. What should be the total value of the credit note?

For a suggested answer, see the 'Answers' section at the end of the book.

4.6 AUTHORISATION AND APPROVAL OF CREDIT NOTES

Authorisation should be given for the preparation of a credit note. The person in authority might indicate that the credit note should be prepared simply by signing or initialling the source document containing details of the sales return.

Credit notes should be checked for accuracy, probably by the accounts supervisor. After a credit note has been approved, it should be sent promptly to the customer.

5 METHODS OF CODING DATA

Sales invoices and credit notes are source documents for recording the details of the transactions in the accounting records of the business.

5.1 CODING REQUIRED FOR A SALES INVOICE

For a **sales invoice**, the coding should be enough to ensure that:

- the transaction can be recorded properly in the general ledger, and

- a record is also made of the money owed by the individual customer.

In a manual system, this will normally require several codes.

- For the general ledger record, the code number for the sales account and for the sales tax account, along with the receivables account code number.

- To record the amount owed by the individual receivable the customer's account code. This might be referred to as the customer's receivables ledger account number.

5.2 CODING REQUIRED FOR A CREDIT NOTE

The **coding required for a credit note** should be sufficient to identify the transaction as a sales return or return from a customer, for recording in the general ledger. In addition, a record should be made of the fact that the debt of the individual customer has now been reduced.

In a manual accounting system, this will normally require several codes:

- For the general ledger account code numbers for the sales returns account, the sales tax account and the receivables ledger account.

- To record the reduction in the amount owed by the individual customer, the customer's account code in the receivables ledger.

5.3 CODING INVOICES AND CREDIT NOTES: GRID BOX STAMP

There are a variety of methods of coding invoices and credit notes. One commonly used method is to use a stamp to put a grid or table on the document, and then fill it in with the code details.

The grid box can go under a variety of names, but essentially it is a box stamped on to the internal copy of an invoice (or credit note) before the invoice details (or credit note details) are entered in the accounting system.

The box is filled in both to make a note of the appropriate account code numbers, and as a checklist to make sure that the appropriate procedures for entering the transaction in the accounting system have been carried out.

Even when an invoice is produced by a computerised integrated accounting system, some checks will still be required to ensure that, for example the correct prices have been charged or that the correct individual receivables ledger account has been updated.

The typical contents of a grid box are as follows:

General ledger account names and codes

Debit	Receivables	5003
Credit	Sales	6002
Additions and calculations checked		✓
Credit note authorisation obtained		Not applicable
Receivables ledger account		S42770
Initial when posted		*RGT*

Here, the general ledger account codes of 5003 and 6002 may be the for the accounts in the general ledger for domestic sales and receivables, and the receivables ledger account number will be the customer account number for the customer to whom the invoice was sent.

When the invoice has been correctly recorded in the accounting system, the final grid box is initialled. It therefore acts as a safeguard to make sure that the transaction is not omitted or duplicated in the accounting system. The copy of the invoice or credit note is then filed.

CONCLUSION

In this chapter we dealt with the information required to raise a sales invoice and a credit notes, along with how and when those accounting records are generated. The chapter also revisited accounting for discounts and sales tax, which are particularly relevant when accounting for sales. The chapter concluded with a brief summary of how sales invoice and credit note mat be coded so that they can be recorded in the general ledger.

KEY TERMS

Credit note – A record issued to a customer confirming that they no longer owe money for certain items, perhaps because goods have been returned.

Receivables ledger – A ledger containing accounts for each individual credit customer/trade receivable.

Settlement discount – A discount for early payment of an invoice.

Tax point – The date on which a transaction is deemed to have taken place for sales tax purposes.

Trade discount – A discount on the price of goods or services, agreed in advance (and often granted to regular customers or for bulk purchases).

Sales invoice – A record of the fact that a customer owes money for the goods or services provided.

SELF TEST QUESTIONS

		Paragraph
1	What is the tax point of a sales invoice?	1.4
2	What customer details do you need to produce a sales invoice?	1.4
3	Explain what a trade discount is.	2.1
4	Explain what a settlement discount is.	2.2
5	Is sales tax levied only on goods, or on both goods and services?	3.1
6	How is a grid stamp used in coding?	5.3

EXAM-STYLE QUESTIONS

1   Jacobs Co provides its customers with individual trade discounts from list price. One customer, Caspian, negotiated a 20% trade discount. Caspian's transactions during March were as follows:

March 12   Purchased goods with a $2,000 list price

March 14   Returned faulty goods with a $400 list price

March 20   Paid half of the net balance on the account.

How much did Caspian owe Jacobs Co at 31 March?

A $627.20

B $640

C $800

D $1,280

2   Alan Co sold a drill priced at $235, a sander at $59.20 and a saw priced at $70. These are all gross figures, inclusive of sales tax at 20%.

How much sales tax is included within this transaction?

A $60.70

B $72.84

C $303.50

D $364.20

3   Asap Co is registered to account for sales tax. On 17 June it sold a cash till with a list price of $4,000. Asap Co allowed a trade discount of 25% and the sales tax rate is 20%.

What is the total of the invoice raised by Asap Co?

A $833

B $1,000

C $3,600

D $4,800

4   Campion Co is not registered to account for sales tax. It provides office services to various farming customers. If customers pay within one month of the invoice date, Campion Co allows settlement discounts as follows:

Cash on receipt of invoice   3%

Payment within 7 days   2%

Payment within 14 days   1%

Payment in 30 days   Nil

How much would a customer be invoiced, and expected to pay, if the sales value of services provided was $520 and the customer was expected to pay 10 days after invoicing?

A $520.00

B $514.80

C $509.60

D $504.40

5   Why are sales invoices authorised?

A   To prevent invoicing someone who has not received the goods or services ordered

B   To ensure that the invoice is paid on time

C   To ensure that the invoice is correctly posted to the correct book of prime entry

D   To indicate the need for a credit note

6   Baz made a sale to a credit customer at a price of $750, less trade discount of 4%. The customer is expected to take advantage of the early settlement discount terms and receive 5% discount for payment within ten days. What accounting entries should Baz make to record this sale?

A   Debit Receivables $684   Credit Sales $684

B   Debit Receivables $720   Credit Sales $720

C   Debit Receivables $712.50   Credit Sales $712.50

D   Debit Receivables $682.50   Credit Sales $682.50

7   Basker made a sale to a customer at a price of $2,500. The customer is entitled to 8% trade discount. Early settlement discount of 4% has been offered to the customer for payment within ten days, but the customer is not expected to take advantage of this offer. What accounting entries should Basker make to record this sale?

A   Debit Receivables $2,200   Credit Sales $2,200

B   Debit Receivables $2,400   Credit Sales $2,400

C   Debit Receivables $2,300   Credit Sales $2,300

D   Debit Receivables $2,208   Credit Sales $2,208

8   Maz made a sale to a credit customer at a list price of $600 plus sales tax of 20%. The customer was entitled to a trade discount of 5%. What accounting entries should Maz make to record this sale?

    A   Debit Receivables $756   Credit Sales $630
                                                          Sales tax $126

    B   Debit Receivables $525   Credit Sales $437.50
                                                          Sakes tax $87.50

    C   Debit Receivables $720   Credit Sales $600
                                                          Credit Sales tax $120

    D   Debit Receivables $684   Credit Sales $570
                                                          Credit Sales tax $114

9   Kaz made a sale to a customer at a list price of $2,000, on which trade discount of 5% will be deducted. Kaz is registered to account for sales tax at the rate of 15%. What accounting entries should Kaz make to record this sale?

    A   Debit Receivables $1,900   Credit Sales $1,900

    B   Debit Receivables $2,185   Credit Sales $1,900
                                                          Credit Sales tax $285

    C   Debit Receivables $2,300   Credit Sales $2,000
                                                          Sales tax $300

    D   Debit Receivables $1,470   Credit Sales $1,470

10   Raz made a sale to a customer at a list price of $2,500. The customer is entitled to 7% trade discount. Raz is registered to account for sales tax at the rate of 10%. What accounting entries should Raz make to record this sale?

    A   Debit Receivables $2,942.50   Credit Sales $2,675.00
                                                          Credit Sales tax $267.50

    B   Debit Receivables $2,557.50   Credit Sales $2,325.00
                                                          Credit Sales tax $232.5

    C   Debit Receivables $2,750   Credit Sales $2,500
                                                          Credit Sales tax $250

    D   Debit Receivables $2,407.50   Credit Sales $2,250.00
                                                          Sales tax $157.50

For suggested answers, see the 'Answers' section at the end of the book.

Chapter 10

RECEIVABLES

This chapter explains the entries in the receivables account in the general ledger, including the relationship with other parts of the accounting system, such as cash receipts.

Any business that offers credit to customers runs the risk of not being paid. A debt which almost certainly will not be paid is described as irrecoverable. A debt which may (or may not) be paid is regarded as doubtful. This chapter explains the accounting treatment to write off an irrecoverable debt and make an allowance for a doubtful debt.

The chapter concludes by briefly explaining reports produced by an accounting system relating to receivables

This chapter covers syllabus area G1.

CONTENTS

1   Trade receivables' in the general ledger

2   Accounting for contras

3   Irrecoverable debts

4   Irrecoverable debts recovered

5   Allowance for receivables

6   Reports produced by the accounting system

LEARNING OUTCOMES

At the end of this chapter, you should be able to:

*   explain the entries in the receivables account in the general ledger

*   define, and distinguish between, irrecoverable debts and the allowance for receivables

*   account for the write-off of irrecoverable debts

*   account for the recovery of a debt previously written-off as irrecoverable

*   explain the need to make an allowance for receivables

*   calculate and account for the allowance for receivables

*   explain the reports produced by an accounting system which assist managers and employees in the course of their work.

---

1 TRADE RECEIVABLES' IN THE GENERAL LEDGER

1.1 INTRODUCTION

Some definitions are a useful introduction to aid understanding.

A **receivable** is any amount due to a business. Examples of receivables include amounts due from customers, repayments due of sales tax or successful claims made against insurance policies where the proceeds have not yet been received.

A **trade receivable** is a customer who owes money to the business as a result of buying goods or services on credit.

1.2 RECEIVABLES' IN THE GENERAL LEDGER

The accounting entries required to record a credit sale are:

Debit   Receivables (to record the gross amount due from the customer)

Credit   Sales (to record the net income earned)

Credit   Sales tax on outputs (if relevant)

If all proceeds as expected, the subsequent cash receipt will be accounted for as follows:

Debit   Cash at bank (to record receipt from the customer)

Credit   Receivables (to clear the amount which is no longer due from the customer)

If a customer returns goods, perhaps because they were faulty or the wrong items were delivered and invoiced, a this also needs to be recorded in the general ledger. The accounting entries required to record goods returned by a credit customer are:

Debit   Sales returns (or Returns inwards) (to record the reduction in net income)

Debit   Sales tax on outputs (if relevant)

Credit   Receivables (to clear the gross amount which is no longer due from the customer)

There are other transactions relating to receivables that will be recorded in the general ledger over a period of time which will be considered in this chapter.

The receivables' general ledger account normally includes the following entries:

Trade receivables

	$		$
Balance b/f	X	Sales returns	X
Credit sales	X	Cash at bank	X
Bank – dishonoured cheques (1)	X	Irrecoverable debts	X
Bank – refunds of credit balances (2)	X	Contra with payables ledger (4)	X
Interest charged (3)	X	Balance c/f	X
	—		—
	X		X
	—		—
Balance b/f (5)	X		

Numbered items above can be clarified as follows:

1   If a payment from a credit customer has been declined by their bank, the trade receivables and cash at bank ledger accounts must be corrected to reflect the fact that the payment has not, in fact, been received and that the amount is still outstanding.

2   If a customer made an overpayment to settle an amount due, the overpayment should be returned to the customer. This will require a bank payment and adjustment in the trade receivables' general ledger account.

3   Some businesses may try to charge their customers interest on overdue amounts. If that is done, this will increase the amount owing from that customer and also increase interest received in the statement of profit and loss.

4   A business may both sell to, and buy from, another business on credit terms. If that is the case, each business will have amounts owing both to and from each other. This is explained further in the following section.

5   The closing balance at the end of an accounting period is the balance which will be included in the statement of financial position compiled at that date.

Remember that, as the general ledger accounts are updated, the memorandum-only receivables ledger account for each customer will also be updated simultaneously using the same information. Therefore, there will be no differences between the trade receivables general ledger account and the total of the memorandum-only individual receivables' ledger customer account balances.

2   ACCOUNTING FOR CONTRAS

2.1   WHAT IS A CONTRA?

Sometimes a business, A, may purchase goods from another business, B, and may also sell goods to B. In this case, A would have a payable to B and also a receivable due from B. These balances can be netted off against each other as the balances are owed to and from the same business.

2.2 ACCOUNTING ENTRIES FOR A CONTRA

You need to reduce the trade receivables' asset i.e. credit to reduce it. You also need to reduce the trade payables' liability i.e. debit to reduce it.

Debit   Payables

Credit   Receivables

Remember also that the individual accounts in the payables' ledger and receivables' ledgers will also be simultaneously updated when this transaction is recorded in the accounting system.

EXAMPLE – ACCOUNTING FOR A CONTRA

At 31 March 20X8, P Ahmed had total receivables' of $73,427 and total payables of $59,012. The receivables total included an amount due from J Singh of $3,500, and the payables total included an amount due to J Singh of $6,250. J Singh and P Ahmed agreed that they should contra the maximum amount possible, rather than making payments to each other.

Prepare P Ahmed's receivables' and payables' general ledger accounts as at 31 March 20X8 having accounted for the contra. Prepare also P Ahmed's memorandum receivables' ledger and payables' ledger accounts with J Singh.

SOLUTION

Receivables

Date		$	Date		$
31 Mar X8	Balance b/d	73,427	31 Mar X8	Contra – payables	3,500
			31 Mar X8	Bal c/d	69,927
		———			———
		73,427			73,427
		———			———
31 Mar X8		69,927			

Payables

Date		$	Date		$
31 Mar X8	Contra – rec'ables	3,500	31 Mar X8	Balance b/d	59,012
31 Mar X8	Balance c/d	55,512			
		———			———
		59,012			59,012
		———			———
			31 Mar X8	Balance b/d	55,512

J Singh – Receivable ledger

Date		$	Date		$
31 Mar X8	Balance b/d	3,500	31 Mar X8	Contra – payables	3,500
			31 Mar X8	Bal c/d	nil
		———			———
		3,500			3,500
		———			———
31 Mar X8		nil			

J Singh – Payable ledger

Date		$	Date		$
31 Mar X8	Contra – rec'ables	3,500	31 Mar X8	Balance b/d	6,250
31 Mar X8	Balance c/d	2,750			
		———			———
		6,250			6,250
		———			———
			31 Mar X8	Balance b/d	2,750

3 IRRECOVERABLE DEBTS

3.1 INTRODUCTION

An **irrecoverable debt** traditionally referred to as a **bad debt** is a debt which is considered to be uncollectable.

If a debt is considered to be uncollectible then it is prudent to remove it totally from the amounts owing to the business and to charge the amount as an expense to the statement of profit or loss. **The original sale remains in the accounting records as this did actually take place.** The debt, however, is removed and an expense is charged to the statement of profit or loss for irrecoverable debts. The accounting entries are:

Debit: Irrecoverable debts expense, and Credit: Trade receivables

The consequence of this is that profit is reduced and receivables in the statement of financial position are also reduced.

ACTIVITY 1

Ab Co have total receivables' at the end of its accounting period of $45,000. Included in this total is an amount of $790 owed by J Singh who has been declared bankrupt and $1,240 due from P Chan who has disappeared.

Required:

Write up the receivables general ledger and irrecoverable debts expense account to reflect the writing-off of these two irrecoverable debts.

For a suggested answer, see the 'Answers' section at the end of the book.

4 IRRECOVERABLE DEBTS RECOVERED

4.1 INTRODUCTION

Sometimes a receivable is written off as irrecoverable in one accounting period, and then payment is (unexpectedly) received in a subsequent accounting period.

4.2 DOUBLE-ENTRY

When a receivable is written off the double-entry is:

Debit   Irrecoverable debts expense

Credit   Receivables

The full accounting entries for payment received relating to that receivable in a subsequent accounting period are:

Debit   Receivables (to reinstate the receivable that had been cancelled when the debt was written off)

Credit   Irrecoverable debts expense (shown as a reduction in the irrecoverable debt expense in the statement of profit or loss)

And, to record the receipt:

Debit   Cash at bank

Credit   Receivables

Note that this is the usual double-entry for payment received from a credit customer.

This two sets of accounting entries above can be simplified to:

Debit   Cash at bank

Credit   Irrecoverable debts expense

The debit and the credit to the receivables general ledger account cancel each other out, leaving the net adjustment to be the receipt of cash and a reduction in irrecoverable debts expense account.

ACTIVITY 2

Ling prepares financial statements to 31 December each year. At 31 December 20X7 there were receivables' of $3,655 and there was also a debt written off from L Moss of $699. During the year to 31 December 20X8 Ling made credit sales of $17,832 and received receipts from credit customers totalling $16,936. During 20X8, Ling also received the $699 from L Moss that had been written off in 20X7.

Write up these transactions in Ling's general ledger accounts for 20X7 and 20X8.

For a suggested answer, see the 'Answers' section at the end of the book.

---

5 ALLOWANCE FOR RECEIVABLES

5.1 INTRODUCTION

The **allowance for receivables** reduces the reported trade receivables general ledger account balance to reflect uncertainties over collectability.

There may be some amounts due from credit customers where there is some cause for concern that not all amounts may be fully recovered but those amounts are not yet regarded as irrecoverable and written-off. Such amounts due may be considered to be 'doubtful' and an allowance is required recognise that such amounts may not be fully recovered.

Any amount regarded as 'doubtful' remains within receivables, but a separate 'allowance for receivables' general ledger account is established. The allowance is a credit balance. This is netted off against the trade receivables general ledger account balance in the statement of financial position to give a net figure for trade receivables that are regarded as probably recoverable.

The allowance should consist only of specific amounts where, for example, the customer is known to be in financial difficulty, or is disputing an invoice, or payment is already overdue, or is refusing to pay for some other reason (e.g. a faulty product sold), and therefore the amount owing may not be fully recovered. Therefore, an allowance can only be established where there is some evidence or indication that a particular receivable may not be recovered in part or in full.

To account for an allowance against receivables, the accounting entries are as follows:

Debit: Irrecoverable debts

Credit: Allowance for receivables

Normally the allowance is assessed and adjusted at each accounting year-end. An **increase** in the allowance from one year-end to another is accounted for as follows:

Debit: Irrecoverable debts expense

Credit: Allowance for receivables

A **decrease** in the allowance from one year-end to another is accounted for as follows:

Debit: Allowance for receivables

Credit: Irrecoverable debts expense

EXAMPLE – SPECIFIC RECEIVABLES' ALLOWANCE

At 1 January 20X6, J Stamp had trade receivables' totalling $68,000 and an allowance for receivables of $3,400. During the year ended 31 December 20X6, J Stamp made credit sales of $354,000 and had receipts from receivables' of $340,000.

At 31 December 20X6, J Stamp reviewed the individual receivables' ledger accounts and identified $2,000 which was to be accounted for as irrecoverable. In addition, at that date, it was estimated that amounts totalling $5,000 were overdue and that an allowance should be made for this amount.

Prepare the trade receivables, irrecoverable debts expense and allowance for receivables' general ledger accounts for the year ended 31 December 20X6.

SOLUTION

General ledger accounts

Receivables

Date		$	Date		$
1 Jan X6	Balance b/d	68,000	31 Dec X6	Irrecoverable debt	2,000
	Sales	354,000		Cash at bank	340,000
			31 Dec X6	Bal c/d	80,000
		422,000			422,000
1 Jan X7		80,000			

Allowance for receivables

Date		$	Date		$
			1 Jan X6	Balance b/d	3,400
31 Dec X6	Balance c/d	5,000	31 Dec X6	Irrecoverable debts	1,600
		5,000			5,000
			1 Jan X7	Balance b/d	5,000

Irrecoverable debts expense

Date		$	Date		$
31 Dec X6	Receivables' w/off	2,000			
	Allowance for receivables	1,600	31 Dec X6	P&L expense	3,600
		3,600			3,600

Note that the change in the allowance for receivables required (from $3,400 to $5,000 = $1,600) is accounted for as follows:

Debit   Irrecoverable debts expense $1,600

Credit   Allowance for receivables $1,600

EXAMPLE – SPECIFIC RECEIVABLES' ALLOWANCE

Izumi had trade receivables' of $11,200 at 31 May 20X4.Of these it was decided to write off an amount of $500 from P Foster as this customer has been declared bankrupt. In addition, there is some doubt as to whether or not an amount of $214 due from A Evans be recovered as that is now overdue for payment.

At 1 June 20X3 Izumi had a balance on the allowance for receivables' account of $230.

SOLUTION

Step 1   Write off the irrecoverable debt of $500 and remove it from the trade receivables general ledger account at 31 May 20X4.

Step 2   Calculate the change in the allowance for receivables required at 31 May 20X4.

	$
Allowance required at 31 May 20X4 re A Evans	214
Allowance at 1 June 20X3	230
Reduction in allowance for the year	16

Step 3   Write up the allowance for receivables account putting in the opening balance of $230 and the closing balance required of $214. The decrease in allowance required of $16 is credited to the irrecoverable debts expense account.

General ledger accounts

Allowance for receivables

20X3/X4	$	20X3/X4	$
31 May Irrecoverable debts expense	16	1 June Bal b/d	230
31 May Bal c/d	214		
	———		———
	230		230
	———		———
		20X4/X5	
		1 June Bal b/d	214

Irrecoverable debts expense

20X3/X4	$	20X3/X4	$
31 May Receivables	500	31 May Allowance for receivable	16
		31 May P&L a/c	484
	———		———
	500		500
	———		———

Conclusion

When a specific allowance for receivables is to be made, the amounts remain due and are not removed from receivables, as in the case of an irrecoverable debt. Note that the change or movement in the allowance for receivables is accounted for in the irrecoverable debts expense account.

ACTIVITY 3

Hinata is preparing annual financial statements for the year ended 30 June 20X9. The balance on the trade receivables general ledger account is $78,635. Included in this figure are $2,385 of customers whose debts are now deemed to be irrecoverable. Hinata has already written off $2,634 of debts during the year. In addition, Hinata wishes to create an allowance for receivables for $3,250 owed by certain customers known to be in financial difficulties. The opening allowance for receivables in July 20X8 was $4,300.

Required:

(a)   Adjust the trade receivables general ledger account in respect of the irrecoverable debts.

(b)   Calculate the change in the allowance for receivables required and prepare the general ledger account for the allowance for receivables.

(c)   Prepare the irrecoverable debts expense account.

For a suggested answer, see the 'Answers' section at the end of the book.

6   REPORTS PRODUCED BY THE ACCOUNTING SYSTEM

6.1   INTRODUCTION

In addition to producing sales invoices, integrated computerised accounting systems will produce a range of documents and reports to assist managers and employees within a business.

When data is entered in the sales system, such as a customer order, this will update the detailed 'sales orders' listing. In an integrated system, the sales ordering system will interact with inventory management system to confirm whether the goods are available and, if not, when they are expected to be available, and this information can be communicated to the customer.

When the goods are despatched, the progress of the sales order can be updated. Upon confirmed delivery of the goods, the system will generate the sales invoice, which will be posted to the sales and trade receivables' accounts in the general ledger. There will also be simultaneous update of the receivables' ledger account for that credit customer. Additional management information, such as the progress of the sales order, the statement of account to be issued to the customer (see 6.2 below) and the aged receivables' analysis (see 6.3 below) will also be updated.

In due course, upon receipt of cash from the customer, there will be a detailed receipts listing used to update the cash at bank and trade receivables' accounts in the general ledger. There will also be update of the individual credit customer account, the individual statement of account and the aged receivables analysis.

6.2 STATEMENTS OF ACCOUNT

A statement of account, often called simply a statement, sets out the transactions that a business had with a particular customer since the previous statement.

A statement covers a specified period of time (e.g. a month) and shows:

- the balance on the account at the start of the period covered by the statement

- invoices issued to the customer during the period

- credit notes issued to the customer during the period

- payments by the customer during the period

- the balance on the account at the end of the period, which is 'now'. In other words, it shows the current balance on the customer's account, stating what the customer currently owes.

Remember that trade discount and early settlement discount expected to be taken by a credit customer will not be included in the statement of account as they are excluded from invoice amounts.

A statement is simply a list of the transactions on the customer's account. The information is readily available from the **customer's account in the receivables ledger**, where all the transactions are recorded.

There are two common reasons for producing statements and sending them to customers:

- It may be the policy of the business to issue statements regularly, perhaps every month, to remind the customer about the position on the account. Sending a statement may prompt the customer to make a payment

- a customer may request a statement, possibly because it wants to check the details of the transactions shown on the account.

6.3 AGED RECEIVABLES' ANALYSIS

Credit customers do not always pay on time, and it may be necessary to remind them that payment is due. In many businesses, there are standard procedures for checking on overdue account balances and taking measures to persuade customers to pay.

Management also need to know how efficient the accounts department has been at collecting debts.

An aged receivables analysis is a report that is both useful for identifying late payers and for providing information about receivables and debt collection efficiency to management.

An aged receivables analysis is a report listing all the receivables of a business, how much they owe, and for how long the money has been owed. Typically, unpaid debts are analysed into amounts that have been outstanding for less than one month, for between one and two months, for between two and three months and for over three months. However, the analysis can vary from one organisation to another.

An analysis is typically presented as follows. In this example, there are just three credit customers, but in reality there could be a large number of them.

Aged receivables analysis as at (date)

Credit customer	Total owing	Outstanding for			
		Less than 30 days	30–60 days	60–90 days	More than 90 days
	$	$	$	$	$
T Grainger	551.86	279.30	272.56	–	–
C N Lawson	713.59	–	–	279.03	434.56
Burden & Co	518.47	219.50	248.30	50.67	–
Total	1,783.92	498.80	520.86	329.70	434.56

Notes

1   Although the columns are headed 'Less than 30 days', '30–60 days' and so on, it is common practice to assume that there are 30 days in a month, so less than 30 days means less than one calendar month and 30–60 days really means between one and two months.

2   For each customer, the total of the unpaid debts in the 'Outstanding for' columns add up to the total amount currently owed by the customer, as shown in the 'Total owing' column.

3   It is usual to show grand total figures at the end of the report, because these provide useful information for management.

If a business normally allows up to 30 days' credit to customers, it will expect most unpaid debts to be in the 'Less than 30 days' column. Most other unpaid debts should be in the 30–60 days column. However, if a business normally allows only 30 days' credit, but it has a large amount of unpaid debts in the '60–90 days' and 'More than 90 days' columns, then its credit control and debt collection procedures are probably poor and inefficient.

6.4   OTHER REPORTS

Other reports produced by a computerised accounting system relating to receivables include:

- detailed listings of sales orders, and their state of progress through to despatch and invoicing

- a transaction listing e.g. sales invoices processed on a particular week or specific date

- a receivable ledger account extract or summary for an individual credit customer which may be issued to the customer clarify and resolve particular queries or problems

- a list of irrecoverable debts written off during a specific period

- a summary of the results of a 'search enquiry' e.g. a list of all invoices processed with a net price of $2,500 or a list of all receivable ledger account balances in excess of $7,500 as at 31 July 20X2.

CONCLUSION

An irrecoverable debts is written off as soon as it is identified. The receivable is removed from the trade receivables general ledger account, and an expense is charged to the statement of profit or loss. An irrecoverable debt can be written back if it is received at a later date.

An allowance is made in respect of receivables that are doubtful. The receivables remain in the books, but the trade receivables' figure reported in the statement of financial position is reduced by the allowance. The increase or decrease in the allowance is charged or credited to the statement of profit or loss.

KEY TERMS

Aged receivables analysis – a report that is both useful for identifying late payers and for providing information about receivables and debt collection efficiency to management. It analyses the total amount outstanding according to how old the debt is as at the date of the report.

Allowance for receivables – an allowance made against receivables that probably will not be collectable; it is netted off the receivables balance in the statement of financial position. The allowance is made against one or more specific receivables when there is objective evidence that the amount due may not be fully recovered.

Irrecoverable debt – a receivable which is considered to be uncollectible.

Statement of account – a statement that sets out the transactions that a business had with a particular customer since the previous statement.

Trade receivable – a customer who owes money to the business as a result of buying goods or services on credit.

SELF TEST QUESTIONS

		Paragraph
1	What are the accounting entries normally recorded in the receivables general ledger account?	1.2
2	What is the double-entry to write off an irrecoverable debt?	2.1
3	How is a receipt in respect of a previously written off debt treated?	3.2
4	What is a doubtful debt?	4.1
5	What is a contra?	5.1
6	What is a statement of account?	6.2
7	Explain what an aged analysis of receivables and explain what it is used for.	6.3

EXAM-STYLE QUESTIONS

1   During the year, C Arthy wrote off $1,400 of trade receivables as irrecoverable. At the end of the year, it was decided to reduce the allowance for receivables' from $3,000 to $2,700. What is the total statement of profit or loss charge in respect of irrecoverable debts?

    A $300

    B $1,100

    C $1,400

    D $1,700

2   At 1 January, H Ellen had a balance on the allowance for receivables' account of $7,900. During the year, irrecoverable debts of $3,600 were written off. At the end of the year, it was decided to increase the allowance for receivables' by $1,500. What accounting entries are needed to increase the allowance?

    A   Debit Irrecoverable debts $1,500, Credit Allowance for receivables $1,500

    B   Debit Irrecoverable debts $5,100, Credit Allowance for receivables $5,100

    C   Debit Allowance for receivables $1,500, Credit Irrecoverable debts $1,500

    D   Debit Allowance for receivables $5,100, Credit Irrecoverable debts $5,100

For suggested answers, see the 'Answers' section at the end of the book.

PRACTICE QUESTION 1

NEED FOR AN ALLOWANCE

Explain the difference between the irrecoverable debts account and the allowance for receivables account.

For suggested answers, see the 'Answers' section at the end of the book.

RECEIVABLES : CHAPTER 10

PRACTICE QUESTION 2

R BENNETT

R Bennett is reviewing the trade receivables balances at the year end 30 June 20X4, which total $18,793 before reflecting the following:

(a)   Irrecoverable debts of $371 are to be written off.

(b) $120 has been received in respect of a debt which was written off in the previous year. No more money is expected to be received from this customer.

(c)   The allowance for receivables' at 1 July 20X3 comprised:

	$
Specific allowances	
R Abra	171
F Jinx	130
	301

The allowance against R Abra's debt is no longer required as the debt is included in the $371 irrecoverable debts to be written off in the period. The allowance against F Jinxs' debt is to remain, and an allowance is required in respect of the debt of E Waters which stands at $620.

Required:

(1)   Open up a trade receivables general ledger account and an irrecoverable debts expense account and record the transactions in (a) and (b) above.

(2)   Calculate the allowance for receivables required at 30 June 20X4.

(3)   Open up an allowance for receivables account and record the allowance at 30 June 20X4.

For suggested answers, see the 'Answers' section at the end of the book.

Chapter 11

PURCHASES AND PURCHASE RECORDS

Most businesses purchase a wide range of goods and services from suppliers. As a general rule, businesses prefer to buy goods and services on credit, although some small items may be purchased with notes and coins using 'petty cash'.

This chapter explains the typical procedures for ordering goods or services on credit, receiving delivery, receiving a purchase invoice, checking the invoice and identifying and resolving any discrepancies. It also covers the recording of purchases and purchase returns in the accounting records.

The chapter covers the syllabus area for purchases and purchase returns.

This chapter covers syllabus area H1.

CONTENTS

1   Buying goods or services

2   Source documents

3   Suppliers' invoices and supporting documents

4   Credit notes

5   Authorising and coding

LEARNING OUTCOMES

At the end of this chapter, you should be able to:

•   identify and recognise source purchase and expenditure documents

•   complete purchase invoices and process credit notes

•   record purchases and purchase returns

•   code purchases and supplier records and data.

---

1 BUYING GOODS OR SERVICES

The procedures for buying goods or services were explained in an earlier chapter but a brief reminder may be useful here.

1.1 PURCHASE REQUISITION

Expenditure by a business must be properly authorised. If there are no rules regarding authorisation of expenditure, there would be nothing to stop any employee using business resources to make any purchase for any reason.

The rules for authorisation vary from one business to another, and it is important to know who can authorise different types and amounts of expenditure.

Expenditure should not be approved for payment unless there is evidence that the initial purchase was properly authorised. Proper authorisation is normally evidenced by a signature from a suitably responsible person, such as a manager. This authorising document is often called a **purchase requisition**. Following authorisation, a purchase requisition becomes an authority to spend.

1.2 METHODS OF PURCHASING

A business may purchase goods or services in different ways.

- Once authority has been obtained, an item can be ordered verbally, by telephone. For example, suppose that there is flooding in a washroom due to a blocked drain. After authority has been obtained to have the fault repaired, a plumber can be contacted by telephone.

- Occasionally, an item may be purchased via the internet after authority has been given, although the person making the purchase will probably be required to pay immediately by credit or debit card and then make a separate claim for reimbursement, perhaps by a petty cash claim.

- Business to business transactions also take place over the internet with customers buying from suppliers.

- For expensive items, a business may ask one or more suppliers to submit a **price quotation**. The business specifies the goods or services that it wants to purchase and suppliers who are invited to 'bid' for the work each submit a price quotation. One of these quotations is then approved – usually the lowest-priced bid, although other factors such as quality of product or service and delivery dates are also considered.

- A common method of ordering goods and services from a supplier is to prepare and submit a written purchase order.

2 SOURCE DOCUMENTS

You will recognise many of the following when studying sales transactions.

2.1 PURCHASE ORDER

A purchase order is a written request by a business for the supply of a specified quantity of goods or a service.

Large businesses may have a specialist purchasing department, with buyers whose job is to process purchase requisitions. They may ask several potential suppliers to submit a price quotation, or they may select a supplier and negotiate a price.

Having agreed the purchase terms with a supplier, the buyer prepares a formal purchase order. One copy goes to the supplier, and is the formal order. At least one other copy is retained, as documentary evidence for use when checking later on.

An example of a purchase order was shown in an earlier chapter.

When services are purchased, the purchase order can take the form of a written contract, specifying the nature of the service and the agreed price.

2.2 DELIVERY NOTE AND GOODS RECEIVED NOTE

When a supplier delivers goods, a **delivery note** (also referred to as an advice note), normally in duplicate, is prepared and accompanies the goods supplied. It is a record of what the supplier has delivered to the purchaser. One copy of the delivery note is retained by the supplier and two copies accompany the goods delivered.

The physical goods received are checked against the delivery note by the person receiving the goods, such as a member of the stores or warehouse team. Any discrepancies between them should be identified and reported. For example, the delivery note may state say that 10 boxes have been delivered, but in fact only 8 boxes have been delivered.

The condition of the goods should also be checked. If some or all of the goods appear to be in a poor or damaged condition, the person accepting the delivery can do one of three things:

- reject the entire consignment of goods and refuse to accept any of them

- reject the goods that appear to be damaged or in poor condition, and accept the remainder

- accept all the goods, but agree with the delivery firm what the condition of the goods is, and make a record of this on all copies of the delivery note.

If goods have been accepted in unsatisfactory condition, or if some goods have been rejected, this fact should be recorded on both copies of the delivery note and signed. One copy is returned to the supplier and the other is retained by the purchaser. This means that both the purchaser and supplier have a signed copy of the delivery note which includes comments regarding the quantity and condition of the good delivered.

2.3 RECORDING SERVICES PROVIDED

When services are provided, a documentary record is often kept to confirm that the work has been done. An example is work carried out by an outside contractor on the customer's premises, such as a plumber or electrician doing repair work.

It is quite common for such services to be charged for according to the time spent by the contractor doing the work. The plumber or electrician will state the time taken to do the repair work, along with any other charges for components.

When services are provided on a time-charged basis, there should be:

- a contract for the work, in which the rate for the work is specified

- a timesheet, showing how many hours have been worked by the individual each day. Typically, a timesheet is prepared each week. It should be checked by a manager or supervisor and signed as confirmation that the stated hours have actually been worked.

An example of a timesheet is shown below. This is a timesheet for work done by an engineer who works for an outside contractor. It is prepared by the engineer's employer, Telesouth Installation Engineers, and checked and confirmed by R Ruan, an employee of the customer, J Forrester Wholesale Supplies.

TIMESHEET			
Telesouth Installation Engineers			
Engineer	D Huan		
Customer site:	**J Forrester Wholesale Supplies**		
Week ending:	Friday 16 June 20X4		
Day	**Hours worked**	**Weekday hours**	**Weekend hours**
Saturday	0		0
Sunday	0		0
Monday	9am – 5pm	8	
Tuesday	9am – 5pm	8	
Wednesday	9am – 5pm	8	
Thursday	9am – 5pm	8	
Friday	9am – 5pm	8	
Total hours		40	0
Signature of customer	R Ruan		

2.4 PURCHASE INVOICE

The supplier usually submits an invoice when the goods or services are delivered, or soon after. The sales invoice issued by the supplier is a purchase invoice to the customer. Whereas a sales invoice represents income to the supplier, purchase invoices represent expenditure to the purchaser.

Invoices are often addressed to the accounts department, and it is at this stage that the accounts staff become involved in checking and recording the items of expenditure.

3 SUPPLIERS' INVOICES AND SUPPORTING DOCUMENTS

You are aware of invoices and credit notes from earlier chapters so this chapter progresses on to processing suppliers' invoices and other documents. If you need to, please refer back to earlier chapters which explain the documents.

3.1 CHECKING INVOICES AGAINST SUPPORTING DOCUMENTATION

When purchase invoices are received from suppliers, they must be checked. If there is any problem with an invoice, it should be followed up with the supplier immediately.

Three types of check may be required:

- that the invoice details are correct

- that there is a document such as a purchase order or authorised price quotation, showing that the goods or services detailed on the invoice were properly ordered

- that the goods ordered were all delivered and in good condition, or that the service was delivered to the buyer's satisfaction.

The individual who does these checks needs to compare the invoice details with other documents, in particular the purchase order (or contract or price quotation) and the signed delivery note from the stores or warehouse team. This means that the accounts department should retain a copy of this supporting documentation. A copy of the appropriate documents should therefore be sent to the accounts department when they are created or received. Within the accounts department, there should be a system of filing these documents so that they can be traced easily when the purchase invoice is received, such as:

- purchase orders for which no invoice has yet been received can be filed in purchase number order.

- the delivery note should be attached to the purchase order when the goods have been delivered. The supplier's delivery note should show the purchase order number, which means that it should be easy to match by number the delivery note with the filed copy of the purchase order.

- the supplier's invoice should also give the purchase order number as a reference, so that the invoice can be matched with the purchase order.

3.2 CHECKING THE INVOICE DETAILS FOR CALCULATION ERRORS

Each purchase invoice should be checked to make sure that its details are correct.

If an invoice has been prepared manually rather than by computer, there is always a chance of an **arithmetic error**. There may be an error in multiplying a quantity by a price, or in adding up a column of figures. Even an invoice generated by a computerised system should be checked, including checking that the correct rate of sales tax has been charges and calculated on the invoice.

The recommended procedure should therefore be to **check all the calculations** on an invoice. If there appears to be an error, the supplier should be contacted, probably by telephone, and asked to confirm the error and issue a credit note or an amended invoice to resolve the problem.

Example

You are asked to check an invoice from Frost Supplies that includes the following details.

Item		Quantity	Price per unit	Total
			$	$
456213	Widgets	250	12.45	3,112.50
478002	Grommits	145	14.67	2,177.15
				5,299.65

The invoice total is incorrect.

Here, there are two errors in the calculations, and if the quantities and unit prices are correct, the invoice should be for the following amount.

Item		Quantity	Price per unit	Total
			$	$
456213	Widgets	250	12.45	3,112.50
478002	Grommits	145	14.67	2,127.15
				5,239.65

To resolve this problem, you should contact the supplier and ask for confirmation that the invoice is incorrect.

- The supplier should agree to send a **credit note** for $60.

- You should write a note on the invoice stating that a credit note for $60 should be expected from the supplier.

- It should be office procedure that the invoice is not be processed further until the credit note has been received. The incorrect invoice and the supporting documentation should be retained together until the credit note is received.

The fact that such errors may be queried gives businesses an incentive to check sales invoices before issuing them to customers. If customers need to delay the recording and processing of an invoice to resolve queries then the payment of the invoice may be delayed. Some businesses only make payments at fixed intervals, such as a fixed day every month, so even a slight delay in processing could lead to an even longer wait for the payment is made.

3.3 CHECKING THE SALES TAX CALCULATION

You may need to take particular care with the calculation of sales tax. Remember that when the supplier offers a settlement discount for early payment of the invoice, the sales tax should be calculated on the assumption that it will not be reduced to account for the settlement discount. Accounting for a reduced amount of sales tax due to settlement discount is excluded from the ACCA FA1 syllabus.

When sales tax is charged, you should also check that the invoice is appropriate for the relevant sales tax. The supplier's sales tax registered number should be shown on the invoice.

ACTIVITY 1

Here is a supplier's invoice. You are required to determine if the calculations have been correctly carried out.

MARCHANT PAPER LTD

74 High Road
Leeds LS14 0NY
Telephone: 0191 328 4813
Tax Reg. No. 947 4565 411

SALES INVOICE

Invoice No: 47914

Customer   J Forrester Wholesale Supplies Ltd
Unit 79b
Oakhampton Industrial Estate
Bristol BS27 4JW

Date/Tax Point: 2 March 20X3

Order No: E9471

Item No.	Description	Quantity	Item value	Discount	Total $
EE27	Envelopes A5	20,000	£8.50 per 1,000	7%	258.10
EE29	Envelopes A4	20,000	£12.75 per 1,000	5%	242.25
RE20	Recycled A4 envelopes	30,000	£11.50 per 1,000	8%	217.40

Total before taxes	717.75
Sales tax at 20%	143.55
Total	861.30

Terms: 5% cash discount for payment within 30 days
Carriage paid
E&OE

For a suggested answer, see the 'Answers' section at the end of the book.

The following is a comprehensive activity to help you revise earlier studies of documents.

ACTIVITY 2

Given below are three purchase invoices and related purchase orders and goods received notes. Should these purchase invoices be passed for payment?

LIGHTING INVENTORY LTD

14 High Road
Crowborough
East Sussex
Telephone 01673 892014
Tax Reg. No. 226 1429 292

SALES INVOICE

Invoice No:	497731
Customer	Fielden Lighting Ltd
	Crowhurst Road
	Wareham
	Kent
Date/Tax Point:	20 May 20X6

Supply of:	Total ($)
27 Brandish light fittings	510.30
14 Farell light fittings	216.44
19 Barnstable wall mounts	240.92
Sub total	967.66
Sales tax at 20%	193.53
Invoice total	1,161.19

Terms: Net cash within 30 days
E&OE

SUMMERHILL SUPPLIES

27 High Road
Knebworth
Herts
Telephone 01985 621058
Tax Reg. No. 221 7438 319

SALES INVOICE

Invoice No:	FL 493
Customer	Fielden Lighting Ltd
	Crowhurst Road
	Wareham
	Kent
Date/Tax Point:	20 May 20X6

	Total ($)
4 PC 21 Light fittings	194.60
11 TL 15 Wall fittings	441.57
12 MT 06 Lamp stands	387.76
	1,023.93
Less: trade discount	56.27
Sub total	967.66
Sales tax at 20%	193.53
Invoice total	1,161.19

Terms: Net cash within 30 days
E&OE

Stonewall Stationery

Merrydown Court
Wadhurst
Telephone: 01673 492492
Tax Reg. No. 496 3211 566

SALES INVOICE

Invoice No: 13382

Customer   Fielden Lighting Ltd
                 Crowhurst Road
                 Wareham
                 Kent

Date/Tax Point: 18 May 20X6

Order No: E5561

Item No.	Description	Quantity	Item value	Discount	Total $
106924	2 Hole Files – A4	25	£1.50	10%	33.75
17240	Lever Arch Files	40	£2.50	15%	85.00
			Total before taxes		118.75
			Sales tax at 20%		23.75
			Total		142.50

Terms: 5% cash discount for payment within 30 days
         Otherwise net 60 days
         E&OE

Fielden Lighting

Crowhurst Road
Wareham
Kent
Telephone: 01673 472841
Tax Reg. No. 742 8287 974

PURCHASE ORDER

Order No: 5566

To: Lighting Inventory Ltd
                14 High Road
                Crowborough
                E. Sussex

Date: 30 April 20X6

Please supply:
    20   Barnstable wall mounts
    20   Brandish light fittings
    14   Farell light fittings

Delivery to: As above

Fielden Lighting
Crowhurst Road
Wareham
Kent
Telephone: 01673 472841
Tax Reg. No. 742 8287 974

PURCHASE ORDER

Order No: 5561

To: Stonewall Stationery
              Merrydown Court
              Wadhurst

Date: 20 April 20X6

Please supply:

25 × 106924

40 × 17240

Delivery to: As above

Fielden Lighting
Crowhurst Road
Wareham
Kent
Telephone: 01673 472841
Tax Reg. No. 742 8287 974

PURCHASE ORDER

Order No: 5568

To: Summerhill Supplies
              27 High Street
              Knebworth
              Herts

Date: 30 April 20X6

Please supply:

12	MT06 Lamp stands
6	PC21 Light fittings
11	TL15 Wall fittings

Delivery to: As above

GOODS RECEIVED NOTE

Supplier	Lighting Inventory Ltd	No. 4615
Supplier DN no.	XX41	
Date:	18 May 20X6	
Time:	1:07pm	

Ref..	Item delivered	Quantity	Condition
	Farell light fittings	14	OK
	Brandish light fittings	20	OK
	Barnstable wall mounts	15	OK

Received in good condition

Signed ...... *PHarman* ....

Print name.... P Harman ....

GOODS RECEIVED NOTE

Supplier	Summerhill Supplies	No. 4621
Supplier DN no.	F316	
Date:	20 May 20X6	
Time:	10:43am	

Ref..	Item delivered	Quantity	Condition
	TL15 wall fittings	11	OK
	PC21 light fittings	4	OK
	MT06 lamp stands	12	OK

Received in good condition

Signed ...... P Harman ....

Print name.... P Harman ....

GOODS RECEIVED NOTE

Supplier	Stonewall Stationery	No. 4617

Supplier DN no.   4411

Date: 10 May 20X6

Time: 5:12pm

Ref..	Item delivered	Quantity	Condition
17240	Files	40	OK
106924	Files	25	6 damaged and returned

Received in good condition

Signed .... P Harman ....

Print name....... P Harman ....

For a suggested answer, see the 'Answers' section at the end of the book.

3.4 CHECKING INVOICES FOR SERVICES

There are fewer items to check on an invoice for services than on an invoice for goods. However:

- invoices for services should be checked for arithmetical accuracy, if they have been manually prepared

- the amount charged should be checked against supporting documentation if it exists. For example, an invoice for the services of temporary office staff should be checked against the time sheets of the individual or individuals.

In many cases, however, there might be insufficient supporting documentation in the accounting department. For example:

- if an invoice is received for quarterly rent of premises or for hire of machinery, the accounts department may not have a copy of the rental or hire agreement and so cannot check the invoice for accuracy

- regular invoices for gas, electricity, telephone charges and water supplies cannot be checked for reasonableness by the accounts staff

- there may be other regular invoices for repeated services, such as monthly invoices for office cleaning services or three-monthly invoices for waste disposal services.

In such cases, the invoice should be referred to a person who is in a position to **authorise the invoice for payment**. This could be an office manager, for example. Authority can be evidenced by signing or initialling the invoice, whatever the established procedure happens to be in the business.

4 CREDIT NOTES

4.1 INTRODUCTION

When there is an error in a purchase invoice, the supplier normally prefers to issue a credit note rather than cancel the original invoice and issue a replacement.

This is normal and accepted practice. However, an incorrect purchase invoice should not be processed for payment until the credit note has been received.

Example

An invoice from Crab Co for 600 units of product PQR costing $4 each, and the invoice net amount is $2,400 plus sales tax of $480, and a total of $2,880.

On checking the documentation, you find that, although 600 units were ordered and delivered, the delivery note contains a hand-written note that 100 units were delivered in a damaged condition.

You should contact the supplier and explain the problem. The supplier's copy of the delivery note should also include a note that 100 units were delivered in a damaged condition, and if this is the case, the supplier should agree not to charge for the 100 units. The supplier should therefore agree to issue a credit note for $400 plus sales tax of $80, or $480 in total.

The invoice should be retained, but not processed, until the credit note has been received. When the credit note is received, it should be checked and if it is acceptable, the invoice and credit note should be processed together.

4.2 CHECKING CREDIT NOTES

When credit notes are received, they should be checked for accuracy.

- Check the accuracy of the arithmetic, particularly if the credit note has been prepared manually.

- Check that the credit note is for the correct amount. The best way to do this is probably to write a note of the discrepancy on the invoice. When the credit note is received, it should then be a reasonably straightforward matter to check that the credit note deals with the discrepancy noted on the invoice.

5 AUTHORISING AND CODING

5.1 AUTHORISING PURCHASE INVOICES

Purchase invoices should be authorised for payment before they are paid. There are two ways in which invoices may be approved.

- The purchase invoices may be checked in the accounts department, against supporting documentation. If the invoice appears to be correct, it should be noted to show that the checks have been carried out, and then approved by a person with the necessary authority in the accounts department. This could be the accounts supervisor.

- If the accounts department is unable to carry out the checks on the invoices, a copy of the invoice should be sent to a person who can check and confirm the accuracy of the invoice. This may be the manager responsible for the expenditure e.g. the purchasing manager.

  When the invoice has been authorised (with a signature of the appropriate person) it should be returned to the accounts department.

If a discrepancy is identified and the supplier has agreed to provide a credit note, the invoice should not be approved until the credit note has been received, and the invoice should then be approved at the same time as the credit note.

This process of approving invoices is important, because unless it is carried out properly and according to established office procedures, there is a risk that payments will be made that should not have been made. Similarly, credit notes should also be authorised prior to processing to ensure that any amounts owed to suppliers are correctly accounted for.

5.2 EXPENSE ACCOUNT CODES, ASSET ACCOUNT CODES AND SUPPLIER ACCOUNT CODES

Asset expenditure (i.e. expenditure on non-current assets, such as plant and equipment) and expense expenditure must be distinguished from each other. In addition, different types of asset expenditure and different types of expense are categorised according to their nature.

There is an account in the general ledger for each category of expenditure. These are commonly referred to as **expense accounts**, each having an identifying name and account number or code.

Asset expenditure results in the purchase of a non-current asset for use in the business, and there are **asset accounts** in the general ledger for different categories of asset expenditure, such as land and buildings, plant and machinery, equipment and motor vehicles.

Just as there are individual accounts in a receivables' ledger for each credit customer, a business also maintains individual accounts for each credit supplier within the **payables' ledger**. Each payables' ledger account has both an identifying name and account number or code. The payables' ledger is not part of the double-entry bookkeeping system, it is memorandum only information and will be updated simultaneously when the general ledger is updated.

When expenditure is recorded in the accounting system, the following reference names or codes are required:

- the general ledger names or codes used to identify and record the transaction using the principles of double-entry bookkeeping

- the payables' ledger name or code identifying the supplier to update the appropriate payables' ledger account.

5.3 NUMBERING PURCHASE INVOICES

It is common practice, for reasons of internal control, to allocate an internal, sequential, reference number to each purchase invoice. This should also apply to credit notes. This number should be recorded on the invoice or credit note itself, in addition to the payable ledger code and general ledger codes.

5.4 GRID BOX STAMP (OR FRONT SHEET)

A purchase invoice should not be entered into the accounting system and processed for payment unless it has been properly authorised. When the invoice is authorised after checks carried out in the 'payables section' of the accounts department, there should be visible evidence that the checks have been completed.

This will result in either:

- the invoice is correct and can be processed, or

- a discrepancy was identified, the supplier contacted and a credit note has been received from the supplier and can now be processed.

Evidence of the check should be:

- written on the invoice, perhaps as an authorising signature

- entered into a grid stamped on to the invoice by the clerks in the purchase ledger section

- written on a front sheet attached to the invoice by the clerks in the purchase ledger section.

The same grid stamp or front sheet can also be used to write in the general ledger code for the expenditure and the supplier account code.

An example of a front sheet is shown on the following page.

The following details should be entered on either the invoice or a front sheet:

- **Date**. This is the date the invoice is received by the accounts department. If a supplier is requesting payment of an invoice, this date can be used to check when the invoice was received, and so how long it has been unpaid.

- **Agreed to purchase order**. There should be evidence that the invoice has been checked and agreed with the purchase order. In the example below, the front sheet does this by having space for the purchase order number and for tick boxes to show that the prices, discounts and credit terms on the invoice are the same as those shown on the purchase order. There could be another tick box to confirm that the quantities delivered are correct.

- **Agreed to delivery note**. There should also be evidence that the invoice has been checked against the delivery note, and that the quantities on the invoice were the quantities delivered in good condition. In the front sheet below, the evidence is provided by entering the delivery note number, and by means of tick boxes for checks on the quantities and their condition.

- **Calculations checked**. There should be evidence to show that the invoice has been checked to make sure that the calculations are correct. In the front sheet below, there are tick boxes to show that specific calculations have been checked.

- **Discrepancies**. If any discrepancies or errors have been identified, a note should be written to explain how they are being resolved. If the supplier has agreed to send a credit note, the details should be noted.

- **Supplier account reference**. The supplier account code should be noted.

- **General ledger account references**. The general ledger account codes for the expenditure should be noted. There may be more than two general ledger account codes if, for example, sales tax on inputs needs to be accounted for or if the purchase invoice includes more than one product, with each requiring a different account code.

- **Discounts**. Trade discounts may be detailed on the invoice and, if so, they should be checked. Remember that trade discounts are excluded from the amounts processed and accounted for in the general ledger. There may be a tick box to identify whether settlement discount terms, if offered, are to be accepted.

- **Signature and date**. When all items have been checked, and the codes obtained, the document should be signed and dated by the checker.

- **Invoice authorised for payment**. After the invoice has been checked, it should be authorised. Authorisation is evidenced by the signature of the person giving the appropriate level of authorisation to approve the invoice.

- **Invoice (and credit note, if there is one) entered in the general ledger.** When the invoice is returned to the accounts department, it will be processed to update the general ledger and the memorandum-only payables ledger. Invoices may be processed in batches or in real-time as soon as all appropriate checks have been completed.

Purchase invoice check list

Date invoice received	31 May 20X4
Purchase order number	19853
Prices	✔
Discounts	✔
Terms	✔
Delivery note number	AB5612
Quantities	✔
Condition	✔
Calculations checked	
Price extensions	✔
Totals	✔
Sales tax	✔
Date discrepancies notified	
To supplier	None
To department manager	None
Payable ledger account reference	P4234
General ledger account codes	Dr 500312; Cr 600753
Signature	G.T. Hobbs Date 8 June 20X4
Approved for payment	B.B Barnes Date 10 June 20X4

ACTIVITY 3

1   A business received a purchase invoice for $400 plus sales tax at 20%. The supplier offers all customers a settlement discount of 2% if payment is received within 7 days of the invoice date.

What is the total of the purchase invoice, including sales tax at 20%?

A $480.00

B $489.60

C $470.40

D $392.00

2   An invoice was received from a non-sales tax registered supplier for $300. When checking against the original order the buyer noted that the agreed trade discount of 20% had been omitted as had a settlement discount of 5%.

What is the correct total of the purchase invoice?

A $228.00

B $240.00

C $252.00

D $285.00

3   A business subscribed for a trade magazine.

How should this invoice be accounted for?

A   It should be paid immediately

B   It should be diarised until the latest date when any settlement discount can be claimed and paid at that point

C   It should be matched with documentation providing evidence of the order, authorised and then paid

D   It should be rejected

For a suggested answer, see the 'Answers' section at the end of the book.

CONCLUSION

After purchase invoices and credit notes have been received and checked, and any discrepancies resolved, the details of the purchase invoices and credit notes should be recorded in the accounting system. The procedures for recording expenditure in the accounts are similar to the procedures for recording credit sales and sales returns which were described in an earlier chapter.

KEY TERMS

Credit note – A document issued by a supplier to a customer to reduce the amount due for goods and/or services previously supplied and invoiced, perhaps because goods received were faulty.

Price quotation – A document sent to a potential customer quoting the price for specified goods and/or services, including the key terms and conditions. If accepted and signed by the purchaser, it becomes a purchase order from the customer.

Purchase invoice – A document issued by a supplier to a customer as a formal request for payment following the supply of goods and/or services.

Purchase order – A request, usually in writing, by a business for the supply of a specified quantity of goods or a service.

Purchase requisition – A document, which when properly compiled and signed, acts as authority to make a purchase and incur expenditure.

SELF TEST QUESTIONS

		Paragraph
1	What is a purchase requisition?	1.1
2	When is a timesheet used?	2.3
3	State three checks to do when receiving a purchase invoice from a supplier.	3.1
4	What would you do if you checked an invoice and found that the goods on the invoice disagreed with the details on the purchase order and delivery note?	3.1
5	What should you check on a credit note when you receive one?	4.2
6	List and explain the different codes you will meet with purchase and expenses documentation.	5.4

EXAM-STYLE QUESTIONS

1   What sometimes takes the place of a purchase order when services are purchased?

   A   A written contract specifying nature of the service and agreed price

   B   A delivery note listing the service and price agreed

   C   A completed timesheet

   D   A purchase requisition

2   A customer purchased 20 units of inventory at $50 per unit their business. The supplier allowed a trade discount of 10% and applied sales tax at 20%.

   What is the total invoice price that the supplier should charge the customer?

   A $900.00

   B $1,000.00

   C $1,080.00

   D $1,200.00

For suggested answers, see the 'Answers' section at the end of the book.

Chapter 12

PAYABLES

When expenditure is incurred, a record should be entered in the accounting system. Purchases on credit are recorded in the general ledger and in a memorandum payables ledger. This chapter explains the procedures for recording credit purchases in the accounting records. It also considers reports relating payables produced by the accounting system. This chapter covers the syllabus area for purchases and credit transactions.

This chapter covers syllabus area H1.

CONTENTS

1   Trade and other payables

2   Accounting for contras

3   Reports produced by the accounting system

LEARNING OUTCOMES

At the end of this chapter, you should be able to:

*   record accounting entries relating to credit purchases including returns outwards and contras

*   describe a computerised payables ledger

*   understand the purpose of and prepare an aged payables analysis.

1 TRADE AND OTHER PAYABLES

1.1 INTRODUCTON

Some definitions are a useful introduction to aid understanding.

Trade payables (often simply referred to as 'payables') are liabilities outstanding relating to the purchase of goods and services used by a business in the normal course of its activities. This may include raw materials and components for a manufacturing business, or finished goods ready for sale for a trading business.

Other payables are amounts outstanding which do not relate directly to trade payables. Examples include:

- output sales tax collected on behalf of the tax authorities but not yet paid over

- non-statutory deductions from employees' wages and salaries (such as trade union subscriptions and charitable donations) which have been deducted from earnings but not yet paid over

- accruals for items such as payment of rent and lease payments due but not yet paid.

In addition, remember that the ACCA FA1 syllabus and exam assumes that computerised accounting systems are used. This means that when, for example, a credit purchase is recorded in the accounting system, it automatically updates the general ledger accounts along with updating the memorandum payables' ledger accounts.

1.2 TRADE PAYABLES IN THE GENERAL LEDGER

The accounting entries required to record a credit purchase are:

Debit — Purchases or other expense or asset account (to record the net expense or asset cost due to the supplier)

Debit — Sales tax on inputs (if relevant)

Credit — Payables (to record the gross liability due to the supplier)

If all proceeds as expected, the subsequent payment will be accounted for as follows:

Debit — Payables (to clear the amount which is no longer to the supplier)

Credit — Cash at bank (to record the payment to the supplier)

If all processed as expected, the subsequent payment will be accounted for as follows:

Debit — Payables (to clear the amount which is no longer to the supplier)

Credit — Cash at bank (to record the payment to the supplier)

If the business decides to take advantage of the settlement terms offered by the supplier, the total liability due to the supplier must be removed from the general ledger, and this is matched by a reduced cash payment plus recording of discount received, a form of income.

The above accounting entries will be modified to record discount received as follows:

Debit   Payables (to clear the amount which is no longer to the supplier)

Credit   Cash at bank (to record the payment of a reduced amount to the to the supplier)

Credit   Discount received (to record the settlement discount received – a form of income)

If goods are returned to the supplier, perhaps because they were faulty or the wrong items were delivered and invoiced, a this also needs to be recorded in the general ledger. The accounting entries required to record goods supplied by a credit supplier are:

Debit   Payables (to record the reduction in liability)

Credit   Purchases (or Returns Outwards) (to record the reduction in expense or asset cost)

Remember that, as general ledger accounts are updated, the memorandum only payables' ledger accounts will be updated simultaneously. Therefore, the total of the payables' ledger balances will agree with the balance on the payables general ledger account.

There are other transactions relating to payables that will be recorded in the general ledger over a period of time.

The payables' general ledger account may include any of the following entries:

Trade payables

Cash at bank	X	Balance b/f	X
Purchases returns	X	Credit purchases	X
Early settlement discounts received	X	Interest on overdue accounts (1)	X
Contra with receivables' ledger (2)	X		
Balance c/f	X		
	—		—
	X		X
	—		
		Balance b/f (3)	X

The numbered items above can be clarified as follows:

1   Suppliers may charge their customers interest on overdue amounts. If so, this will increase the amount owing to that supplier and also increase interest payable in the statement of profit and loss.

2   One business may both sell to, and buy from, another on credit terms. If that is the case, each business will have both amounts owing both to and from each other. Rather than make payments in full to each other, the two businesses may agree to offset (or 'contra') an agreed amount against the balances due to each other.

The following accounting entries will have the effect of reducing both the receivables' and payables' general ledger accounts in each business:

Debit: Payables $X

Credit: Receivables $X

3   The closing balance at the end of an accounting period is the balance which will be included in the statement of financial position compiled at that date. The balance will be classified as a current liability.

Remember that, as the general ledger accounts are updated, the memorandum-only individual payables ledger accounts will also be updated at the same time using the same information. Therefore, there will be no differences between the payables general ledger account and the total of the memorandum individual payables' ledger accounts.

2   ACCOUNTING FOR CONTRAS

2.1   WHAT IS A CONTRA?

Sometimes a business, A, may purchase goods from another business, B, and may also sell goods to B. In this case, A would have a payable to B and also a receivable due from B. These balances can be netted off against each other as the balances are owed to and from the same business.

2.2   ACCOUNTING ENTRIES FOR A CONTRA

You need to reduce the trade receivables' asset i.e. credit to reduce it. You also need to reduce the trade payables' liability i.e. debit to reduce it.

Debit   Trade payables

Credit   Trade receivables

Remember also that the individual accounts in the payables' ledger and receivables' ledgers will also be simultaneously updated when this transaction is recorded in the accounting system.

EXAMPLE – ACCOUNTING FOR A CONTRA

At 31 March 20X8, J Singh had total receivables' of $58,000 and total payables of $47,250. The receivables total included an amount due from P Ahmed of $6,250, and the payables total included an amount due to P Ahmed of $3,500. J Singh and P Ahmed agreed that they should contra an amount of $3,500, being the maximum that could be accounted for in this way.

Prepare J Singh's receivables' and payables' general ledger accounts as at 31 March 20X8 having accounted for the contra. Prepare also J Singh's memorandum receivables' ledger and payables' ledger accounts with P Ahmad.

SOLUTION

Trade receivables

Date		$	Date		$
31 Mar X8	Balance b/d	58,000	31 Mar X8	Contra – payables	3,500
			31 Mar X8	Bal c/d	54,500
		———			———
		58,000			58,000
		———			———
31 Mar X8		54,500			

Trade payables

Date		$	Date		$
31 Mar X8	Contra – rec'ables	3,500	31 Mar X8	Balance b/d	47,250
31 Mar X8	Balance c/d	43,750			
		———			———
		47,250			47,250
		———			———
			31 Mar X8	Balance b/d	47,250

P Ahmed – Receivable ledger

Date		$	Date		$
31 Mar X8	Balance b/d	6,250	31 Mar X8	Contra – payables	3,500
			31 Mar X8	Bal c/d	2,750
		———			———
		6,250			6,250
		———			———
31 Mar X8		2,750			

P Ahmed – Payable ledger

Date		$	Date		$
31 Mar X8	Contra – rec'ables	3,500	31 Mar X8	Balance b/d	3,500
31 Mar X8	Balance c/d	Nil			
		———			———
		3,500			3,500
		———			———
			31 Mar X8	Balance b/d	Nil

3 REPORTS PRODUCED BY THE ACCOUNTING SYSTEM

3.1 INTRODUCTION

In addition to recording purchase invoices, input sales tax, discount received and returns outwards, computerised accounting systems will produce a range of documents and reports to assist managers and employees within a business, such as transactions listings, or individual payables' ledger accounts for specific suppliers if there is a query to be resolved.

Depending upon how large or complex an organisation is, the purchase of goods or services is normally initiated by a purchase requisition. This is a request for goods or services to be ordered when a business need has been identified. Upon approval of the requisition, a supplier can be selected based upon appropriate criteria (cost, delivery date etc.) and a purchase order raised and issued to that supplier.

Upon receipt of the goods or services, they will be checked to confirm they are complete and in good condition and the progress of the purchase order can be updated. Receipt of the invoice from the supplier will enable the general ledger purchases and trade payables' accounts to be updated. Simultaneously, the memorandum information of the individual credit supplier account will be updated, along with the aged payables' analysis (see 3.2 below) and other management reports (see 3.3 below).

The cycle will be completed in due course when payment is made for the goods and services received. This will be evidenced by a detailed listing of bank payments which is used to update the general ledger accounts and the memorandum management information.

3.2 AGED PAYABLES' ANALYSIS

In exactly the same way as customer balances can be analysed in terms of their age, so too can suppliers' balances. We refer in this case to an aged payables analysis.

An aged payables analysis is a report showing amounts owed to credit suppliers, analysed in terms of the number of days each amount has been outstanding.

An aged debt analysis relating to credit customers is an important tool of management control. By referring to amounts overdue, managers can initiate appropriate action to chase slow payers. This is obviously not an important consideration in the reverse situation (money owed to credit suppliers) and as a result, most businesses make less use of their payables analysis than of their receivables analysis.

Despite this, there are good reasons why managers should pay attention to the aged payables analysis. One reason is the need to maintain good relationships with trusted suppliers. If an organisation is consistently late in paying its debts, suppliers may retaliate by reducing the level of customer service, withdrawing favourable trading terms, or, in the last resort, refusing to make further supplies. To avoid this issue, it makes sense to monitor suppliers' balances to ensure that debts due are paid in good time.

It is also a good idea for a business to monitor amounts owed to ensure that settlement discounts are claimed and not missed.

An aged payables' analysis is prepared exactly the same way as the aged receivables' analysis. The layout of the report, also, is the same as we have already seen in the aged receivables' analysis. The only difference, obviously, is that the starting point is the ledger accounts for credit suppliers rather than credit customers. In addition the time periods used may be shorter, to indicate time periods within which payments must be made if discount received on early settlement of amounts due is to be earned.

An analysis is typically presented as follows. In this example, there are just three credit suppliers, but in reality there could be any number of them.

Aged payables analysis as at (date)

Credit supplier	Total due	Outstanding for			
		Less than 10 days	10–30 days	30–60 days	More than 60 days
	$	$	$	$	$
Box Co	3,557.22	950.00	2,468.19	139.03	–
Carton Co	2,963.45	–	1,778.07	830.00	355.38
Crate Co	1,418.47	129.50	748.30	216.27	324.40
Total	7,939.14	1,079.50	4,994.56	1,185.30	679.78

Notes

1   Although the columns are headed 'Less than 10 days', '10–30 days' and so on, it is common practice to assume that there are 30 days in a month, so less than 30 days means less than one calendar month and 30–60 days really means between one and two months.

2   For each supplier, the total due in the 'Outstanding for' columns add up to the total amount currently owed to each supplier, as shown in the 'Total due' column.

3   It is usual to show total figures at the end of the report, because these provide useful information for management.

3.3   OTHER REPORTS

Other reports produced by a computerised accounting system relating to payables include:

- purchase requisitions record, including progress towards order placement

- purchase orders record, including progress towards completion, which may be in several stages if there are multiple deliveries of goods, or if damaged goods are returned

- a transaction listing e.g. purchase invoices processed in a particular week or on a specific date or a list of bank payments made to individual credit suppliers

- a payable ledger account extract or summary for an individual credit supplier which may be used to reconciled with statements issued by the supplier to confirm that the payable ledger account balance is fairly stated

- a summary of the results of a 'search enquiry' e.g. a list of all invoices processed with a net cost of $2,500 or a list of all payable ledger account balances in excess of $7,500 as at a specific date.

ACTIVITY 1

1   XZ Co purchased goods at a cost of $450, including sales tax of 20%. What accounting entries should XZ Co make to record this transaction in the general ledger?

    A   Debit: Purchases $450   Credit: Payables $540
            Debit: Sales tax $90

    B   Debit: Purchases $375   Credit: Payables $450
            Debit: Sales tax $75

    C   Debit: Payables $450   Credit: Purchases $375
                                              Credit: Sales tax $75

    D   Debit: Payables $375   Credit: Purchases $450
            Debit: Sales tax $75

2   PR Co purchased goods at a cost of $450, on which sales tax at 20% was added. PR Co was offered settlement discount of 5% if payment was made within 10 days of the invoice date. PR Co made the payment within 10 days. What accounting entries should PR Co make to record this payment?

    A   Debit: Payables $450   Credit: Bank $540
            Debit: Sales tax $90

    B   Debit: Payables $450   Credit: Bank $540
            Debit: Sales tax $90

    C   Debit: Payables $540   Credit: Bank $513
                                              Credit: Discount received $27

    D   Debit: Bank $513   Credit: Payables $540
            Debit: Discount received $27

3   GH Co purchased goods at a net cost of $680, on which sales tax at 15% was added. GH Co was offered settlement discount of 5% if payment was made within 10 days of the invoice date. GH Co made the payment within 10 days. What accounting entries should GH Co make to record this payment?

    A   Debit: Payables $646   Credit: Bank $680
            Debit: Discount received $34

    B   Debit: Bank $742.90   Credit: Payables $782.00
            Discount received $39.10

    C   Debit: Payables $782.00   Credit: Bank $646
                                            Credit: Sales tax $102
                                            Credit: Discount received $34

    D   Debit: Payables $782.00   Credit: Bank $742.90
                                            Credit: Discount received $39.10

For a suggested answer, see the 'Answers' section at the end of the book.

CONCLUSION

Credit purchase transactions are recorded in the general ledger and the memorandum payables ledger. This chapter explained the accounting entries required to account for credit purchases and related transactions such as receipt of credit notes from supplier, payments to suppliers, discount received and contra entries.

Other reports produced by a computerised accounting system were also considered, such as an aged payables' listing to monitor the total payable liability outstanding and when payments are expected to fall due.

KEY TERMS

Trade payables (often simply referred to as 'payables') are liabilities outstanding relating to the purchase of goods and services used by a business in the normal course of its activities.

Other payables are amounts outstanding which do not relate directly to trade payables, such as output sales tax collected on behalf of the tax authorities but not yet paid.

Aged payables' analysis – List of payables, analysed according to how long it is until payment is due.

Contra – A reduction in the receivables' and payables general ledger account balances of a business when goods and services are both sold to, and purchased from, another business.

Payables ledger – A memorandum ledger containing ledger account records for individual credit suppliers.

SELF TEST QUESTIONS

		Paragraph
1	Provide examples of payables, other than trade payables.	1.1
2	What accounting entries are required in the general ledger to record purchases returns?	1.2
3	Wat accounting entries are required in the general ledger to record a contra?	2.2
4	What is an aged payables analysis?	3.2
5	Why should management be interested in an aged payables analysis?	3.2

EXAM-STYLE QUESTIONS

1   Which of the following will appear as a debit entry in the general ledger?

   A   Contra entry in the payables' account

   B   Settlement discount in the discount received account

   C   Contra entry in the receivables' account

   D   A payment to a credit supplier in the cash at bank account

2   Which is not a reason for maintaining an aged payables analysis?

   A   To avoid customers' unduly delaying payment

   B   To take advantage of settlement discounts

   C   To check that payments are made on time

   D   To avoid suppliers withdrawing credit terms

3   KL Co made a purchase of goods from a credit supplier. The list price of the goods purchased was $1,000, on which trade discount of 10% was allowed and sales tax of 15% applied. What was KL Co's total liability to the supplier?

   A $1,035

   B $1,150

   C $1,265

   D $935

4   OP Co made a purchase of goods from a supplier. The list price of the goods purchased was $2.500, on which trade discount of 10% was allowed and sales tax of 15% applied. How much input sales tax did OP Co record in its general ledger on this transaction?

   A $375

   B $337.50

   C $412.50

   D $125

5   Yu Co made a payment to a credit supplier. The list price of the goods purchased was $800, on which trade discount of 20% was allowed and sales tax of 5% applied. What was YU Co's input tax liability on this transaction?

   A $40

   B $120

   C $32

   D $31

For suggested answers, see the 'Answers' section at the end of the book.

Chapter 13

RECONCILIATIONS

The purpose of this chapter is to explain how the entries in the bank general ledger account can be checked against a bank statement in order to identify and correct any errors or omissions in the bank general ledger account. It also explains how this checking process is summarised in a bank reconciliation statement. In addition, the procedure to reconcile individual supplier account balances to supplier statements is explained and illustrated. This chapter covers the syllabus area of reconciliations.

This chapter covers syllabus areas I1, I2, I3.

CONTENTS

1   General bank services and operation of the bank clearing system

2   Function and form of banking documentation

3   Bank reconciliation statement

4   Errors and omissions in the bank general ledger account

5   Supplier statement reconciliations

LEARNING OUTCOMES

At the end of this chapter, you should be able to:

- recognise the need to reconcile the bank general ledger account with the bank statement periodically

- identify the main reasons for any discrepancies between the bank general ledger account and the bank statement, such as errors, unanticipated receipts and payments and timing differences

- correct errors and/or omissions in the bank general ledger account

- reconcile the corrected bank general ledger account balance with the bank statement through adjustments for uncleared and uncredited cheques

- reconcile individual payable ledger account balances with supplier statements, including making correcting entries in the general ledger when necessary.

---

1 GENERAL BANK SERVICES AND OPERATION OF THE BANK CLEARING SYSTEM

This content was covered in more detail in an earlier chapter but it will be useful to have a brief recap before moving on to dealing with bank reconciliations.

A business uses the bank general ledger account to record every receipt and payment that passes through its bank account. In theory, the balance on the bank general ledger account should be the same as the balance as per the bank's record of the bank account as documented by the bank statement. In practice, however, this is not always the case and the two records need to be reconciled to ensure that there are no errors or omissions.

There are several reasons for differences between the bank general ledger account and the bank statement which are explained below. However, do remember that with the use of modern technology, many of the differences which may arise between the cash at bank general ledger account and the bank statement are perhaps less significant than they used to be as receipts and payments are now processed much quicker than they used to be.

1.1 CHEQUES, RECEIPTS, ELECTRONIC PAYMENTS, CHARGES AND INTEREST

With cheques and credit transfers, there are timing differences between recording the receipt or payment in the bank general ledger account and the transfer of cash into or out of the bank account.

- **Making payments by cheque.** When a business pays a supplier by cheque, the payment will be recorded in the bank general ledger account and the cheque issued to the supplier. The supplier should receive the cheque through the post a day or so later, but may not pay the cheque into their bank immediately. When the cheque is paid in, the transfer of money from the payer's bank account to the payee's bank account does not happen instantly. There is a further delay, perhaps of two or three days, due to the time it takes for the cheque payment to be 'cleared' through the banking system. Thus, it could take a week or more from the recording of a cheque payment in the business's' general ledger account to appear on the bank statement.

- **Receiving payments by cheque.** Similarly, when a business receives a payment by cheque, it should record the receipt in the bank general ledger account, and it is good business practice to pay the cheque into the bank as soon as possible (ideally, on the same day). Even so, the lodging of cheques into the bank account will take two or three days, due to the 'clearing' delay and so there will be a further difference between the business's record and the bank statement.

- **Dishonoured cheques.** When a customer pays by cheque, the payer's bank may refuse to honour it. When a cheque 'bounces', it is returned with a message 'refer to drawer', but it can take a few days before this happens. As far as the business is concerned, payment has been received from the customer and entered in the bank general ledger account. When it discovers that the cheque has been returned and/or dishonoured, it will have to reflect this in the bank general ledger account. In the meantime, both the bank and the business will have different balances due to the timing of the recording of the dishonoured cheque.

- **Receiving payments by credit transfer.** A similar delay occurs when payments are received from customers by credit transfer.

- **Receipts by direct debit, standing order or BACS.** A business may record the transactions in its bank general ledger account on the dates that the payments are due. However, if it does this, it will need to check that the cash has actually been received into its bank account. A customer may, for example, cancel a standing order payment.

  When this occurs, the entry of a cash receipt in the bank general ledger account would be wrong. A business may therefore wait for confirmation from the bank that the direct debits and standing order transactions have been processed by the bank before recording them in the bank general ledger account.

- **Payments by standing order.** A business that makes payments by standing order may record the payments in the bank general ledger account on the due payment dates. (The details of the payments can be obtained from the schedule the business should maintain.) When a business makes payments by direct debit, however, the amount of the payment can vary. For example, if telephone bills are paid by direct debit, the amount payable each time will depend on usage of the telephone during the billing period. Direct debit payments cannot therefore be recorded in the bank general ledger account until the notification from the supplier or the bank of the amount paid has been received.

- **Electronic receipts and payments.** Increasingly, businesses may pay and receive funds electronically, say through BACS. Receipts are particularly difficult to predict as to when they will arrive in the bank account. A business may wait for confirmation from the bank that such transactions have taken place before recording them in the general ledger.

- **Bank charges.** Individuals may not pay any bank charges on personal accounts provided they keep their account 'in credit'. For a business bank account, however, a bank usually makes charges for its services. Bank charges are deducted from the account balance, and notified to the business on the next bank statement. Until it receives a bank statement, the business does not know how much the bank charges are and so cannot record them in the bank general ledger account. Bank charges are recorded as a cash payment in the bank general ledger account when the bank statement is received. The same is true of bank interest paid for, say, loans and overdrafts.

  Similarly, if a business has a deposit or savings account and received interest on this bank account, the amount of interest receivable is not known, and so cannot be recorded, until after a bank statement has been received.

2 FUNCTION AND FORM OF BANKING DOCUMENTATION

Business bank account holders receive regular statements of account from the bank, perhaps every month or even every week. With computerised banking systems, it is now possible to request and download a bank statement without the need for it to be requested and delivered using the postal service.

A bank statement shows all the payments and receipts processed through the account by the bank since the previous bank statement.

A bank statement may look something like this:

		Paid out $	Paid in $	Balance $	
	SouthEast Bank plc				
	High Street, Borchester BO1 2ER				
Account Name: ABC Co					
Account number 22353712					
2 July	Balance b/f			345.00	
3 July	Cheque 23457	100.00		245.00	
5 July	Cheque 23454	278.00		33.00	o/d
6 July	BGC T J Smith		425.00	392.00	
9 July	DD Cheshire Gas	45.00		347.00	
9 July	Bank charges	56.00		291.00	
10 July	BAC Fullaway Limited		230.00	521.00	
11 July	SO BV Properties	400.00		121.00	
12 July	BGC Reach plc		314.00	435.00	
12 July	Cheque 23455	499.00		64.00	o/d
15 July	Balance c/f			64.00	o/d

Notes relating to the bank statement

1   When a business has cash in its bank account, it regards it as an asset. Assets are shown as a debit balance in the cash at bank general ledger account. To the bank, however, the situation is a 'mirror image' opposite. To the bank, when a business has cash in its account, the bank 'owes' that amount to the account-holder who can withdraw the cash at any time. From the bank's perspective, the customer's bank balance is therefore a liability and in the accounting system of the bank, this is reflected as a credit balance (it is a liability of the bank) in the customer account and the bank statement.

When a bank account is overdrawn, the business owes cash to the bank. In the business general ledger account, this is recorded as a credit balance. To the bank, the situation is again the opposite. The account holder owes the bank money, and is therefore a receivable of the bank. Receivables are assets and, to the bank, bank the overdrawn balance is an asset. In the customer account and bank statement this is presented as a debit balance and by o/d (i.e. overdrawn).

2   For each transaction, the bank statement shows the date it was processed by the bank and the cash was actually paid into or out of the account. The amount of the receipt or payment is shown, together with the resulting balance on the account.

3   For payments by cheque, the cheque number is shown.

4   Payments and receipts by standing order, direct debit and BACS are usually shown by the letters SO, DD and BAC respectively.

5   Receipts by cheque are shown by the letters BGC or the words 'bank giro credit', together with some description to identify the receipt or the payment.

6   More modern forms of electronic payment or cash transfer may identify the name of the person or business transferring cash, perhaps as payment of an invoice.

3 BANK RECONCILIATION STATEMENT

3.1 INTRODUCTION

For the reasons explained earlier, the balance on the account shown by the bank statement will rarely be the same as the current balance in the cash at bank account in the general ledger.

A bank statement is used to check that the general ledger account is not misstated in any way. This is done by checking the details on the bank statement and the details in the general ledger account, and making sure that they are in agreement with each other. If the balance in the bank statement and the balance in the general ledger account is different, this exercise involves checking the difference in the two balances, and making sure that the differences can be properly reconciled and explained.

Bank reconciliations are important because they are a check on the accuracy of the cash at bank general ledger account. In particular:

- if any errors have been made they should be identified and corrected

- the cash at bank general ledger account should be updated to include any receipts or payments that have not yet been recorded, such as standing order and direct debit payments, BACS receipts and bank charges.

ACTIVITY 1

1   Why does a business reconcile its cash at bank general ledger account with the bank statement periodically?

   A   It is a legal requirement.

   B   It speeds up the posting of transactions to the general ledger accounts.

   C   It is a control measure checking for errors and omissions.

   D   It enables the business to correct mistakes with the accurate bank records.

2   The cash at bank account balance in the general ledger is $165.40 in hand. Reference to the bank statement shows that a standing order of $10.00 to a supplier has not been recorded in the general ledger account but that every other item is the same in both the general ledger account and the bank statement. The omitted standing order is then recorded in the cash at bank general ledger account.

   What are the balances shown in the cash at bank general ledger account and on the bank statement after updating has taken place?

   A   Cash at bank general ledger $155.40 Cr; Bank statement: $155.40 Dr

   B   Cash at bank general ledger $155.40 Dr; Bank statement: $155.40 Cr

   C   Cash at bank general ledger $175.40 Cr; Bank statement: $175.40 Dr

   D   Cash at bank general ledger $175.40 Dr; Bank statement: $175.40 Cr

For a suggested answer, see the 'Answers' section at the end of the book.

3.2 PREPARING A BANK RECONCILIATION

The procedure to perform a bank reconciliation is explained and illustrated below. The procedure is then used in an illustrative example later in the chapter so you can see each stage of the procedure in action.

Step 1

The opening balance on the bank statement and the opening balance in the cash at bank general ledger account should be agreed or reconciled. (The two opening balances may be different, for the same reasons that the two closing balances may be different!)

This is done by looking for receipts or payments during the period that explain the difference. For example, if the opening balance on the bank statement is $3,000 credit and the opening balance in the cash at bank general ledger account is $4,500 debit, the difference may be explained by a receipt (bank giro credit or BGC) for $1,500 during the period. This may be a receipt that was recorded in the cash at bank general ledger account in the previous period, but which was not processed and cleared by the bank until the current period. In other words, the difference in the two opening balances should be explained by 'timing differences' between when a payment or receipt was recorded in the cash at bank general ledger account and when the payment or receipt was processed by the bank.

Transactions that explain the difference between the two opening balances should be ticked on the bank statement to signify that they have been explained and matched in both documents.

Step 2

Individual transactions in the cash at bank general ledger account should be matched with the same transactions on the bank statement. If there are matching transactions in the two documents, we can tick the items in both documents as being matched.

Step 3

The difference in the two closing balances must be explained by transactions on the bank statement and transactions in the cash at bank general ledger account that have not yet been ticked (i.e. explained and matched).

There may be some receipts or payments shown in the bank statement that are not yet recorded in the cash at bank general ledger account. These items could be standing order payments, direct debit payments, BACS transactions or bank charges.

For standing orders and direct debits, the schedule of payments or receipts should be checked, to make sure that they have all been made as expected.

Update the cash at bank general ledger account to record all of these transactions on the date the reconciliation takes place. When items on the bank statement are entered in the cash at bank general ledger account, they should be ticked on the bank statement to show that they have been matched and dealt with.

Step 4

After updating the cash at bank general ledger account, it will have an amended balance, but it may still differ from the balance on the bank statement. There may be some items recorded in the general ledger account that have not yet been ticked because they do not appear on the bank statement.

These items will be:

- cash receipts received and entered in the general ledger account, but not yet appearing on the bank statement because the bank has not yet processed them. These transactions are commonly referred to as **outstanding lodgements**

- payments by cheque entered in the general ledger account but not yet appearing on the bank statement because the bank has not yet processed them. These transactions are termed **unpresented cheques**.

Outstanding lodgements and unpresented cheques should explain the difference between the updated cash at bank general ledger account balance and the bank statement balance. These transactions should appear on the next bank statement, and will be used to reconcile the two opening balances when the next bank reconciliation is performed.

Step 5

Prepare the bank reconciliation statement. This is a simple statement that sets out the reasons for the differences between the two closing balances.

Bank reconciliation statement as at [date]		
	$	$
Closing balance per the bank statement		3,451.00
Unpresented cheques		
Cheque 13578	45.00	
Cheque 13580	291.00	
Cheque 13583	138.00	
	———	
		(474.00)
		———
		2,977.00
Outstanding lodgements		
Receipt VBF Limited	200.00	
Receipt S Dowding	37.00	
	———	
		237.00
		———
Closing balance per the cash at bank general ledger account		3,214.00
		———

Study this sample reconciliation carefully to ensure that you understand why unpresented cheques have been subtracted and outstanding lodgements have been added.

- Unpresented cheques are payments recorded in the general ledger account but not yet on the bank statement. This balance will therefore be lower than the bank statement balance, by the amount of these payments.

- Outstanding lodgements are receipts recorded in the general ledger account but not yet on the bank statement. This balance will therefore be higher than the bank statement balance, by the amount of these receipts.

3.3 ILLUSTRATIVE EXAMPLE

The following example is quite long, but try to follow the procedure carefully to perform the bank reconciliation. It uses a typical computerised accounts format for the cash at bank general ledger account.

Shown below is the cash at bank general ledger account of Bradley Trading for the week ended 31 May 20X5, together with the bank statement at 31 May 20X5. You are also given a bank reconciliation statement for the week ended 24 May 20X5, and details of bank paying-in slips for the week.

Cash at bank general ledger account

Date	Details	Reference/	Receipts	Payments	Balance
20X5		Cheque number	Debit	Credit	
May			$	$	$
27	Opening balance				6,194.33
27	Cumnor Ltd		76.93		6,271.26
27	Holmes & Sons		119.11		6,390.37
27	Cash sales		490.68		6,881.05
27	Skipper Ltd	12791		44.80	6,836.25
27	Wessex Water	SO		294.00	6,542.25
27	Hill & Co	12792		117.23	6,425.02
27	GW Rail	12793		87.00	6,338.02
28	Wood House		29.48		6,367.50
28	Cash sales		251.09		6,618.59
28	W R Smith	12794		32.89	6,585.70
28	Binder & Sons	12795		918.20	5,667.50
29	Cash sales		365.70		6,033.20
29	Wills Insurance	DD		750.00	5,283.20
29	GW Rail	12796		111.00	5,172.20
29	Shatter & Co	12797		98.60	5,073.60
30	Temple & Co		48.60		5,122.20
30	Grove Ltd		194.20		5,316.40
30	Cash sales		208.45		5,524.85
30	P W Resistor	12798		59.21	5,465.64
30	Proffice	12799		115.34	5,350.30
31	Cash sales		441.92		5,792.22
31	Scroll & Sons	12800		643.12	5,149.10
31	GW Rail	12801		17.90	5,131.20
31	Trapp Garage	12802		33.23	5,097.97

Statement of Account

NATIONAL WESTERN BANK   Sheet number 27

66 The Long Way

Bristol BS2 4NY

Account number 17742001

Date	Details	Payments	Receipts	Balance
20X5				
27 May	Balance b/f			6,347.33
27 May	SO: Wessex Water	294.00		6,053.33
28 May	12790	153.00		5,900.33
29 May	Wills Insurance	750.00		5,150.33
30 May	3729: CC		686.72	
	12791	44.80		5,792.25
31 May	3730: CC		280.57	
	12793	87.00		
	Bank charges	14.00		5,971.82

SO standing order   DD direct debit

CC cash and/or cheques   O/D Overdrawn

Bank reconciliation statement for the week ended 24 May 20X5

	$
Balance as per bank statement	6,347.33
Unpresented cheques:	
12790	153.00
Balance as per cash at bank general ledger	6,194.33

Paying-in slip details

27 May 20X5

Cheques: $

Cumnor Ltd   76.93

Holmes & Sons   119.11

                              196.04

Cash sales   490.68

                              686.72

28 May 20X5

Cheques: $

Wood House   29.48

Cash sales   251.09

                              280.57

29 May 20X5

	$
Cash sales	365.70

30 May 20X5

Cheques:	$
Temple & Co	48.60
Grove Ltd	194.20
	242.80
Cash sales	208.45
	451.25

31 May 20X5

	$
Cash sales	441.92

Required:

Task 1

Compare the entries in the two documents, ticking off each item in turn as it is correctly matched.

Task 2

Update the cash at bank general ledger account to include the transactions shown on the bank statement that are not yet in the general ledger account.

Task 3

Calculate the closing balance on the cash at bank general ledger account as at 31 May.

Task 4

Prepare a bank reconciliation statement as at 31 May.

3.4 SOLUTION

Tasks 1, 2 and 3

First of all, reconcile the opening balance on the bank statement with the opening balance in the general ledger account. We know from the previous week's bank statement that the difference was due to an unpresented cheque, number 12790. This is shown in the bank statement for the current week, so we can tick off this item on the bank statement.

Next we need to match and tick off the corresponding transactions during the week that appear in both the general ledger account and the bank statement. Here, the receipts need to be checked first of all by comparing the paying in slips with the bank statement, and then identifying the receipts in the general ledger account.

The only item on the bank statement that is not in the general ledger account is $14 for bank charges. This should be recorded in the general ledger account. The general ledger entries to record bank charges will be: Debit Bank charges, and Credit Cash at bank.

Having entered the bank charges, the cash at bank ledger account can be 'balanced off'.

Statement of Account

NATIONAL WESTERN BANK   Sheet number 27

66 The Long Way

Bristol BS2 4NY

Account number 17742001

Date	Details	Payments	Receipts	Balance
20X5				
27 May	Balance b/fwd			6,347.33
27 May	SO: Wessex Water	✓ 294.00		6,053.33
28 May	12790	✓ 153.00		5,900.33
29 May	Wills Insurance	✓ 750.00		5,150.33
30 May	3729: CC		✓ 686.72	
	12791	✓ 44.80		5,792.25
31 May	3730: CC		✓ 280.57	
	12793	✓ 87.00		
	Bank charges	14.00		5,971.82

SO standing order	DD direct debit
CC cash and/or cheques	O/D Overdrawn

Paying-in slip details

27 May 20X5

Cheques:	$	
Cumnor Ltd	76.93	✓
Holmes & Sons	119.11	✓
	196.04	
Cash sales	490.68	✓
	686.72	✓

28 May 20X5

Cheques:	$	
Wood House	29.48	✓
Cash sales	251.09	✓
	280.57	✓

29 May 20X5

	$
Cash sales	365.70

30 May 20X5
Cheques: $
Temple & Co   48.60
Grove Ltd   194.20
                                                              ————
                                                              242.80
Cash sales   208.45
                                                              ————
                                                              451.25
                                                              ————

31 May 20X5
                                                                   $
Cash sales   441.92
                                                              ————

Cash at bank general ledger account

Date	Details	Reference/	Receipts	Payments	Balance
20X5		Cheque number	Debit	Credit	
May			$	$	$
27	Opening balance				6,194.33
27	Cumnor Ltd	✓	76.93		6,271.26
27	Holmes & Sons	✓	119.11		6,390.37
27	Cash sales	✓	490.68		6,881.05
27	Skipper Ltd	✓12791		44.80	6,836.25
27	Wessex Water	✓ SO		294.00	6,542.25
27	Hill & Co	12792		117.23	6,425.02
27	GW Rail	✓ 12793		87.00	6,338.02
28	Wood House	✓	29.48		6,367.50
28	Cash sales	✓	251.09		6,618.59
28	W R Smith	12794		32.89	6,585.70
28	Binder & Sons	12795		918.20	5,667.50
29	Cash sales		365.70		6,033.20
29	Wills Insurance	✓ DD		750.00	5,283.20
29	GW Rail	12796		111.00	5,172.20
29	Shatter & Co	12797		98.60	5,073.60
30	Temple & Co		48.60		5,122.20
30	Grove Ltd		194.20		5,316.40
30	Cash sales		208.45		5,524.85
30	P W Resistor	12798		59.21	5,465.64
30	Proffice	12799		115.34	5,350.30
31	Cash sales		441.92		5,792.22
31	Scroll & Sons	12800		643.12	5,149.10
31	GW Rail	12801		17.90	5,131.20
31	Trapp Garage	12802		33.23	5,097.97
31	**Bank charges**		–	**14.00**	**5,083.97**
	Column totals		**8,420.49**	**3,336.52**	

Task 4

Bank reconciliation statement
for the week ended 31 May 20X5

	$	$
Balance as per bank statement		5,971.82
Unpresented cheques:		
12792	117.23	
12794	32.89	
12795	918.20	
12796	111.00	
12797	98.60	
12798	59.21	
12799	115.34	
12800	643.12	
12801	17.90	
12802	33.23	
		(2,146.72)
Outstanding lodgements		
29 May	365.70	
30 May	451.25	
31 May	441.92	
		1,258.87
Balance as per cash at bank general ledger account		5,083.97

4 ERRORS AND OMISSIONS IN THE BANK GENERAL LEDGER ACCOUNT

The main reason for comparing the cash at bank general ledger account and the bank statement is to identify any errors or omissions and to correct them. When the reason for an error or omission is not clear, the problem should be brought to the attention of the appropriate person in the business.

4.1 CASH AT BANK GENERAL LEDGER ACCOUNT ERRORS

Errors may occur because a cash receipt or payment is entered as the wrong amount. This should be discovered when comparing the general ledger account with the bank statement. When an error occurs, the general ledger account should be amended, and the correct amount entered.

4.2 CASH AT BANK GENERAL LEDGER ACCOUNT OMISSIONS

It is also possible that some items on the bank statement may not yet have been entered in the general ledger account. For example, bank charges, standing order payments and direct debit payments (or receipts) and receipts by BACS transfer may not have been recorded in the general ledger account. It should be updated and these entries recorded.

Occasionally, a transaction may have been omitted from the general ledger account in error. The bank statement should provide enough information to track down the omitted item to be able to record it correctly in the general ledger accounts.

ACTIVITY 2

A bank reconciliation identified that two additional receipts which total $300 are shown on the bank statement but do not appear in the cash at bank general ledger account.

The receipts comprise $200, dividend receipts from owning shares in another company and $100, interest received from the bank on current account balances.

How should these omissions be dealt with?

For a suggested answer, see the 'Answers' section at the end of the book.

ACTIVITY 3

Given below is the cash at bank general ledger account for a business and the most recent bank statement, together with the previous bank reconciliation statement as at 31 March 20X7.

Bank reconciliation statement as at 31 March 20X7

	$
Balance as per bank statement	65.60
Unpresented cheques:	
144680	100.00
Balance as per cash at bank ledger	34.40 OD

Cash at bank general ledger account

Date	Details	Reference/	Receipts	Payments	Balance
20X7		Cheque number	Debit	Credit	
April			$	$	$
1	Opening balance			34.40	34.40 Cr
1	Turner Ltd		110.29		75.89
1	Collins & Co	144682		41.28	34.61
1	Long Ltd	144683		25.67	8.94
1	Jimmy Dino	144684		171.93	162.99 Cr
2	Danton & Co	144685		231.71	394.70 Cr
3	Water rates	SO		98.20	492.90 Cr
4	Simone Ltd		338.97		153.93 Cr
5	M Smith		10.15		143.78 Cr
10	Grossman	144686		319.06	462.84 Cr
19	Butch Ltd	144687		86.21	549.05 Cr
21	Grape & Co		430.06		118.99 Cr
22	Mothball Ltd		341.36		222.37
25	Betty Ltd	144688		89.24	133.13
28	South Ltd	144689		303.13	170.00 Cr
29	Oak & Sons	144690		475.00	645.00 Cr
30	ABC & Co		549.19		95.81 Cr
30	P D Plant	144691		61.35	157.16 Cr

Statement of Account

Larry Bank   Sheet number 247
5 High Cross
Edinburgh EH1 2WS

Account number 34267115

Date	Details	Payments	Receipts	Balance
20X7				
1 April	Balance b/f			65.60
2 April	BGC: 47619		110.29	175.89
3 April	SO: Tartan Water	98.20		77.69
4 April	144684	171.93		
	144682	41.28		
	144680	100.00		235.52 O/D
7 April	144683	25.67		
	BGC: 47620		338.97	77.78
8 April	BGC: 47621		10.15	
	144685	231.71		143.78 O/D
13 April	144686	319.06		462.84 O/D
24 April	BGC: 47622		430.06	
	144687	86.21		118.99 O/D
25 April	BGC: 47623		150.00	
	BGC: 47624		341.36	372.37
30 April	Bank interest		3.40	
	Bank charges	27.50		
	Balance c/f			348.27

SO standing order	DD direct debit
BGC bank giro credit	O/ D Overdrawn

Task 1

Reconcile the opening balances on the bank statement and in the general ledger account. Then compare all the entries in the two documents and tick off the matching items.

Task 2

Identify any errors and other discrepancies. Explain how the BGC item dated 25 April for $150.00 should be dealt with.

Task 3

Correct any errors or omissions identified in the cash at bank general ledger account, and enter any transactions that have been omitted.

Task 4

Balance off the cash at bank general ledger account. Show the balance carried down at 30 April 20X7 and the balance brought down as at 1 May.

Task 5

Prepare a bank reconciliation statement as at 30 April.

For a suggested answer, see the 'Answers' section at the end of the book.

5 SUPPLIER STATEMENT RECONCILIATIONS

5.1 INTRODUCTION

The objective of a supplier statement reconciliation is to provide assurance that the payable ledger account balance for that supplier is fairly stated. This is achieved by reconciling any differences between:

- the memorandum-only payable account for a supplier i.e. the business's record of its account and balance outstanding with that supplier, and

- the supplier statement balance, i.e. the supplier's record of transactions and the balance outstanding at a specific date.

Note that, as with a bank statement, debits and credits are reversed on the supplier statement as the supplier will record transactions from its own perspective. It may be that, depending upon presentation of the statement, it may use terminology other than debit or credit, such as 'invoice', 'receipt' etc.

Whilst the payables' ledger account in the general ledger may provide some confidence in the integrity of the double-entry system involving transactions with payables, it cannot reveal whether all purchase invoices, credit notes and payments to suppliers have been recorded correctly in the general ledger. However, many suppliers send a monthly statement to their customers detailing the movements on their account during that month. Therefore, it is possible to use this statement to check whether all transactions are included correctly by comparing the statement from the supplier with the business's own payables ledger account for that supplier.

5.2 THE APPROACH TO RECONCILIATION OF A SUPPLIER STATEMENT

This is a very similar procedure to the preparation of a bank reconciliation. The objective is to gain assurance that the payable account is fairly stated, after accounting for any errors or omissions identified when doing the reconciliation.

This is best illustrated by examples.

EXAMPLE 1

The following transactions occurred with a new supplier, MNP, during May and June.

6 May: Purchased goods on credit, costing $987 including sales tax at 20%.

24 May: Purchased goods on credit for which the invoice price is $1,168 including sales tax. The supplier has offered an early settlement discount of 4% ($40) on this invoice.

5 June: Purchased goods on credit for which the invoice price is $1,752. The supplier has offered an early settlement discount of 4% ($60) on this invoice.

12 June: Purchased goods on credit for $141 including sales tax.

12 May: Received a credit note for $188 for damaged goods returned to the supplier.

3 June: Paid the supplier $1,927. Part of this payment was to settle the 24 May invoice, and the settlement discount of $40 was taken.

The payable ledger account number for this supplier is 71003.

Task

Show the supplier's account for May and June, and carry forward the balance on the account at the end of June.

SOLUTION 1

			MNP account				**71003**
Date	Details	Folio	$	Date	Details	Folio	$
12/05	Purchase returns	PR	188	6/05	Purchases	PU	987
3/06	Bank	BK	1,927	24/05	Purchases	PU	1,168
3/06	Disc. rec'd	BK	40	5/06	Purchases	PU	1,752
30/06	Balance c/d		1,893	12/06	Purchases	PU	141
			4,048				4,048
				1/07	Balance b/d		1,893

Notes

1   The closing balance on the account is calculated by totalling the total of the entries on the debit side ($2,155) and the total of all the entries on the credit side ($4,048). The credit entries exceed the debit entries by $1,893 ($4,048 – $2,155), so there is a credit balance of $1,893 on the account.

2   The credit balance in this example represents the unpaid invoices of 5th and 12th June: ($1,752 + $141 = $1,893).

3   The account is ruled off by entering the closing balance to carry forward on the debit side, to make the two column totals equal above the line, and to bring forward the balance below the line, on the credit side of the account.

EXAMPLE 2

W Mossop received the following statement of account from a supplier, MHB:

MHB
Statement of account
Customer: W Mossop   **5 May 20X8**

Date	Description	Dr	Cr	Balance
		$	$	$
14 April	Balance b/f			1,729.46
26 April	Invoice 314/X5	397.42		2,126.88
29 April	Invoice 386/X5	927.04		3,053.92
3 May	Cheque received		1,529.46	1,524.46
4 May	Invoice 019/X6	1,062.96		2,587.42
5 May	Credit note CR174		123.26	2,464.16
			Now due	**2,464.16**

MHB's account in the payables' ledger shows a balance due of $2,804.16. Upon investigation, W Mossop finds the following:

- invoice 019/X6 was actually for $1,602.96

- a cheque for $200 was sent to MHB on 5 May, having been entered in W Mossop's general ledger accounts.

Reconcile the supplier statement to the balance per the payables' ledger.

SOLUTION 2

Begin the reconciliation by identifying the balance at the end of the month covered by the supplier statement.

Then tick-off or match items which appear in the supplier statement and also the payable ledger account for that supplier.

Next, identify unticked or unmatched items in the supplier statement – any such items are likely to form part of the reconciliation. It may be, for example, an invoice issued by the supplier but which had not been received and processed prior to the month-end.

Then, identify any unticked or unmatched items in the payable ledger account – any such items are likely to form part of the reconciliation. It may be, for example, cash paid and recorded but which had not yet been received and recorded by the supplier prior to the month-end.

	$
Balance per supplier statement	2,464.16
Cheque not yet received by MHB	(200.00)
Error in recording invoice 019/X6	
($1,602.96 – $1,062.96)	540.00
	————
Revised balance (agreed to ledger)	2,804.16

However, differences between the supplier statement and the individual payable ledger account do arise for a number of reasons.

In addition to the situations noted in the example, other instances of differences arising include:

- discount received recorded in the general ledger but not yet recorded in the supplier statement, or vice versa

- goods returned to the supplier for a refund or credit note but not yet included in the supplier statement

- differences in monetary amounts recorded in the payables' ledger account when compared with the supplier statement e.g. invoice amount per statement is, say, $345.00 and the amount recorded in the general ledger and individual payable's ledger account is $435.00. The correct amount needs to be investigated and confirmed. If the error is in the supplier statement, the supplier should be informed and a revised statement requested.

- If, following investigation an amendment is required, remember that any amendment required to an individual payable account, it will also require amendment in the purchases and payables general ledger accounts. Remember that, as the general ledger is updated, there will also be simultaneous update of the individual payable ledger accounts.

ACTIVITY 4

Hermes Co receives a supplier statement from Albus. Hermes Co extracts details from the payables ledger for Albus so that a supplier statement reconciliation can be prepared.

All items on the statement could be agreed with the payable ledger account for Albus, except for the following:

(a)   The supplier statement shows an outstanding balance of $1,715 for an invoice which was settled. The remaining balance relates to an early settlement discount that Hermes Co was eligible for and therefore settled the invoice net of this.

(b)   In the payables ledger an invoice for $205 has been incorrectly recorded as a credit note.

(c)   Hermes Co paid $63 by cheque prior to year-end. This amount has not yet been recognised on the supplier statement.

Briefly explain what action, if any, Hermes Co should take relating to the three issues noted above.

For a suggested answer, see the 'Answers' section at the end of the book.

CONCLUSION

Bank reconciliations are used to compare the bank account as recorded in the business's' general ledger against the bank's records of the bank account. The reconciliation highlights any timing differences between the two records along with any discrepancies such as errors and omissions. These are investigated and any necessary corrections made in the general ledger as appropriate. If an error has been made by the bank, then the business communicates this to the bank.

When the cash at bank general ledger account has been updated, the bank reconciliation statement is prepared to reconcile the closing balances in the cash at bank general ledger account and the bank statement. It is usually necessary to include any unpresented cheques and outstanding lodgements in the reconciliation statement.

Supplier statement reconciliations are similar in nature to a bank reconciliation. They help to provide assurance that the payables ledger balance for that supplier is stated fairly as at the date of the reconciliation. As with a bank reconciliation, it may be necessary to update the general ledger and the memorandum payable ledger account if they contain errors or omissions.

KEY TERMS

Bank reconciliation statement – A statement which reconciles the bank balance as per the bank statement with the balance per the cash at bank general ledger account.

Cash at bank ledger account – a general ledger account that is a record of transactions that have passed through the bank account.

Dishonoured cheques – cheques which cannot be paid by the bank due to insufficient funds being available in an account – 'bounced cheques'.

Outstanding deposits (lodgements) – cheques paid into the bank which have not yet passed through the bank's clearing system and so do not show on the bank statement.

Outstanding (unpresented) cheques – cheques written which have not yet gone through the bank's clearing system and so do not show on the bank statement.

Supplier statement reconciliation – an exercise carried out periodically to ensure that the balances on the individual supplier accounts in the memorandum-only payables ledger agree with the statements received from suppliers.

SELF TEST QUESTIONS

		Paragraph
1	What information appears on a bank statement?	2
2	What are outstanding lodgements?	3.2
3	What are unpresented cheques?	3.2
4	What is the general format of a bank reconciliation statement?	3.2
5	What is the objective of performing a supplier statement reconciliation?	5.1

EXAM-STYLE QUESTIONS

1   The bank reconciliation statement of High Co shows outstanding lodgements of $2,300 and outstanding cheques to suppliers of $2,000. High Co's cash at bank general ledger account shows a debit balance at $12,500.

What was the bank balance on the bank statement of High Co at 31 May?

A $12,200

B $12,500

C $12,800

D $16,800

2   After checking a business cash at bank general ledger account against the bank statement, which of the following items could require an entry in the general ledger?

(i)   Bank charges

(ii)   A cheque from a customer, which was dishonoured

(iii)   A cheque not presented

(iv)   A deposits not credited

(v)   Credit transfer entered in bank statement

(vi)   Standing order entered in bank statement

A   (i), (ii), (v) and (vi)

B   (iii) and (iv)

C   (i), (iii), (iv) and (vi)

D   (iii), (iv), (v) and (vi)

3   The balance on the cash at bank general ledger account of Mane at 31 May was a debit of $269.36. It was then discovered on receipt of the bank statement that a standing order for $40 had been omitted from the cash at bank general ledger account and that bank interest on a deposit account of $15.20 had been credited to the business account.

What is the correct balance on Mane's cash at bank general ledger account at 31 May?

A $324.56

B $294.16

C $244.56

D $214.16

4   ABC Co's accounting records show that its cash at bank general ledger account is overdrawn by $1,000. The balance on the bank statement only $500 overdrawn.

Assuming there are no errors on the bank statement, what could account for the difference?

A   Bank charges of $500 charged by the bank

B   A decrease in bank overdraft of $500

C   Unpresented cheques posted to suppliers totalling $500

D $500 paid into the bank has yet to be included in the bank statement

5   Which one of the following does not appear on a supplier statement?

A   Balance b/f

B   Balance c/f

C   Payments/Bank

D   Trade discount

For suggested answers, see the 'Answers' section at the end of the book.

Chapter 14

THE TRIAL BALANCE

The purpose of this chapter is to demonstrate the drafting of an initial trial balance as a check on the accuracy of the general ledger accounts. The trial balance highlights arithmetical errors and the chapter explains how to identify and correct these. There are some errors which the trial balance cannot identify and these are also explained. This chapter covers the syllabus area for the trial balance.

This chapter covers syllabus areas J1, J2.

CONTENTS

1   Initial trial balance

2   Types of error in double-entry

3   Suspense accounts

LEARNING OUTCOMES

At the end of this chapter, you should be able to:

*   compile an initial trial balance

*   identify errors which would be highlighted by the extraction of a trial balance

*   identify and explain different types of errors, in particular, distinguishing between those which may or may not occur in a computerised accounting system

*   distinguish between compensating and non-compensating errors

*   explain the function of a suspense account

*   correct errors using journal entries.

1 INITIAL TRIAL BALANCE

1.1 COMPUTERISED ACCOUNTING SYSTEMS

A **trial balance** is a list of all general ledger account balances at a specific date, classified as either debit balances or credit balances. The total of debit balances should equal the total of credit balances.

In a computerised accounting system, a trial balance can be produced automatically 'on demand'. It should contain an equal value of debits and credits. However, this is not a guarantee that there are no errors or omissions in the trial balance as, for example, a transaction could be posted to the wrong ledger account. Equally, a computerised system is unlikely to allow a transaction to be partially recorded by posting only one half of the double-entry required.

Computerised accounting systems are designed to prevent the following errors which may occur in a manual accounting system:

- processing a single-sided accounting entry

- processing an unequal value of debits and credits when recording a transaction

- processing transactions which affect the payables or receivables general ledger accounts but not updating the individual payables' and receivables' ledger accounts

- processing the payables or receivables general ledger accounts and updating the individual payables' and receivables' ledger accounts incorrectly or incompletely.

Note, however, that a computerised system will permit posting of a transaction if one part of the double-entry is posted to the suspense account. This may occur, for example, if the person processing the transaction is unsure of the accounting entries required to record the transaction; one part of the transaction can be recorded in the suspense account pending further review or investigation. When the query resolved, the suspense account can be cleared by making a correcting journal adjustment. Suspense accounts are considered in more detail in this chapter.

Therefore, much of the content of this chapter relates to a manual accounting system, although these processes would be performed automatically by a computerised accounting system. It is important that you understand the underlying principles of what a trial balance is and how it is produced.

In a manual accounting system, accounts are 'ruled off' or 'balanced off' from time to time, perhaps at each month end, and the balance on each account is carried forward as an opening balance at the start of the next period.

- A debit balance on an account is shown as an opening balance brought down on the debit side of the account.

- Similarly, if there is a credit balance on an account, the opening balance brought down at the start of a period should be on the credit side of the account.

When preparing a trial balance, remember that account balances in the general ledger are:

	Balance
Assets	Debit
Liabilities	Credit
Capital	Credit
Drawings (withdrawals of capital)	Debit
Income (sales)	Credit
Discounts received, purchases returns	Credit
Expenses	Debit
Wages, heat and light, sales returns, irrecoverable debts	Debit

Within the general ledger, all transactions are recorded using the principles of double-entry bookkeeping with a debit entry in one account and a credit entry in another account, and the total value of debit entries and credit entries must always be the same. If they are not, something has gone wrong.

A trial balance checks whether the ledger accounts are correct, insofar as the total debit balances and total credit balances are equal.

The format of a trial balance is a list of accounts with a column for debit balances and a column for credit balances.

Trial balance at (date)

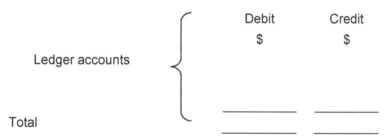

A trial balance is a memorandum listing of all the general ledger account balances. It does not form part of the double-entry bookkeeping system.

1.2 REASONS FOR PRODUCING A TRIAL BALANCE

There are three principal reasons for producing a trial balance.

- At the end of the financial year, a trial balance is used as a starting point for preparation of the annual financial statements comprising a statement of comprehensive income and a statement of financial position. This is something you will encounter in your subsequent studies.

- A trial balance shows the current balances on all the asset, liability, capital, income and expense accounts. This can provide useful information to management.

- In a manual accounting system, preparing a trial balance is a procedure for identifying certain types of errors in the accounting records.

  If the total of debit balances and the total of credit balances are not equal, there must have been one or more errors or omission when entering transactions in the ledger accounts. When the existence of an error has been identified, the next step is to carry out an investigation, and try to find where the double entry mistake or mistakes have happened. When the error has been found, it should be corrected.

Errors recording transactions as double-entry items in the ledgers are much more likely to occur in a manual accounting system than in a computerised accounting system. This is because in a computerised system, most transactions are recorded as double-entry items automatically, without the risk of human error.

Each business will have its own procedures for preparing a trial balance, and some will produce a trial balance more frequently than others. A business with a manual accounting system, however, should produce a trial balance frequently, perhaps monthly or weekly, so that if any errors have been made, their existence will be identified sooner rather than later, and tracking down the cause of the error or errors should be a quicker process.

1.3   PRODUCING AN INITIAL TRIAL BALANCE

An initial trial balance is a trial balance produced by listing all the ledger accounts in the general ledger with their debit or credit balances. It is referred to as an 'initial' trial balance because:

- if the total debits and total credits are not equal, the initial trial balance will have to be corrected

- a trial balance is used to prepare a statement of comprehensive income and a statement of financial position and in this process, a final trial balance will be prepared as the final stage towards producing the annual financial statements.

There are two stages in preparing an initial trial balance.

Step 1   Balance off all the accounts in the general ledger.

Step 2   List all accounts in the ledger, with their debit or credit balance, and total the total debit balances and the total credit balances.

Remember that the trial balance includes only the accounts within the double-entry system. It does not include memorandum accounts such as the individual receivables ledger or payables ledger accounts, for example.

Example

If you think you understand the procedure for preparing an initial trial balance, you may like to attempt preparing your own solution to this example before you review the answer and explanation provided.

The general ledger accounts of Avalon as at 31 December 20X4 are noted below. Balance the accounts, bring down the balances and show all the balances in a trial balance.

Cash at bank account

Date	Details	$	Date	Details	$
(1)	Capital	1,000	(2)	Motor car	400
(4)	Sales	300	(3)	Purchases	200
(8)	Receivables	100	(7)	Payables	200
(11)	Loan	600	(9)	Drawings	75
			(10)	Rent	40
			(12)	Insurance	30

Capital account

Date	Details	$	Date	Details	$
			(1)	Cash at bank	1,000

Motor car account

Date	Details	$	Date	Details	$
(2)	Cash at bank	400			

Purchases account

Date	Details	$	Date	Details	$
(3)	Cash at bank	200			
(5)	Payables	400			

Sales account

Date	Details	$	Date	Details	$
			(4)	Cash at bank	300
			(6)	Receivables	250

Payables account

Date	Details	$	Date	Details	$
(7)	Cash at bank	200	(5)	Purchases	400

Receivables account

Date	Details	$	Date	Details	$
(6)	Sales	250	(8)	Cash at bank	100

Drawings account

Date	Details	$	Date	Details	$
(9)	Cash at bank	75			

Rent account

Date	Details	$			$
(10)	Cash at bank	40			

Loan account

Date	Details	$	Date	Details	$
			(11)	Cash at bank	600

Insurance account

Date	Details	$	Date	Details	$
(12)	Cash at bank	30			

SOLUTION

Step 1   Balance each account and bring down the balances.

Cash at bank account

Date	Details	$	Date	Details	$
(1)	Capital	1,000	(2)	Motor car	400
(4)	Sales	300	(3)	Purchases	200
(8)	Receivables	100	(7)	Payables	200
(11)	Loan	600	(9)	Drawings	75
			(10)	Rent	40
			(12)	Insurance	30
				Balance c/d	1,055
		2,000			2,000
	Balance b/d	1,055			

Capital account

Date	Details	$	Date	Details	$
			(1)	Cash at bank	1,000

Motor car account

Date	Details	$	Date	Details	$
(2)	Cash at bank	400			

Purchases account

Date	Details	$	Date	Details	$
(3)	Cash at bank	200		Balance c/d	600
(5)	Payables	400			
		600			600
	Balance b/d	600			

Sales account

Date	Details	$	Date	Details	$
	Balance c/d	550	(4)	Cash at bank	300
			(6)	Receivables	250
		550			550
				Balance b/d	550

Payables account

Date	Details	$	Date	Details	$
(7)	Cash at bank	200	(5)	Purchases	400
	Balance c/d	200			
		400			400
				Balance b/d	200

Receivables account

Date	Details	$	Date	Details	$
(6)	Sales	250	(8)	Cash at bank	100
				Balance c/d	150
		250			250
	Balance b/d	150			

Drawings account

Date	Details	$	Date	Details	$
(9)	Cash at bank	75			

Rent account

Date	Details	$	Date	Details	$
(10)	Cash at bank	40			

Loan account

Date	Details	$	Date	Details	$
			(11)	Cash at bank	600

Insurance account

Date	Details	$	Date	Details	$
(12)	Cash at bank	30			

Step 2 Prepare the trial balance showing each of the balances in the ledger accounts.

Avalon – Trial balance as at 31 December 20X4

Account	Debit – $	Credit – $
Cash at bank	1,055	
Capital		1,000
Motor car	400	
Purchases	600	
Sales		550
Payables		200
Receivables	150	
Drawings	75	
Rent	40	
Loan		600
Insurance	30	
	2,350	2,350

The total debit balances and the total credit balances are equal at $2,350. It therefore appears that double-entry bookkeeping has been used consistently to record transactions in the accounting system.

Remember: A trial balance is simply a memorandum listing of all the ledger account balances. It is not part of the double-entry process to maintain and update the general ledger.

The initial trial balance may be regarded as the starting point in the process to prepare the annual financial statements. Normally, there will be year-end adjustments to account for, including clearing any temporary suspense account balance along with rectifying any known errors before the annual financial statements are prepared.

ACTIVITY 1

The following are the ledger accounts of Ali's business for the year ended 31 May 20X5.

Tasks

1   Balance each of the general ledger accounts.

2   Prepare a trial balance.

Bank

Date	Details	$	Date	Details	$
	Capital	10,000		Van	2,400
	Loan	5,000		Purchases	700
	Sales	600		Expenses	200
	A Singh	1,200		K James	400
				Drawings	400

Capital

Date	Details	$	Date	Details	$
				Bank	10,000

Loan

Date	Details	$	Date	Details	$
				Bank	5,000

Van

Date	Details	$	Date	Details	$
	Bank	2,400			

Purchases

Date	Details	$	Date	Details	$
	Bank	700			
	K James	400			
	K James	1,600			

K James

Date	Details	$	Date	Details	$
	Bank	400		Purchases	400
				Purchases	1,600

Sales

Date	Details	$	Date	Details	$
				Bank	600
				A Singh	1,200
				T Edwards	1,400
				A Singh	650

A Singh

Date	Details	$	Date	Details	$
	Sales	1,200			Bank	1,200
	Sales	650				

T Edwards

Date	Details	$	Date	Details	$
	Sales	1,400				

Expenses

Date	Details	$	Date	Details	$
	Bank	200			

Drawings account

Date	Details	$	Date	Details	$
	Bank	400			

For a suggested answer, see the 'Answers' section at the end of the book.

2 TYPES OF ERROR IN DOUBLE-ENTRY

2.1 INTRODUCTION

In a manual accounting system, the trial balance is a good initial source of confirmation that an equal value of debits and credits have been posted into the general ledger accounts. However, it may still contain errors or omissions. This section considers the different types of error and whether they affect the trial balance.

Note that a computerised accounting system is unlikely to permit errors involving posting an unequal value of debits and credits when recording a transaction, and neither is it likely to permit a single-sided accounting entry. However, it will permit posting an entry to a suspense account, pending review of the transaction to ensure that it is correctly posted in due course.

For example, an invoice from a supplier may contain technical product specifications or references which an accounts clerk may not fully understand, other than recognising that it is an invoice from a supplier that has granted a credit period. It may be the purchase of a non-current asset, or an asset repair, or a purchase of a product for resale to customers.

Therefore, the accounts clerk may make the following posting to the general ledger, pending further investigation into the nature of the invoice:

Debit: Suspense

Credit: Payables

If, following investigation, it is confirmed that the invoice relates to the purchase of a new item of equipment. The suspense account can now be cleared as follows:

Debit   Non-current assets – equipment

Credit: Suspense

The end result is that the correct accounting entries have been made and the suspense account now has a nil balance.

2.2 ERRORS WHERE THE TRIAL BALANCE STILL BALANCES

2.2.1 ERROR OF OMISSION

This error occurs when a transaction has been completely omitted from the accounting system. As both the debit and credit entries have been omitted, the trial balance will still balance. For example, if a purchase invoice was omitted from the accounting records – both purchases and payables will be understated, but the trial balance will agree.

2.2.2 ERROR OF COMMISSION

An error of commission occurs when a transaction has been recorded in the correct **category or classification** of account, but in the wrong account.

For example, the purchase of a computer should be recorded in the tangible non-current asset account, office equipment. If the purchase was recorded in the motor vehicles asset account then this is the correct type of account (tangible non-current assets – cost account) but the wrong account within this category.

2.2.3 ERROR OF PRINCIPLE

An error of principle occurs when the transaction is recorded in completely the wrong category of account.

For example the receipt of a loan should be recognised as a liability in the statement of financial position. If it was recorded as income in the statement of profit or loss then this is an error of principle.

If a sale (in the statement of profit or loss) was recorded as a trade payable (in the statement of financial position) then this would also be an example of an error of principle.

2.2.4 COMPENSATING ERRORS

Compensating errors occur when two (or more) transactions have been recorded incorrectly, but by coincidence they are incorrect by the same amount and cancel one another out. For example, a repair expense of $670 was recorded in the general ledger as $760, and an insurance expense of $1,100 was recorded in the general ledger as $1,010. One expense was overstated by $90, and the other expense understated by the same amount. These errors are usually very difficult to locate.

2.2.5 ERROR OF ORIGINAL ENTRY: DEBIT AND CREDIT EQUAL BUT WRONG AMOUNTS

Original entry errors occur when there has been an error in the posting of the monetary value of a transaction. An example of this arises if a purchase invoice for $400 is posted to the correct general ledger accounts, but with the wrong monetary value, say $40.

2.2.6 ERROR OF TRANSPOSITION

These errors arise when two numbers within a balance are reversed when entering a transaction into the general ledger, such as $360 is entered instead of $630. For example, the purchase of a machine which cost $4,500 was entered in the general ledger using the correct general ledger accounts as $5,400.

2.2.7 ERROR OF COMPLETE REVERSAL

These errors arise when the double-entry is correct in every aspect other than the fact that the debit and credit are posted the wrong way round. For example, cash sales of $200 should be recorded as a debit to cash at bank and a credit to sales. If an error of complete reversal has occurred, the debit entry would be to sales and the credit entry to cash at bank.

2.3 CORRECTION OF ERRORS NOT LEADING TO AN IMBALANCE IN THE TRIAL BALANCE

Errors that do not lead to an imbalance in the trial balance will generally involve transfers between accounts, creation of the complete double-entry which had been omitted, or amendments to the amounts already accounted for. These corrections will be recorded by journal adjustments.

General approach to correction of errors

The best way to approach the correction of errors is to consider:

- what double-entry should have been posted

- what double-entry was posted

- what entry is required to move from the entry posted to the entry that should have been posted.

To deal with **errors of commission and principle**:

Step 1   Set up the general ledger accounts (T-accounts) affected by the error and put in the balances from the trial balance.

Step 2   Perform the double-entry required to remove the transaction from one account to the other.

Step 3   Produce the required journal. This will describe the double-entry in Step 2.

To deal with **errors of complete omission**, follow the same procedure except that the accounts affected may not yet exist in the trial balance and thus new ones may need to be created.

To deal with **original error entries where the debit and credit are equal but wrong**:

- If the original entry was for too small an amount, perform the double-entry to the same accounts (i.e. the debit and credit to the same accounts as the original entry) for the extra amount required.

- If the original entry was for too great an amount, reverse the excess amount posted. This will involve debiting the account originally credited and crediting the account originally debited.

To deal with **errors of complete reversal** the original entry should be reversed and then the correct double-entry posted. The net effect of this is to debit **double** the amount of the transaction to the account that should have been debited in the first place and credit **double** the amount to the account that should have been credited in the first place.

2.4 ERRORS RESULTING IN AN IMBALANCE ON THE TRIAL BALANCE

Errors that may occur in a manual accounting system, such as posting single-sided entries, or recording transactions with an unequal value of debits and credits are not possible in a computerised accounting system. Similarly, other errors which may occur using a manual accounting system such as miscasting transactions to arrive at an incorrect ledger account balance, omitting a balance when extracting a trial balance or recording a balance wrongly in the trial balance cannot occur in a computerised system.

Note that, in a computerised system, a trial balance will be produced with an equal value of debits and credits. This may include a suspense account when, for example, one part of the double-entry has been posted to a suspense account pending further enquiry. Upon resolving the query, the suspense account can be cleared by using a journal adjustment.

ACTIVITY 2

Prepare the journal entries necessary to correct the following errors in the general ledger (narrative not required).

(a) A payment of $150, which was initially posted to suspense account was, in fact, to meet a personal expense of the proprietor.

(b) The proceeds from the sale of an old computer, $500, had been credited to the equipment cost account.

(c) An invoice received for the purchase of a replacement computer for office use, which cost $2,500, had been omitted from the accounting records.

For a suggested answer, see the 'Answers' section at the end of the book.

2.5 SUMMARY

All errors noted above need to be corrected before financial statements are produced. Any corrections made should be recorded in the journal as part of the process to update the general ledger.

The correction of the errors requires a sound knowledge of what the correct accounting entries should be and then, having determined that, the required journal to correct the original entries.

The section on suspense accounts and error correction highlights the need for this knowledge of the correct entries.

ACTIVITY 3

The trial balance below does not balance.

Trial balance as at [date]

Account	Debit $	Credit $
Motor vehicles		25,800
Bank	16,600	
Receivables	45,100	
Payables		23,200
Capital		47,000
Loans		8,000
Sales	41,100	
Purchases	21,400	
Expenses	4,300	
Drawings		5,000
Petty cash		200
	128,500	109,200

You have been asked to check for errors in the calculation of account balances and in the preparation of the trial balance itself. Upon checking the ledger account balances, you find that the bank account and the payable account have been balanced off as follows:

Bank

Date	Details	$	Date	Details	$
	Balance b/d	5,700		Payable	1,200
	Receivable	14,200		Motor car	14,700
	Sales	800		Purchases	300
	T Brown	20,100		Payable	12,500
	Loan	3,000		Drawings	5,000
	F Abdul	11,800		Expenses	4,300
				Balance c/d	16,600
		55,600			55,600
	Balance b/d	16,600			

Payables

Date	Details	$	Date	Details	$
				Opening balance b/d	15,600
	Bank	1,200			
	Bank	12,500		Purchases	8,950
	Closing balance c/d	23,200		Purchases	12,450
		———			———
		36,900			36,900
		———			———
				Opening balance b/d	23,200

Tasks

1 Check the account balances for bank and payables and make any necessary corrections.

2 Prepare a corrected trial balance.

For a suggested answer, see the 'Answers' section at the end of the book.

ACTIVITY 4

1 Which of the following items would appear on opposite sides of a trial balance?

    A   Capital and sales

    B   Purchases and discounts received

    C   Inventory and expenses

    D   Motor vehicles and cash

2 Which of the following would be identified as an error by a trial balance?

    A   Overstating the balance on the receivables ledger account and the payables ledger account by $100

    B   Omitting an invoice which had fallen behind a filing cabinet from the general ledger

    C   Recording a cash purchase in bank and inventory accounts

    D   Recording $100 commission received as commission paid

3 A purchase of goods has been posted to motor vehicles account. What kind of error is this?

    A   Error of commission

    B   Compensating error

    C   Error of principle

    D   Transposition error

4 Which of the following indicates a complete reversal of entries?

    A   Dr Sales; Cr Bank

    B   Dr Purchases; Cr Cash

    C   An invoice for $50 has not been posted to the general ledger

    D   Crediting $100 discount received in the sales general ledger account

For a suggested answer, see the 'Answers' section at the end of the book.

3 SUSPENSE ACCOUNTS

3.1 INTRODUCTION

When there is an imbalance between total debits and total credits in the initial trial balance, the failure of the trial balance to 'balance' should be reported and there should be established procedures within the business for investigating and correcting the errors. The first step is to open a special account in the ledger called a suspense account. The account should be opened by entering a balance in the account, such that if the suspense account is added to the trial balance, total debits and total credits will be equal.

Example – manual system

A draft initial trial balance has been prepared, and total debits are $145,600 and total credits are $127,100.

The calculation of the account balances and the trial balance itself are checked, but no errors are found in the preparation of the trial balance. The error or errors are therefore somewhere in the ledger accounting entries.

A suspense account should therefore be opened. Total debits exceed total credits by $18,500 ($145,600 – $127,100). The opening balance in the suspense account should therefore be a **credit** balance of $18,500, to make total debits and total credits equal.

Suspense

Date	Details	$	Date	Details	$
				Opening balance	18,500

ACTIVITY 5

You have prepared a draft initial trial balance, with total debits of $267,109 and total credits of $295,133. The calculation of the account balances and the trial balance itself are checked, but no errors were found in the preparation of the trial balance. The error or errors are therefore somewhere in the ledger accounting entries. As the first step in the process of identifying and correcting the errors, open up a suspense account.

For a suggested answer, see the 'Answers' section at the end of the book.

In a computerised accounting system, many of the errors or omission that may occur in a manual accounting system simply cannot occur in a computerised system. One of the more common uses of the suspense account in a computerised system is for it to be used as a temporary account to record one part of the accounting entries to record a transaction, pending clarification and amendment of the item in due course.

3.2 INVESTIGATING THE ERRORS

The balance on a suspense account is the amount by which total debit balances and total credit balances on the ledger accounts are different. It therefore represents the effect of one or more errors where debit entries and credit entries have not matched each other.

The next step is to identify the reasons for the errors, and having identified the errors, put them right.

*   The process of looking for the errors involves going back through all the records of accounting transactions posted to the ledger since the previous trial balance was prepared, looking for errors that have been made. This can be a very long and time-consuming process. This is why it is usually a good idea to prepare a trial balance regularly. If an imbalance occurs, there will not be so many transactions to check, since the error must have occurred since the previous trial balance was checked and verified.

*   Although the search is for mistakes where the debit entry and the credit entry for a transaction have not matched each other, the checking process could reveal other errors too, that have not resulted in a mismatch between debits and credits. If any such errors are found, these should be corrected too, although the correction will not affect the suspense account.

3.3 CORRECTING ERRORS

Most errors, when found, are corrected by recording a double entry adjustment in the ledger accounts.

*   When an error is a cause of an imbalance between total debits and total credits, the double entry adjustment to correct it will involve either a debit entry or a credit entry in the suspense account.

*   When an error is found that has not caused an imbalance between total debits and total credits, the double entry adjustment to correct it will not involve an entry in the suspense account.

The procedure for correcting errors is as follows:

1   Having found an error, think about what has gone wrong.

    (a)   Is there an error or omission in any of the ledger accounts? If not, correcting the error will not affect the ledger or the trial balance.

    (b)   If the error means that one or more ledger accounts are incorrect, has it caused an imbalance between total debits and total credits? If it has not caused an imbalance, correcting the error will not affect the suspense account. If it has caused an imbalance, correcting the error will affect the suspense account.

2   If there is an error or omission in any ledger accounts which has not caused an imbalance between total debits and total credits, think about what needs to be done to correct it. The correction will involve a debit entry in one account and a credit entry in the other.

    (a)   If there is an omission from the accounts, it can be corrected by entering a record of the transaction in the accounts, with an appropriate debit and credit entry.

(b)   If a transaction has been debited to the wrong account, you should credit this account with the value of the transaction, and debit the transaction to the correct account.

(c)   If a transaction has been credited to the wrong account, you should debit this account with the value of the transaction, and credit the transaction to the correct account.

3   If there is an error or omission in any ledger accounts that has caused an imbalance between total debits and total credits, think about what needs to be done to correct it.

(a)   Which ledger account is incorrect? Is a debit entry or a credit entry needed to correct the balance on this account? What is the amount by which the account balance has to be corrected? Remember that when an error is due to a transaction having been recorded as a debit when it should have been a credit in the account, or as a credit when it should have been a debit, the adjustment to correct the error will be twice the size of the transaction.

(b)   Having decided how the ledger accounts should be corrected, with a debit or a credit adjustment, the matching credit or debit should be made to the suspense account.

(c)   All the errors have not been properly corrected until the balance on the suspense account is zero.

(d)   Following correction of errors and clearance of the suspense account, a new trial balance should be extracted to ensure that the trial balance is in agreement before financial statements are prepared.

4   Before making any corrections in ledger accounts, the details of the correction should be recorded first of all in the journal, and then posted from the journal to the ledger. The journal entries will provide a record of the corrections that have been made, for future reference if required.

Example – manual system

A trial balance has been produced, but the total debits and total credits are unequal.

Trial balance as at 30 June

Account	Debit	Credit
	$	$
Equipment	20,700	
Bank	540	
Receivables	8,820	
Payables		3,100
Capital		14,700
Sales		56,270
Purchases	29,200	
Expenses	14,500	
Sales returns	760	
	———	———
	74,520	74,070
	———	———

An investigation of the accounting records reveals the following errors:

(a) The business had purchased $2,400 of new equipment, paying by cheque. The payment has been correctly entered in the bank but has not been posted to any other ledger account.

(b) Purchases on credit of $800 have been debited to the payables account.

(c) Sales returns of $760 have been debited to the receivables account.

(d) Cash sales of $1,250 were posted from the cash book (bank account) to the sales account as $1,520.

    1 Open up a suspense account and enter the balance.

    2 Show how each of these errors should be corrected.

    3 Make the correcting entries in the suspense account.

    4 Prepare a corrected trial balance.

Although the ACCA FA1 syllabus and exam presumes that a computerised accounting system is used, this example is helpful to explain and illustrate the methodical approach required to identify and resolve errors in the accounting records.

Solution

Task 1

Total debits exceed total credits by $450 ($74,520 – $74,070), so we open a suspense account and enter a credit balance of $450.

Suspense

Date	Details	$	Date	Details	$
			30/6	Opening balance	450

Task 2

Error (a)

This error has caused an imbalance between total debits and total credits, because the cash account has been correctly credited with a payment of $2,400, but there has been no matching debit entry in the equipment account.

To correct:

Journal entry

Dr Equipment $2,400

  Cr Suspense $2,400

Correction of error of single entry on cash purchase of equipment

Error (b)

Credit purchases should be credited to the payables account, not debited. This error has therefore caused an imbalance between total debits and total credits. To correct the error we need to credit the payables account with $800 to reverse the incorrect debit and then credit the account with another $800 to enter the transaction correctly.

To correct:

Journal entry

Dr Suspense $1,600

 Cr   Payables account $1,600

Correction of error, purchases debited to C(P)LCA, now credited

Error (c)

Sales returns should be credited to the receivables account, not debited. This error has therefore caused an imbalance between total debits and total credits. To correct the error we need to credit the receivables account with $760 to reverse the incorrect debit and then credit the account with another $760 to enter the transaction correctly.

To correct:

Journal entry

Dr Suspense   Dr $1,520

 Cr Receivables ledger account $1,520

Correction of error, sales returns incorrectly credited to receivables, now credited

Error (d)

This error has caused an imbalance between total debits and total credits, because the sales account should have been credited with $1,250, not $1,520. The credit entry is therefore $270 too much. To correct this, we have to debit the sales account with $270.

To correct:

Journal entry

Dr Sales $270

 Cr Suspense $270

Transposition error, sales incorrectly credited with $1,520, corrected to $1,250.

Task 3

The correcting entries in the suspense account are as follows:

Suspense

Date	Details	$	Date	Details	$
	Payables	1,600	30/6	Opening balance	450
	Receivables	1,520		Equipment	2,400
				Sales	270
		3,120			3,120

There is no remaining balance so the error has been corrected.

Task 4

A revised trial balance can now be prepared. Remember that the corrections have adjusted the balances on other ledger accounts. Here, the equipment account, receivables account, payables account and sales account all have altered balances.

Check these amended balances in the trial balance below, to make sure that you agree with how they have been calculated.

- A debit entry to an account increases the debit balance or reduces the credit balance.

- A credit entry to an account increases the credit balance or reduces the debit balance.

Corrected trial balance as at 30 June

Account	Debit $	Credit $
Equipment (20,700 + 2,400)	23,100	
Bank	540	
Receivables (8,820 – 1,520)	7,300	
Payables (3,100 + 1,600)		4,700
Capital		14,700
Sales (56,270 – 270)		56,000
Purchases	29,200	
Expenses	14,500	
Sales returns	760	
	75,400	75,400

CONCLUSION

This chapter looked at how to prepare an initial trial balance of all ledger accounts in the general ledger. The trial balance proves that accounting entries have been completed with arithmetical accuracy. However, there are a number of errors which are not highlighted by the trial balance. These are errors within the general ledger which do not lead to a difference between debit column and credit column totals in the trial balance. Any errors need to be investigated and resolved using the journal to record adjustments. If, initially, the trial balance columns do not equate, a temporary suspense account is used. When errors have been resolved the suspense account is closed.

In computerised accounting systems, many of the potential errors that may occur in a manual accounting system cannot occur. However, a trial balance extracted may still contain errors and omission which need to be identified and corrected.

A suspense account may be used in a computerised system to record one part the double-entry to record a transaction whilst the nature of the other part of the double entry is confirmed.

KEY TERMS

Suspense account – Temporary account used to identify the difference between trial balance column totals. When errors have been identified and corrected, the suspense account is closed. The suspense account may also be used to record part of an accounting transaction in the accounting system pending review and correction.

Trial balance – A memorandum listing of all the general ledger account balances.

SELF TEST QUESTIONS

		Paragraph
1	What is a trial balance?	1.1
2	Give two reasons for preparing a trial balance.	1.2
3	How is a trial balance prepared?	1.3
4	Name and explain three types of error not revealed by a trial balance.	2.2
5	State the three-step procedure to correct an error.	2.3
6	Explain the purpose and use of a suspense account.	3.1

EXAM-STYLE QUESTIONS

1 The following are balances in Lim Soon's general ledger at the end of the year:

	$
Sales	21,500
Purchases	8,000
Motor van	11,000
Bank overdraft	4,000
Inventory	9,500
Capital	3,000

What is the total of each column in Lim Soon's trial balance?

A $22,500

B $28,500

C $31,500

D $57,000

2 The following are the year-end balances in the general ledger of a business:

	$
Fee income	58,900
Expenses	21,200
Receivables	?
Payables	3,300
Capital	20,000
Bank	24,500
Office equipment	7,500

Assuming the trial balance balances, what is the missing figure for receivables?

A $29,000

B $53,200

C $67,700

D $82,200

3 Which of the following errors is identified by a trial balance?

A A complete reversal of entries

B Error of principle

C Error of single entry

D Transposition error

4   Which of the following errors requires a suspense account to be opened in a manual accounting system?

   A   Error in addition of individual supplier account balances

   B   Error of commission

   C   Cash sale recorded as $50, not $55 in the sales account and bank ledger account

   D   Cash purchases of $25 credited to the purchases account and credited in the bank ledger account

5   WRT Co posted a purchase invoice as follows: Debit: payables 1,200, Credit purchases $1,000, Credit Sales tax $200. What adjustment is required to record the transaction correctly in the general ledger?

   A   Debit: Purchases $1,000   Credit: Payables $1,200
         Debit: Sales tax $200

   B   Debit: Purchases $2,000   Credit: Payables $2,400
         Debit: Sales tax $400

   C   Debit: Payables $2,400   Credit: Purchases $2,400

   D   Debit: Payables $2,000   Credit: Purchases $2,000

6   When processing a number of purchase invoices, the accounts assistant at WRT Co had an invoice which had only the payables general ledger account code noted on the invoice. The invoice total of $360 was correctly posted to the payables general ledger account, and the other half of the transaction was posted to suspense account pending further investigation. Upon investigation, it was found that the purchase invoice was for a new machine component which, when fitted, restored the machine to its normal level of operational efficiency. WRT Co is not registered to account for sales tax. What accounting entries are required to clear the suspense account and record the transaction correctly in the general ledger?

   A   Debit: Suspense $360   Credit: Repairs $360

   B   Debit: Non-current assets $360   Credit: Suspense $360

   C   Debit: Repairs $360   Credit: Suspense $360

   D   Debit: Suspense $360   Credit: Non-current assets $360

7   When processing a sales invoice, the accounts assistant at WRT Co omitted to account for sales tax on the transaction. Instead, the full value of the sale was recorded in the sales and receivables' general ledger accounts. The gross value of the sale was $275, which included sales tax at 10%. What accounting entries are required to clear correct the error?

   A   Debit: Purchases $27.50   Credit: Sales tax $27.50

   B   Debit: Sales tax $25   Credit: Payables $25

   C   Debit: Sales tax $27.50   Credit: Purchases $27.50

   D   Debit: Sales tax $25   Credit: Purchases $25

For suggested answers, see the 'Answers' section at the end of the book.

ANSWERS TO ACTIVITIES AND EXAM-STYLE QUESTIONS

CHAPTER 1

ACTIVITY 1

1   **D**   The client has purchased the service of receiving a haircut.

2   **A**   The client has paid immediately by cash for the service 'sold' or provided by the hairdresser.

ACTIVITY 2

1   **A**   Paying for electricity is for the provision of a service rather than a purchase of goods. Answers C and D relate to income rather than payments.

2   **B**   This is a small payment made for convenience as it prevents the need for a full stationery order. The car repairs (A) is personal expenditure and is not a business payment. Petty cash expenditure is on cash terms so paying for goods supplied on credit (C) cannot be correct. Wages and salaries (D) are for larger amounts than would be paid by petty cash.

3   **C**   These are all payroll-related items although not all may apply in all countries.

ACTIVITY 3

1   It is important to keep records of receipts and payments in order to correctly account for the costs associated with the project. Also, it will assist in the evaluation of the project in terms of whether the money has been well spent.

2   A system of authorisation and control will help to prevent the spending of money that is not within the terms of the project.

3   It is important to make any payments on time to avoid problems with suppliers. Any receipts should also be recorded and paid into the bank promptly to avoid the risk of loss. Timely recording enables management to continuously review the up-to-date position. For example, if expenses are not included in the accounting records of the business until after the project ends it may appear that the project was less expensive than it really was.

ANSWERS TO EXAM-STYLE QUESTIONS

1   **C**   The business needs to keep track of the amounts due to credit suppliers. This means that they need to record all purchases on credit when goods are received and all payments to suppliers. A consignment of goods that has been purchased will not necessarily be sold in a single transaction and so the consumption of inventory will not be recorded in the manner described in the question.

2   **B**   Because the Internet Service Provider gives its clients the service of access to internet facilities. A, the sale of goods is trading in goods. C, paying the employee is employing them for labour. It is a payroll payment. D is money invested by shareholders.

3   **A**   Petty cash is available for small payments and is more convenient than obtaining cash from the bank each time it is needed. The other options are related to the bank account of the business.

4   **C**   It is always important to maintain records in case of query. It is also important to ensure that the customer pays for the goods actually received. This is a credit transaction and not a cash transaction and it is not expenditure by the stationery business.

5   **B**   The payroll department in an organisation has responsibility for paying salaries in most organisations. In the smallest businesses, it may be the business owner who pays wages and salaries.

CHAPTER 2

ACTIVITY 1

A sales order form is produced by the seller, and confirmed by a signature of the customer.

A purchase order is generated by the buyer and sent to the supplier.

ACTIVITY 2

The sales invoices of a business all have the same format, size and colour and have the name of the business clearly stated at the top. Sales invoices are sequentially numbered. The name of the customer will be different for each sales invoice.

Purchase invoices will look different, because they come from different suppliers. They could be printed on paper of different sizes and colours, they are laid out in different ways and they have different business names at the head of the document. The invoice numbers vary and have little or no relevance to the purchaser.

ACTIVITY 3

| Sales order | In some cases, a business may record the details of a customer's order on a sales order form. A sales order form is produced by the seller, and confirmed by a signature of the customer. |

| Delivery note | When goods are delivered to the customer, the customer is normally asked to sign a delivery note, as evidence that the delivery has been made. In the same way, the provider of a service, such as a telephone engineer visiting a customer's premises, may ask the customer to sign a document as evidence that the work has been completed. |

| Sales invoice | When the goods have been delivered, or the service provided, the seller sends an invoice to the customer. A sales invoice is a demand for payment, issued by the business to its customer, giving details of the items sold and the amount owing. The invoice also includes a date, and the customer is then required to pay the invoice within the credit period that has been agreed. |

| Remittance advice | Some businesses attach a tear-off payment slip to their invoices and ask the customer to return it with their payment. These tear-off payment slips are often called remittance advices. When a remittance advice is received with the payment, it is easier for the business to identify what the payment is for – in other words, it is easier to match the payment with the invoice. |

| Purchase order | A business places an order to buy goods or a service with a supplier. Whereas a sales order is generated by the seller, a purchase order is generated by the buyer. The purchase order is sent to the supplier.

(Purchase orders are sometimes placed by word of mouth, for example by telephone. However, there needs to be a high level of trust between the buyer and seller to rely this, so that the buyer will not later disagree with the supplier about the order details.) |

| Goods received note | When the goods are delivered, the buyer will receive a delivery note from the supplier. The delivery note may be used to prepare a goods received note. A goods received note sets out the details of the delivery in a standard form for the buyer. |

| Purchase invoice | The supplier will send an invoice to the buyer. Invoices received by a business from its suppliers are called purchase invoices.

The purchase invoice is checked against a copy of the purchase order and the goods received note, and is authorised by a manager of the purchasing business. At the appropriate time, the invoice is paid. |

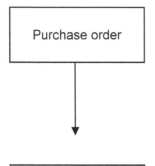

ACTIVITY 4

1   **A**   Credit note, which serves to decrease the amount owed. A debit note would be raised by the customer and sent to the supplier to request that the amount owed is reduced because, for example, they have returned goods. The credit note is notification that the amount owing from the customer has been reduced.

2   **D**   Statement of account. It includes details of invoices issued and amounts received by the supplier. The cheque requisition is an internal document used within the customer's business. The advice note is issued before delivery.

ACTIVITY 5

Sales invoices are numbered sequentially, and it is probably best to file sales documents in invoice number order. As long as the invoice number is known, the documents can be easily retrieved.

Purchase orders are not necessarily numbered sequentially, so it may be appropriate to file documents relating to purchases in date order, probably purchase invoice date order rather than by purchase order date or due date.

However, you may find that in your own business, documents are filed in a different sequence.

ACTIVITY 6

When a business holds personal data about an individual, the business must comply with the data protection principles. These include not disclosing personal data to others without appropriate authority or for a reason required by law. Therefore, you cannot give the bank manager any details relating to your customer. If you did disclose information, the customer may have the right to take legal action against you.

ANSWERS TO EXAM-STYLE QUESTIONS

1   **B**   The manufacturer provides, rather than asks for, information. The quotation is accepted by the customer who is supplied with the goods after making a deposit. This is followed by the invoice from the manufacturer to indicate the amount outstanding.

2   **A**   The delivery note lists the goods supplied. It does not include any costs. All of the other documents include prices or amounts paid/received.

3   **B**   Follows the order of a purchase from a supplier. The other options are out of sequence.

4   **B**   This reduces the amount owing. The advice note is simply advice of forthcoming delivery.

5   **D**   This omission would require an increase in the amount due from the customer, perhaps by raising a new invoice for postage and packaging charges. All other options require a reduction in the amount owed.

6   **B**   This provides a standard or common document to be used within the business rather than dealing with a number of different purchases invoices.

7   **C**   A quotation does not involve any transfers of funds or of obligations. The bookkeeping records will only be updated if the customer subsequently orders the goods for which a quote was issued.

CHAPTER 3

EXAM-STYLE QUESTIONS

1   **C**   Vulnerability because it can be subject to vandalism, attacks by viruses and so on.

CHAPTER 4

ACTIVITY 1

The figures in brackets are used here to indicate the transaction number in the activity. They can be used to match the debit entry for the transaction with the corresponding credit entry.

Capital

	$		$
		Cash at bank (1)	150,000

Property

	$		$
Cash at bank (2)	140,000		

Purchases

	$		$
Cash at bank (3)	5,000		
Cash at bank (5)	8,000		

Sales

	$		$
		Cash at bank (4)	7,000
		Cash at bank (7)	15,000

Sundry expenses

	$		$
Cash at bank (6)	100		

Wages payable

	$		$
Cash at bank (8)	2,000		

Postage costs

	$		$
Cash at bank (9)	100		

Cash at bank

	$		$
Capital (1)	150,000	Property (2)	140,000
Sales (4)	7,000	Purchases (3)	5,000
Sales (7)	15,000	Purchases (5)	8,000
		Sundry expenses (6)	100
		Wages payable (8)	2,000
		Postage costs (9)	100
		Closing balance c/f	16,800
	172,000		172,000
Opening balance b/f	16,800		

ACTIVITY 2

Transactions in the general ledger

Journal   **Date 25/9/20X4**

Journal No.		Details	General ledger account reference	Dr $	Cr $
(i)	1	Dr: Van asset	GL10 (made up)	10,000	
		Cr: Payables	GL12 (made up)		10,000
(ii)	2	Dr: Wages	GL50	1,000	
		Cr: Cash at bank	GL100		1,000
(iii)	3	Dr: Receivables	GL25	696	
		Cr: Sales	GL2		696

Conclusion   It is important that you get used to the idea of writing double-entry in journal form, as the examiner may use it as a less time consuming way than ledger accounts to test your knowledge of double-entry bookkeeping.

ACTIVITY 3

The balance brought down is $8,950 credit.

Cash at bank

	$		$
Capital	10,000	Purchases	1,000
Sales	300	Rent	2,500
Balance c/d	8,950	Electricity	750
		New van	15,000
	19,250		19,250
		Balance b/d	8,950

ACTIVITY 4

(a)

Cash at bank

		$			$
1 June	Balance b/d	4,200	3 June	Purchases	1,600
3 June	Sales	3,700	8 June	Telephone expenses	850
10 June	Sales	6,100	15 June	Equipment	2,000
15 June	Sales	4,900	28 June	Purchases	3,700
26 June	Sales	8,800	29 June	Salaries payable	14,200
			30 June	Balance c/d	5,350
		27,700			27,700
1 July	Balance b/d	5,350			

(b) A credit balance on the bank account would indicate that the business has an overdraft on its account with the bank, because payments out of the account have exceeded receipts into the account. A bank overdraft is a liability, because it represents money owed to the bank. As a liability, it is a credit balance in the account.

ACTIVITY 5

Receivables

	$		$
Sales	1,000	Cash at bank	1,000

Sales account

	$		$
		Receivables	1,000

Cash at bank account

	$		$
Receivables	1,000		

Remember to deduct trade discount at the point of sale before accounting for the sale. The net amount of the sale is therefore $1,000 ($1,250 – ($1,250 × 20%)). The settlement discount is ignored as the customer was not expected to take advantage of the discount terms, and subsequent payment was received outside of the discount period.

ACTIVITY 6

Receivables

	$		$
Sales	975	Cash at bank	975

Sales account

	$		$
		Receivables	975

Cash at bank account

	$		$
Receivables	975		

Remember to deduct trade discount at the point of sale before accounting for the sale. The net amount of the sale is therefore $1,000 ($1,250 – ($1,250 × 20%)). If the customer is expected to take advantage of the settlement discount terms, this is also deducted before accounting for the transaction. Therefore the transaction should be accounted for at $975 ($1,000 – ($1,000 × 2.5%)).

ACTIVITY 7

Receivables

	$		$
Sales	975	Cash at bank	975

Sales account

	$		$
		Receivables	975
		Cash	25

Cash at bank account

	$		$
Receivables	1,000		

Remember to deduct trade discount at the point of sale before accounting for the sale. The net amount of the sale is therefore $1,000 ($1,250 – ($1,250 × 20%)). If the customer is expected to take advantage of the settlement discount terms, this is also deducted before accounting for the transaction. Therefore the transaction should be accounted for at $975 ($1,000 – ($1,000 × 2.5%)). However, if the customer does not take advantage of the settlement discount, the full amount of $1,000 is due, with the 'excess cash' received treated as a cash sale.

ACTIVITY 8

Receivables

	$		$
Sales	1,000	Cash at bank	975
		Sales account	25

Sales account

	$		$
Receivables	25	Receivables	1,000

Cash at bank account

	$		$
Receivables	975		

Remember to deduct trade discount at the point of sale before accounting for the sale. The net amount of the sale is therefore $1,000 ($1,250 – ($1,250 × 20%)). The settlement discount is initially ignored as the customer is not expected to take advantage of the discount terms. However, when the customer subsequently pays promptly, revenue is reduced and receivables are reduced to reflect that fact that a reduced amount has been received in full settlement of the amount due. The final journal adjustment to clear the receivable balance and reduce sales revenue is as follows:

Debit: Sales account $25

Credit Receivables $25

ACTIVITY 9

Payables

	$		$
Cash at bank	490	Purchases	500
Discounts received	10		

Discounts received account

	$		$
		Payables	10

Notice how an extra double-entry in addition to the cash at bank entry has to be made to account for the settlement discount received.

ACTIVITY 10

	Supplies	Tax element
(a)	$120 gross	Tax = $20
(b)	$480 gross	Tax = $80
(c)	$200 net	Tax = $40
(d)	$1,272 gross	Tax = $212
(e)	$17,484 gross	Tax = $2,914

EXAM-STYLE QUESTIONS

1   **C**

2   **B**   The journal may include a record of year-end accounting adjustment and corrections of errors in the general ledger. In addition to this, it will also include any other non-routine transactions to be recorded in the general ledger.

3   **C**   The value of the sale has been agreed at $1,900 as the customer was expected to take advantage of the discount terms offered.

4   **A**   Remember that the customer was expected to take the discount offered, so the initial sale and receivable is recorded after deducting settlement discount. When the amount is paid after the discount period the full amount is due and the 'excess cash' received is accounted for as a cash sale.

PRACTICE QUESTION 1

ELEMENTS OF THE FINANCIAL STATEMENTS

An asset is a present economic resource controlled by the business as a result of past events. For example, a building that is owned and controlled by an entity and used to house its operations and to generate revenues would be classified as an asset.

A **liability** is a present obligation of the business to transfer an economic resource as a result of past events. A bank loan or overdraft are examples of a liability.

Equity or capital is the residual interest that the owner has in the assets of the business after all liabilities have been settled. The term 'equity' is normally used in relation to a limited company, whereas 'capital' is the term normally used for an unincorporated business such as a sole trader or a partnership.

Assets, liability and capital are the elements which are used to compile the statement of financial position.

Expenses consists of decreases in assets or increases in liabilities which result in a reduction of capital due to the owner. Examples of expenses include wages paid to employees, repairs and maintenance, insurance.

Income is consists of increases in assets or decreases in liabilities that result in an increase in capital due to the owner. The principal source of income for most entities is revenue earned from the sale of goods and services.

Income and expenses are the elements used to compile the statement of profit or loss.

PRACTICE QUESTION 2

COMPONENTS OF THE FINANCIAL STATEMENTS

The statement of profit or loss summarises the revenues earned and expenses incurred by a business during an accounting period, usually one year.

The statement of financial position is a statement of assets, liabilities and capital of a business as at a specific point in time, usually the end of an accounting period.

There are also notes and disclosures to support and explain the information in the financial statements. For example, there may be analysis of some of the monetary values in the financial statements, such as a summary of changes to property plant and equipment during the year, identifying additions and disposals during the year.

CHAPTER 5

ACTIVITY 1

1   **D**   Customers must not be careless in handling their own money. The bank is merely looking after it for them.

2   **A**   Provides instances when a bank is entitled to return the cheque. If it is six months out of date it may be that the underlying contract has been resolved in another way and the cheque has been forgotten about. An unsigned cheque may indicate carelessness or a decision not to make payment. Banks agree to pay cheques up to the balance of the customer's account or an agreed credit facility but not beyond so if there are insufficient funds on the account it is entitled to return the cheque. A payee who pays in an 'account payee' cheque is following the instructions written on the cheque.

3   **B**   The endorsement 'account payee' is a restriction on who can pay the cheque into a bank account. In this case, it can only be done by the payee.

ACTIVITY 2

	Cheque no.	Amount	Signed by:
		$	
(a)	11723	5,379.20	any two of the three directors
(b)	11724	1,406.29	T Tims and S Simon, the managers
(c)	11725	293.50	either T Tims or S Simon
(d)	11726	20,501.80	F Freud, the managing director and
			G Gammage, the finance director

ACTIVITY 3

1   **D**   A debit card provides an immediate form of payment and from the bank account of the customer rather than from a credit facility which would be typical of a credit card or a separate account as in the case of a charge card. Payment by cheque may have a delay between making payment to the seller and the cheque being presented for payment.

2   **A**   BACS is a medium for the electronic transfer of funds and is more appropriate for wages and salaries than a standing order or a credit transfer.

3   **B**   If the limit would be exceeded the customer will not be able to make payment so will need to provide cash, a cheque or some other form of payment. The other options are all valid.

ACTIVITY 4

Cash paid in

Notes	Number	Amount $		Coins	$
				10c	30.70
$50	1	50.00		5c	10.95
$20	2	40.00			———
$10	17	170.00			41.65
$5	51	255.00			———
$2	40	80.00		2c	7.62
$1	89	89.00		1c	2.45
50c	258	129.00			———
20c	391	78.20			10.07
10c	307	30.70			———
5c	219	10.95			
2c	381	7.62			
1c	245	2.45			

Cheques, POs, etc				Brought forward	712	20	Brought forward	972	11
Unifloss Ltd	279	30		North Bank					
A Armad	27	18		vouchers	259	91			
H Knight	55	19							
P Dilip	104	72							
N C Fishes	31	95							
L Lister	82	82							
Z Sgolai	131	04							
Total carried forward	712	20		Total carried forward	972	11			
Date _____				Account _____			Carried over $	972	11

Bank Giro Credit

Date:	16 July 20X5		$50	50	00

Code No.	16 39 64	$20	40	00
Bank	Aylesford Bank	$10	170	00
Branch	Brighton	$5	255	00
Account in the name of		$2	80	00
Account No.	1 7 2 3 4 5 5 2	$1	89	00
		50c	129	00
Number of cheques	7	20c	78	20
		Silver	41	65
Fee	Paid in by / Ref:	Bronze	10	07
		Total cash	942	92
	PLEASE DO NOT WRITE BELOW THIS LINE	Cheques POs, etc.	972	11
		$	1,915	03

C3 0D92157A   C77

Tutorial note: The actual items that would accompany this paying-in slip to the bank would be:

- the notes and coins suitably packaged and bagged
- the cheques
- the copy card vouchers
- the copy card summary.

When this is paid into the bank the person paying them in would sign the paying-in slip.

ANSWERS TO EXAM-STYLE QUESTIONS

1   **B**   This facilitates the payments and receipts between customers and suppliers between their different banks.

2   **A**   Every bank customer an individual bank account number. Every cheque issued by a bank customer has a different number but each customer's cheques could run the same sequence. The drawee is the bank and branch and each branch has its own identifying sort code.

3   **D**   The parent is making the payment direct from their bank account to the child's bank account and has control over it. If the child was claiming the amount it would be a direct debit. BACS is used by companies rather than individuals.

4   **B**   The partnership has, in effect, not paid the amount due and is still liable to pay it. No-one else takes over liability without a separate agreement.

5   **C**   Consistency causes potential difficulty. For example, if criminals become aware that the same person deals with the banking all the time they could apply pressure on that individual in some way.

CHAPTER 6

ACTIVITY 1

1   **D**   Wages and salaries plus employer's pension contributions.

2   **A**   Wages and salaries less deductions paid by employees.

ACTIVITY 2

1   **D**   Pension details are provided separately.

2   **A**   BACS provides for transfer of funds from the employer's bank account to those of the employees.

ACTIVITY 3

C $(100 × \$3) + (9 × \$4) = \$336$

ACTIVITY 4

The bonuses they will receive will be:

Employee B

	$
Scheme 1: Sales exceed $100 million by $2m.	
Bonus 2 × $10	20
Scheme 2: Less than 1,000 boxes	—
Scheme 3: Department's output exceeded 10,000 boxes 10% × $120	12
	—
Total bonus	32
	—

Employee C

	$
Scheme 1: Sales exceed $100 million by $2m.	
Bonus 2 × $10	20
Scheme 2: 30 excess boxes @ $5 for 10 boxes	15
Scheme 3: Department's output exceeded 10,000 boxes 10% × $130	13
	—
Total bonus	48
	—

ACTIVITY 5

Employee K earns commission of:

	$
Total sales	35,000
Less: cancellations $(1,500 + 2,500)	(4,000)
Commissionable sales	31,000
Commissionable payable	
First $20,000 × 5%	1,000
Next $11,000 × 7.5%	825
Total commission	1,825

ACTIVITY 6

Wages and salaries payable account

	$		$
Bank	4,697.04	Wages and salaries expense	
Tax authority	1,963.36	Gross pay	6,172.20
(488.20 + 1,029.96 + 445.20)		Employer's state benefit	488.20
	6,660.40		6,660.40

Wages and salaries expense account

	$		$
Wages and salaries payable account:			
Gross wages and salaries	6,172.20		
Employer's state benefit	488.20		

Tax authority account

	$		$
		Wages and salaries payable account:	
		Income tax and state benefit	1,963.36

Bank account

	$		$
		Wages and salaries payable account:	
		Net wages and salaries	4,697.04

ACTIVITY 7

Wages and salaries payable account

	$		$
Bank	569.38	Wages and salaries expense	
Tax authority		Gross pay	801.25
(122.69 + 72.18 + 80.53)	275.40	Employer's state benefit	80.53
Pension payable	67.00	Employer's pension contribution	30.00
(37.00 + 30.00)			
	———		———
	911.78		911.78
	———		———

Wages and salaries expense account

	$		$
Wages and salaries payable account:			
Gross wages and salaries	801.25		
Employer's state benefit	80.53		
Employer's pension contributions	30.00		

Tax authority account

	$		$
		Wages and salaries payable account:	
		Income tax and state benefit	275.40

Pension payable account

	$		$
		Wages and salaries payable account:	
		Pension contributions	67.00

Bank account

	$		$
		Wages and salaries payable account:	
		Net wages and salaries	569.38

If you total up all the debits and credits made in these accounts, you will find that they add up to the same total. This shows that the double-entry is complete.

ANSWERS TO EXAM-STYLE QUESTIONS

1   **C**   Each item completed counts towards pay.

2   **D** $2,000 + $100 bonus less $350 income tax less $180 contributions.

3   **C** $(35 \times \$5) + (8 \times \$5 \times 1.5) = \$235$.

4   **A**   Like all other payments they are made from either cash or bank accounts ultimately.

CHAPTER 7

ACTIVITY 1

Date	Reference	Account number	Total	Receivables	Cash sales	Sales tax
1 June			$	$	$	$
	A C Bhatt	1037	265.40	265.40		
	Flowers Limited	1002	319.64	319.64		
	E Murphy	1053	396.61	396.61		
	P Taylor	1025	236.98	236.98		
	F Willis	1129	326.89	326.89		
	Young Fashions	1042	115.79	115.79		
	Perry & Co	1079	163.26	163.26		
	L Connor Ltd	1023	115.37	115.37		
	O McGovern	1152	327.36	327.36		
	J Shepard	1116	372.45	372.45		
	Cole and Porter	1014	325.67	325.67		
	P Smith	1046	235.89	235.89		
	D Smith	1103	117.80	117.80		
	Cash sales		2,480.95	–	2,067.46	413.49
			5,800.06	3,319.11	2,067.46	413.49

ACTIVITY 2

Cash receipts record

Date	Description	Total	Receivable	Cash sales	Sales tax	
		$	$	$	$	
20 April	Cash sales	798.91	–	665.76	133.15	
20 April	D Middleton, a/c 5469	884.84	884.84			
	Totals	1,683.75	884.84	665.76	133.15	

Bank

Date	Details	Folio	$	Date	Details	Folio	$
20 April	Sales	CR?	798.91				
20 April	D Middleton	CR?	884.84				

Sales

Date	Details	Folio	$	Date	Details	Folio	$
				20 April	Bank	CR?	665.76

Sales tax

Date	Details	Folio	$	Date	Details	Folio	$
				20 April	Bank	CR?	133.15

Receivables

Date	Details	Folio	$	Date	Details	Folio	$
				20 April	Bank	CR?	884.84

D Middleton (receivable ledger account)

Date	Details	Folio	$	Date	Details	Folio	$
				20 April	Bank	CR?	884.84

ACTIVITY 3

Analysed cash payments record

Date	Cheque number	Payee/account number	Total	Payables	Sales tax	Wages and salaries	Other	Discount received
			$	$	$	$	$	$
23/7/X4	1003	N Hudson, P4153	4,230	4,230				130
24/7/X4	1004	G Fazaal, P4778	2,350	2,350				
28/7/X4	1005	Purchases	960		160		800	
30/7/X4	1006	Salary	2,500			2,500		

Note: There is no entry for sales tax for payment of the credit invoices, because the sales tax on the invoices was accounted for when the purchase invoice was recorded in the general ledger.

ACTIVITY 4

Date	Cheque number	Payee/account number	Total	Payables	Sales tax	Wages and salaries	Other	Discount received
			$	$	$	$	$	$
23/7/X4	1003	N Hudson, P4153	4,230	4,230				130
24/7/X4	1004	G Fazaal, P4778	2,350	2,350				
28/7/X4	1005	Purchases	960		160		800	
30/7/X4	1006	Salary	2,500			2,500		
			10,040	6,580	160	2,500	800	130

Arithmetic accuracy check:	$
Other	800
Wages	2,500
Sales tax	160
Payables	6,580
Total column total	10,040

The **discounts received** column total is a memorandum only column and is not included in this total.

ACTIVITY 5

Date	Narrative	Cheque No	Folio Ref (PL)	Bank $		Payables $		Sales Tax $		Non-current Assets $		Telephone and Postage $		Travel Expenses $		Sundry $		Discounts received $	
22/6	Step Wholesale Supplies	114321	PL56	200	00	200	00												
22/6	Northern telephone	114322	–	419	23			69	87			349	36						
22/6	Computer Supplies	114323	PL32	618	26	618	26											32	54
				1,237	49	818	26	69	87			349	36					32	54

ACTIVITY 6

1 **B** Receipts are recorded as debits in the general ledger. This transaction is by cheque and so appears in the bank account.

2 **B** $250 plus 20% = $300. Sales tax = $50.

ANSWERS TO EXAM-STYLE QUESTIONS

1 **C** As this is a cash transaction, there is no need to refer to Georgio Caterers.

2 **D** Discount is received from settling payables before their normal due date.

3 **C** Sales tax is recorded when the actual transaction takes place.

CHAPTER 8

ACTIVITY 1

Petty Cash Voucher		No. _105_	
Date _30/5/X7_			
For what required		AMOUNT $	¢
Stationery		19	00
Sales tax @ 20%		3	80
Total		22	80
Supporting documentation			
Till receipt			
Signature _T. Jones_			
Authorised _R. Smith_			

Net goods amount = $22.80 × (100/120) = $19.00. The sales tax amount is $19.00 × 20% = $3.80.

ACTIVITY 2

The vouchers total $4.67 + $12.90 + $2.99 + $5.06 + $16.25 = $41.87. The amount required to top up the petty cash float to $100 is therefore $41.87.

There should be $58.13 ($100 − $41.87) in notes and coins left in petty float before it is topped up. The cash float should be totalled to check that this is the case.

ACTIVITY 3

Petty cash log – May

Date	Receipts $	Voucher/ Reference No	Details $	Total payment $		Sales tax $		Travel expenses $		Office expenses $		Client entertaining $		Stationery $		Sundry $	
1/5	100.00		Bank														
1/5		832	Printing	31	50	5	25							26	25		
1/5		833	Taxi	7	40			7	40								
3/5		834	Tea, coffee	8	23					8	23						
4/5		835	Stationery	12	49	2	08							10	41		
5/5		836	Taxi	11	30	1	88	9	42								
5/5		837	Train fare	6	50			6	50								
8/5	77.42		Bank														
				77	42	9	21	23	32	8	23			36	66		

ACTIVITY 4

Step 1   Prepare a petty cash log.

Step 2   Record the transactions for the month.

Step 3   Total the columns.

Step 4   Calculate the imprest top up.

Step 5   Post the petty cash log totals to the general ledger.

Date	Receipts $	Details	Total payment $		Sales tax $		Cleaning $		Repairs $		Sundry $	
1/9	50.00	Balance b/d										
2/9		Coffee	1	89							1	89
4/9		Light switch	12	00	2	00			10	00		
10/9		Taxi	5	00							5	00
15/9		Cleaner	15	00			15	00				
25/9		Repairs	5	88	0	98			4	90		
30/9	39.77	Imprest top up										
			39	77	2	98	15	00	14	90	6	89

Petty cash

Date	Details	Folio	$	Date	Details	Folio	$
1/9	Balance b/f		50.00	Sept		PCB	39.77
30/9	Bank	PCB	39.77	30/9	Balance c/f		50.00
			———				———
			89.77				89.77
			———				———
1/10	Balance b/f		50.00				

Bank

Date	Details	Folio	$	Date	Details	Folio	$
				30/9	Petty cash		39.77

Sales tax

Date	Details	Folio	$	Date	Details	Folio	$
30/9	Petty cash	PCB	2.98				

Cleaning

Date	Details	Folio	$	Date	Details	Folio	$
30/9	Petty cash	PCB	15.00				

Repairs

Date	Details	Folio	$	Date	Details	Folio	$
30/9	Petty cash	PCB	14.90				

Sundry office expenses

Date	Details	Folio	$	Date	Details	Folio	$
30/9	Petty cash	PCB	6.89				

ACTIVITY 5

Total cash:	$	Total of petty cash vouchers:	$
4 × $20 notes	80.00	731	15.90
2 × $10 notes	20.00	732	6.73
2 × $5 note	10.00	733	21.90
5 × $1 coins	5.00	734	35.60
3 × 50¢ coins	1.50		———
7 × 20¢ coins	1.40		80.13
15 × 10¢ coins	1.50		———
6 × 5¢ coins	0.30		$
4 × 2¢ coins	0.08	Cash	119.87
9 × 1¢ coins	0.09	Petty cash vouchers	80.13
	———		———
	119.87	Imprest amount	200.00
	———		———

ACTIVITY 6

Total cash:	$	Petty cash vouchers:	$
1 × $5 note	5.00	1142	6.50
2 × $1 coins	2.00	1143	7.00
6 × 50p coins	3.00	1144	21.00
5 × 20¢ coins	1.00	1145	1.20
3 × 10¢ coins	0.30	1146	1.66
2 × 5¢ coins	0.10		
24¢ in small denomination coins	0.24		———
	———		37.36
	11.64		———
	———		

	$
Cash	11.64
Vouchers	37.36
	———
	49.00
	———

The petty cash float is short by $1. Although this amount may seem insignificant it is important that the reason for the difference is discovered. Possible reasons could be:

(a) $1 too much cash was paid out on one of the petty cash claims

(b) one of the petty cash vouchers has been made out for $1 too little although the correct amount was paid out in cash

(c) $1 has been advanced to an employee by the petty cashier but no voucher or IOU has been completed, or

(d) $1 has been stolen from the petty cash float.

ANSWERS TO EXAM-STYLE QUESTIONS

1 **D** The imprest amount equals cash in the petty cash float plus the vouchers which indicate how much has been spent.

2 **A** Total of vouchers is $35.22. Net amount is $35.22 \times \dfrac{100}{120} = \$29.35$.

   Sales tax = $29.35 × 20% = $5.87

3 **A** It is the amount spent, represented by the petty cash vouchers.

CHAPTER 9

ACTIVITY 1

1 **B** Indicates that this is the price 'at the factory gates'. Additional costs would be added for delivery.

2 **D** Copies are needed to assist in communicating with the customer, as evidence for posting transactions to the accounts and as a record for possible future use.

3 **D** This links the credit note with the invoice and, therefore, the transaction in the strongest way. Credit notes are numbered sequentially so that number alone would not assist. The amount and reason for issue of the credit note may or may not be of some assistance depending on the number of returns between customer and supplier.

4 **C** 3 × $77 = $231

   $231 – (10% × $231) = $207.90

5 **A** $500 × 0.95 = $475.00 after trade discount deducted.

$475.00 × 0.96 = $456 after early settlement deducted as the customer is expected to pay promptly to take up the discount offer.

6 **B** $750.00 × 94% = $705.00 after trade discount deducted. Note that early settlement discount is not deducted as the customer is not expected to take advantage of the settlement discount offer.

7 **C** $1,500 × 0.94 = $1,410.00 after trade discount deducted.

$1,410.00 × 0.97 = $1,367.70 after early settlement discount deducted as the customer is expected to pay promptly to take up the discount offer. The initial sale transaction is recorded as follows:

Debit Receivables $1,367.70   Credit Revenue $1.367.70

When the customer does not pay promptly, the full amount of $1,410.00 is due, and when the cash is received, it is accounted for as follows:

Debit Cash $1,410.00   Credit Revenue $42.30

Credit Receivables $1,367.70

8 **B** $600 × 90% = $540 × 96% = $518.40 40 after trade discount and early settlement discount is deducted. Note that early settlement discount is deducted as the customer is expected to take advantage of the settlement discount offer.

9 **D** $1,500 × 98% = $1,470.00 after trade discount deducted. As the customer is not expected to take advantage of the early settlement terms, early settlement discount is not deducted to arrive at the invoice price.

ACTIVITY 2

Step 1   Calculate the net amount (the sub total) less the discount.

	$
Net amount	443.00

Very important note: This amount is not shown on the invoice but is used to calculate the sales tax.

Step 2   Calculate the sales tax based on the net amount

Sales tax = $443.00 ×20/100

= $88.60

Remember to round down to the nearest 1c.

Step 3   The invoice will show:

	$
Sub-total	443.00
Sales tax at 20%	88.60
Amount payable	531.60

ACTIVITY 3

PRINTING UNLIMITED

80 New High Street
Exeter
Devon EX4 2LP
Telephone 01233 464409
Tax Reg. No. 486 4598 220

SALES INVOICE

Invoice No:	33826
Customer	P J Freeman
	New Street
	Plymouth
	Devon PL4 7ZU
Customer ref:	F12
Date/Tax Point:	22 June 20X4
Order No:	E10947

Supply of:	$
10,000 A5 economy plain manila envelopes at $6.20 per 1,000	62.00
10,000 A4 white window envelopes at $8.80 per 500	176.00
Less: early settlement discount ($62 + $176) × 3%	(7.14)
Sub total	230.86
Sales tax at 20%	46.17
Invoice total	277.03

Terms: 3% for payment within 10 days. Net 30 days.

Note that early settlement discount is deducted as the customer is expected to take up the early settlement discount offered.

PRINTING UNLIMITED

80 New High Street
Exeter
Devon EX4 2LP
Telephone 01233 464409
Tax Reg. No. 486 4598 220

SALES INVOICE

Invoice No:	33827
Customer	DU Enterprises
	Finch Estate
	Dartmouth
	EX55 99R
Customer ref:	D46
Date/Tax Point:	22 June 20X4
Order No:	E10948

	$
200 Suspension files at $26.70 per 50	106.80
500 Document wallets (paper) at $4.21 per 50	42.10
400 Document wallets (plastic) at $15.80 per 100	63.20
Total for goods before discount	**212.10**
Less trade discount at 5%	(10.61)
Sub total	201.49
Sales tax at 20%	40.29
Invoice total	241.78

Terms: Net 30 days

PRINTING UNLIMITED

80 New High Street
Exeter
Devon EX4 2LP
Telephone 01233 464409
Tax Reg. No. 486 4598 220

SALES INVOICE

Invoice No:	33828
Customer	Tab Design
	22 Fairmount Road
	Tavistock
	Devon TA4 8BB
Customer ref:	T03
Date/Tax Point:	22 June 20X4
Order No:	E10949

Supply of:	$
3 Whiteboard marker sets (10) at $8.30	24.90
1 Personal lockable file at $28.30	28.30
7 Accordian expanding files at $3.40	23.80
3,000 Plain self-seal envelopes at $7.99 per 500	47.94
	124.94
Less: 10% trade discount	(12.49)
Sub total	112.45
Sales tax at 20%	22.49
Invoice total	134.94

Terms: 4% for payment within 10 days
Net 30 days

Note that early settlement discount is not deducted as the customer is not expected to take up the early settlement discount offered.

ACTIVITY 4

	$
Credit note sub-total	28.30
Sales tax at 20%	5.66
Credit note total	33.96

ANSWERS TO EXAM-STYLE QUESTIONS

1 **B** ($2,000 – $400) – (20% ($2,000 – $400)) = $1,280. If half of the net balance is outstanding, that is $640.

2 **A** £364.20 $\times \dfrac{20}{120}$ = $60.70

3 **C** $4,000 – (25%× $4,000) = $3,000. Sales tax is $3,000 × 20% = $600. The total is $3,600.

4 **B** The entitlement is to 1% discount. Therefore, invoice value and expected cash receipt would be: $520 × 1% = $5.20. $520.00 – $5.20 = $514.80.

5 **A** It is important only to charge customers when appropriate to maintain goodwill.

6　　**A**　　The net value of the invoice is: $750 × 96% × 95% = $684. Trade discount is always deducted and settlement discount is also deducted if the customer is expected to take advantage of the early settlement discount terms.

7　　**C**　　The net value of the invoice is: $2,500 × 92% = $2,300. Trade discount is always deducted and settlement discount is also deducted only if the customer is expected to take advantage of the early settlement discount terms.

8　　**D**　　The net value of the invoice is: $600 × 95% = $570. Sales tax of $570 × 20% = $114 is added to this to give a gross receivable of $684.

9　　**B**　　The net value of the invoice is: $2,000 × 95% = $1,900. Sales tax of $1,900 × 15% = $285 is added to this to give a gross receivable of $2,185.

10　　**B**　　The net value of the invoice is: $2,500 × 93% = $2,325. Sales tax of $2,325 × 10% = $232.50 is added to this to give a gross receivable of $2,557.50.

CHAPTER 10

ACTIVITY 1

Step 1　　Enter the opening balance in the trade receivables' general ledger account. As trade receivables are an asset then this will be on the debit side of the ledger account.

Trade receivables

	$		$
Opening balance	45,000		

Step 2　　As the two debts are considered to be irrecoverable then they must be removed from the trade receivables general ledger account by a credit entry to that account and a corresponding debit entry to the irrecoverable debts expense account.

Trade receivables

	$		$
Opening balance	45,000	Irrecoverable debts expense – J Singh	790
		Irrecoverable debts expense – P Chan	1,240

Irrecoverable debts expense

	$		$
TRLC account – J Singh	790		
TRLC account – P Chan	1,240		

Step 3　　The trade receivables general ledger account must now be balanced and the closing balance (of $42,970 in this case) would appear in the statement of financial position as the net trade receivables figure at the end of the accounting period.

Trade receivables

	$		$
Opening balance	45,000	Irrecoverable – J Singh	790
		Irrecoverable – P Chan	1,240
		Balance c/d	42,970
	45,000		45,000
Balance b/d	42,970		

Step 4 Finally the irrecoverable debts expense account should be balanced and the balance written off to the statement of profit or loss as an expense of the period.

Irrecoverable debts expense

	$		$
TRLC account – J Singh	790	Statement of profit or loss	2,030
TRLC account – P Chan	1,240		
	2,030		2,030

Conclusion When a debt is considered to be irrecoverable then it is written out of the accounts completely by removing it from the trade receivables general ledger account and charging the amount as an expense to the statement of profit or loss in the accounting period in which the debt was determined to be irrecoverable.

ACTIVITY 2

Step 1 Write up the trade receivables general ledger account and irrecoverable debts expense account at 31 December 20X7.

Trade receivables

20X7	$	20X7	$
31 Dec Bal b/d	3,655	31 Dec Irrecoverable	699
		31 Dec Bal c/d	2,956
	3,655		3,655
20X8			
1 Jan Bal b/d	2,956		

Irrecoverable debts expense

20X7	$	20X7	$
31 Dec Trade receivables	699	31 Dec Statement of profit or loss	699
	699		699

Step 2 Write up the trade receivables' ledger account for 20X8 showing the credit sales and cash received from trade receivables.

Trade receivables

20X8	$	20X8	$
1 Jan Bal b/d	2,956	31 Dec Cash	16,936
31 Dec Sales	17,832		

Step 3   Record the entry for the irrecoverable debt recovered.

Irrecoverable debts expense

20X8	$	20X8	$
		31 Dec Cash at bank	699

Step 4   Balance the trade receivables general ledger account and transfer the balance on the irrecoverable debts expense account to the statement of profit or loss.

Trade receivables

20X8	$	20X8	$
1 Jan Bal b/d	2,956	31 Dec Cash	16,936
31 Dec Sales	17,832	31 Dec Bal c/d	3,852
	———		———
	20,788		20,788
	———		———
20X9			
1 Jan Bal b/d	3,852		

Irrecoverable debts expense

20X8	$	20X8	$
31 Dec Statement of profit or loss	699	31 Dec Cash at bank	699
	———		———
	699		699
	———		———

ACTIVITY 3

(a)

Trade receivables

20X8	$	20X8	$
30 Jun Bal b/d	78,635	30 Jun Irrecoverable debts	2,385
		30 Jun Bal c/d	76,250
	———		———
	78,635		78,635
	———		———
20X8			
1 Jul Bal b/d	76,250		

(b)   **Calculate the change in the allowance for receivables required at 30 June 20X9.**

	$
Allowance required at 1 July 20X8	4,300
Allowance required at 30 June 20X9	3,250
	———
Reduction in allowance for the year	1,050
	———

Allowance for receivables

20X8	$	20X8	$
30 Jun Irrecoverable debts	1,050	30 Jun Bal b/d	4,300
20X9			
30 Jun Bal c/d	3,250		
	4,300		4,300
		20X9	
		1 Jul Bal b/d	3,250

(c)   **Irrecoverable debts**

20X9	$	20X9	$
30 Jun Trade receivables w/off	2,634	30 Jun Allowance for receivables	1,050
30 Jun Trade receivables w/off	2,385	30 Jun P&L a/c	3,969
	5,019		5,019

Note that the irrecoverable debt written off earlier in the year is included. It has already been removed from the trade receivables general ledger account

EXAM-STYLE QUESTIONS

1   **B**   The irrecoverable debts written off minus the decrease in the receivables allowance.

2   **A**   The increase in the allowance is $1,500, although the full cost of irrecoverable and doubtful debts charged to the statement of profit or loss for the year will be $3,600 + $1,500 = $5,100.

PRACTICE QUESTION 1

NEED FOR AN ALLOWANCE

The irrecoverable debts account is used to write off customer balances that are no longer considered collectable. This normally occurs when there are serious doubts about whether the customer will pay anything. The allowance for receivables account is used to adjust the trade receivables general ledger account balance in the statement of financial position to reflect the fact that the recoverable value of receivables' balances may be less than the total amount that is owed.

The balance on the allowance for receivables account is offset against the gross value of receivables in the statement of financial position to show an estimate of the amount that the entity is likely to collect.

PRACTICE QUESTION 2

R BENNETT

(1)

Trade receivables

20X4		$	20X4		$
30 June	Balance b/d	18,793	30 June	Irrecoverable debts expense	371
			30 June	Balance c/d	18,422
		18,793			18,793
1 July	Balance b/d	18,422			

Irrecoverable debts expense account

20X4		$	20X4		$
30 June	Trade receivables	371	30 June	Cash at bank	120
30 June	Receivables allowance (from task 3)	449	30 June	Statement of profit or loss	700
		820			820

(2)   Receivables allowance at 30 June 20X4

	$
Specific allowances	
F Jinx	130
E Walters	620
	750

(3)

Allowance for receivables

20X4		$	20X3		$
30 June	Balance c/d	750	1 July	Balance b/d	301
			20X4		
			30 June	Irrecoverable debts expense	449
		750			750
			1 July	Balance b/d	750

CHAPTER 11

ACTIVITY 1

Calculation errors identified:	$
Item EE27 20,000 × $8.50 per 1,000 =	170.00
Less: 7% trade discount (7% × $170.00)	11.90
	158.10
Item RE20 30,000 × $11.50 per 1,000 =	345.00
Less: 8% trade discount (8% × $345.00)	27.60
	317.40

The net total should be: $158.10 + $242.25 + $317.40 = $717.75

Sales tax is calculated before taking account of settlement discount = $717.75 × 20% = $143.55

The corrected invoice is presented below for completeness:

MARCHANT PAPER LTD

74 High Road
Leeds LS14 0NY
Telephone: 0191 328 4813
Tax Reg. No. 947 4565 411

SALES INVOICE

Invoice No: 47914

Customer   J Forrester Wholesale Supplies Ltd
Unit 79b
Oakhampton Industrial Estate
Bristol BS27 4JW

Date/Tax Point: 2 March 20X3

Order No: E9471

Item No.	Description	Quantity	Item value	Discount	Total $
EE27	Envelopes A5	20,000	$8.50 per 1,000	7%	158.10
EE29	Envelopes A4	20,000	$12.75 per 1,000	5%	242.25
RE20	Recycled A4 envelopes	30,000	$11.50 per 1,000	8%	317.40

Total before taxes	717.75
Sales tax at 20%	143.55
Total	861.30

Terms: 5% cash discount for payment within 30 days
Carriage paid
E&OE

ACTIVITY 2

Invoice from Lighting Inventory Ltd

Brandish light fittings – 20 ordered and delivered but 27 invoiced. There is a problem to resolve.

Farell light fittings – 14 ordered, delivered and invoiced. This is fine.

Barnstable wall mounts – 20 ordered, 15 delivered but 19 invoiced. There is a problem resolve.

There are two problems with the invoice, both of which must be resolved before it is passed for payment.

Invoice from Summerhill Supplies

PC21 light fittings – 6 ordered, 4 delivered, 4 invoiced. This is fine.

TL15 wall fittings – 11 ordered, delivered and invoiced. This is fine.

MT06 lamp stands – 12 ordered, delivered and invoiced. This is fine.

This invoice can be passed for payment, but whether and when the remaining 2 PC21 light fittings will be delivered should be followed up.

Invoice from Stonewall Stationery

106924 2 Hole Files – 25 ordered, delivered and invoiced but 6 were damaged. There is a problem to resolve.

17240 Lever Arch Files – 40 ordered, delivered and invoiced. This is fine.

The damaged goods situation must be resolved; therefore this invoice cannot be passed for payment.

ACTIVITY 3

1 **A** $400 + [$400 × 20] = $480.00

2 **B** [$300 – (20% × $300)] = $240. This is the amount net of the trade discount. The settlement discount does not appear on the face of the invoice. The settlement discount will only be accounted for at the point the buyer decides to take advantage of the early settlement terms.

3 **C** Only by checking the original documentation, such as the subscription order form, is it possible to confirm whether the transaction is valid.

ANSWERS TO EXAM-STYLE QUESTIONS

1 **C** This is evidence of work done which is charged for the service. A written contract does not provide evidence that the work has been done, only that there is an agreement between two parties for work to be done.

2 **C** First, determine total price of the goods 20 × $50 = $1,000, and then deduct 10% of that amount for trade discount ($1,000 – 10% = $900). Finally, increase this amount by 20% to arrive at the invoice total ($900 × 120% = $1,080.00.

CHAPTER 12

ACTIVITY 1

1   **B**   Debit: Purchases $375   Credit: Payables $450
Debit: Sales tax $75

The gross amount of the payable must be split between the net purchase cost and sales tax as follows:

Sales tax = $450 × 20/120 = $75

Net cost = $450 × 100/120 = $375

To record a liability requires a credit entry in the payables account.

2   **C**   Debit: Payables $540   Credit: Bank $513
Credit: Discount received $27

The net cost needs to be grossed up to recognise sales tax on the transaction.

Sales tax = $450 × 1.20 = $540

This gross cost needs to be split between the net payment and the discount received as follows = $540 × 0.95 = $513 payment required.

Discount received of $540 × 0.05 = $27

A payment reduces the liability in the payables account.

3   **C**   Debit: Payables $540   Credit: Bank $513
Credit: Discount received $27

The net cost needs to be grossed up to recognise sales tax on the transaction.

Sales tax = $680 × 1.15 = $782

This gross cost needs to be split between the net payment and the discount received as follows = $782 × 0.95 = $742.90 payment required.

Discount received of $540 × 0.05 = $39.10

A payment reduces the liability in the payables account.

ANSWERS TO EXAM-STYLE QUESTIONS

1   **A**   This will have the effect of reducing the liability due to credit suppliers.

2   **A**   Aged payables' analysis is concerned with payables rather than receivables and will analyse amounts due for payment within particular time periods.

3   **A**   Trade discount is deducted by the supplier before the invoice is prepared – the net value of the invoice will be: $1,000 × 0.90 = $900, on which sales tax of 15% is applied: $900 × 1.15 = $1,035 total liability due to the supplier.

4   **B**   Trade discount is deducted by the supplier before the invoice is prepared – the net value of the invoice will be: $2,500 × 0.90 = $2,250, on which sales tax of 15% is applied: $2,250 × 0.15 = $337.50 input sales tax on this transaction.

5   **C**   Trade discount is deducted by the supplier before the invoice is prepared – the net value of the invoice will be: $800 × 0.80 = $640, on which sales tax of 5% is applied: $640 × 0.05 = $32, to give a gross liability of $672.

CHAPTER 13

ACTIVITY 1

1   **C**   The bank statement offers an external check on the accounting records of the cash at bank general ledger account. The reconciliation enables the cash at bank general ledger account to be updated and any omissions or errors in the accounting records to be identified and rectified. It may be that there are errors or omission on the bank statement due to bank errors, so the bank statement cannot always be relied upon to be accurate.

2   **B**   A positive bank account balance (i.e. cash in the bank) is a credit on the bank statement and a debit balance in the cash at bank general ledger account. The standing order payment is a credit in the cash at bank general ledger account and therefore reduces the debit balance. When the standing order is recorded in the cash at bank general ledger account, it will reduce the cash in hand.

ACTIVITY 2

The cash at bank general ledger account requires amendment for these additional receipts. When the cash at bank general ledger account has been updated, a revised account balance should be obtained. The accounting entries required to record these two items in the general ledger are as follows:

Dr   Cash at bank $200

Cr   Dividends received $200

Dr   Cash at bank $100

Cr   Interest received $100

ACTIVITY 3

Tasks 1, 2, 3 and 4

The difference between the two opening balances is explained by cheque 144680, which appears on the bank statement and so can be ticked off.

When you match the transactions on the bank statement with those in the general ledger account, you should find three discrepancies (unticked items) on the bank statement.

• A credit transfer of $150.00 shown as a receipt on the bank statement. This receipt should be investigated and the payer identified. The general ledger account and the individual receivable account should be amended to reflect this receipt.

• Bank interest of $3.40 should be entered into the cash at bank general ledger account as a receipt (debit) and credited to the bank interest received account in the general ledger.

• Bank charges of $27.50 should be entered into the cash at bank general ledger account as a payment (credit) and also debited to the bank charges account in the general ledger.

Statement of Account

Larry Bank

5 High Cross

Edinburgh EH1 2WS

Sheet number 247

Account number 34267115

Date	Details	Payments	Receipts	Balance
20X7				
1 April	Balance b/f			65.60
2 April	BGC: 47619		✓ 110.29	175.89
3 April	SO: Tartan Water	✓ 98.20		77.69
4 April	144684	✓ 171.93		
	144682	✓ 41.28		
	144680	✓ 100.00		235.52 O/D
7 April	144683	✓ 25.67		
	BGC: 47620		✓ 338.97	77.78
8 April	BGC: 47621		✓ 10.15	
	144685	✓ 231.71		143.78 O/D
13 April	144686	✓ 319.06		462.84 O/D
24 April	BGC: 47622		✓ 430.06	
	144687	✓ 86.21		118.99 O/D
25 April	BGC: 47623		150.00	
	BGC: 47624		✓ 341.36	372.37
30 April	Bank interest		3.40	
	Bank charges	27.50		
	Balance c/f			348.27

SO standing order

BGC bank giro credit

DD direct debit

O/ D Overdrawn

Cash at bank general ledger account

Date	Details	Reference/	Receipts	Payments	Balance
20X7		Cheque number	Debit	Credit	
April			$	$	$
1	Opening balance			34.40	34.40 Cr
1	Turner Ltd		✓ 110.29		75.89
1	Collins & Co	144682		✓ 41.28	34.61
1	Long Ltd	144683		✓ 25.67	8.94
1	Jimmy Dino	144684		✓ 171.93	162.99 Cr
2	Danton & Co	144685		✓ 231.71	394.70 Cr
3	Water rates	SO		✓ 98.20	492.90 Cr
4	Simone Ltd		✓ 338.97		153.93 Cr
5	M Smith		✓ 10.15		143.78 Cr
10	Grossman	144686		✓ 319.06	462.84 Cr
19	Butch Ltd	144687		✓ 86.21	549.05 Cr
21	Grape & Co		✓ 430.06		118.99 Cr
22	Mothball Ltd		✓ 341.36		222.37
25	Betty Ltd	144688		89.24	133.13
28	South Ltd	144689		303.13	170.00 Cr
29	Oak & Sons	144690		475.00	645.00 Cr
30	ABC & Co		549.19		95.81 Cr
30	P D Plant	144691		61.35	157.16 Cr
30	**[Detail to be added]**		**150.00**		**7.16 Cr**
30	**Interest received**		**3.40**		**3.76 Cr**
30	**Bank charges**			**27.50**	**31.26 Cr**

Note: Here there is an overdraft closing balance.

Task 5

Bank reconciliation statement as at 30 April 20X7

	$	$
Balance as per bank statement		348.27
Unpresented cheques:		
144688	89.24	
144689	303.13	
144690	475.00	
144691	61.35	
	———	
		(928.72)
Outstanding lodgements		
ABC & Co		549.19
		———
Balance as per cash at bank general ledger account		(31.26)
		———

ACTIVITY 4

In relation to the supplier statement reconciliation, the following is relevant:

(a)   The supplier statement is incorrect as the discount has not been applied. The supplier should be contacted but no adjustment is required in Hermes Co's accounting records.

(b)   This item does require amendment in Hermes Co's accounting records as a purchase invoice has been incorrectly accounted for as a credit note. An adjustment is required to reverse the incorrect credit note and recognise correct invoice as follows:

Dr Purchases $410 (205 × 2),   Cr Payables $410

(c)   This is purely a timing difference. The amount has been paid, and it is correct to have recognised this reducing the payables balance. The payment should appear in the supplier statement for the following month.

ANSWERS TO EXAM-STYLE QUESTIONS

1   **A** $12,500 – $2,300 + $2,000 = $12,200

2   **A**   Each item listed appears in the bank statement but not the cash at bank general ledger account. This must be updated and to lead to an updated general ledger account balance.

3   **C** $269.36 – $40.00 + $15.20 = $244.56

4   **C**   The cheques have been recorded in the cash at bank general ledger but not yet shown on the bank statement. When they are presented it will increase the bank overdraft.

5   **D**   Trade discount appears on invoices, but not in the accounts. As statements are a reflection of ledger accounts, trade discount does not appear on statements.

CHAPTER 14

ACTIVITY 1

Step 1 Balance each of the ledger accounts.

Bank

Date	Details	$	Date	Details	$
	Capital	10,000		Van	2,400
	Loan	5,000		Purchases	700
	Sales	600		Expenses	200
	A Singh	1,200		K James	400
				Drawings	400
				Balance c/d	12,700
		16,800			16,800
	Balance b/d	12,700			

Capital

Date	Details	$	Date	Details	$
				Bank	10,000

Loan

Date	Details	$	Date	Details	$
				Bank	5,000

Van

Date	Details	$	Date	Details	$
	Bank	2,400			

Purchases

Date	Details	$	Date	Details	$
	Bank	700			
	K James	400			
	K James	1,600		Balance c/d	2,700
		2,700			2,700
	Balance b/d	2,700			

K James

Date	Details	$	Date	Details	$
	Bank	400		Purchases	400
	Balance c/d	1,600		Purchases	1,600
		———			———
		2,000			2,000
		———			———
				Balance b/d	1,600

Sales

Date	Details	$	Date	Details	$
				Bank	600
				A Singh	1,200
				T Edwards	1,400
	Balance c/d	3,850		A Singh	650
		———			———
		3,850			3,850
		———			———
				Balance b/d	3,850

A Singh

Date	Details	$	Date	Details	$
	Sales	1,200		Bank	1,200
	Sales	650		Balance c/d	650
		———			———
		1,850			1,850
		———			———
	Balance b/d	650			

T Edwards

Date	Details	$	Date	Details	$
	Sales	1,400			

Expenses

Date	Details	$	Date	Details	$
	Bank	200			

Drawings

Date	Details	$	Date	Details	$
	Bank	400			

Step 2   List each account name and balance then total up the debits and the credits.

Ali – Trial balance as at 31 May 20X5

Account	Debit	Credit
	$	$
Bank	12,700	
Capital		10,000
Loan		5,000
Van	2,400	
Purchases	2,700	
Payable – K James		1,600
Sales		3,850
Receivable – A Singh	650	
Receivable – T Edwards	1,400	
Expenses	200	
Drawings	400	
	20,450	20,450

ACTIVITY 2

		Debit	Credit
		$	$
(a)	The entry **should** have been:		
	Drawings	150	
	Cash at bank		150
	The **actual** entry was		
	Suspense	150	
	Cash at bank		150
	The **correcting** entry required is therefore		
	Drawings	150	
	Suspense		150
(b)	Equipment cost	500	
	Non-current asset disposals		500
(c)	Equipment cost	2,500	
	Payables		2,500

The best approach in determining the appropriate correcting journal is to think what **should** have happened (write the double entry as it originally should have been) and compare this with what **did** happen (again in double entry) and thus determine the necessary entry to move from the wrong version to the right one.

ACTIVITY 3

Task 1

The account balances should be calculated as follows:

Bank

Date	Details	$	Date	Details	$
	Opening balance b/d	5,700		Payables	1,200
	Receivables	14,200		Motor car	14,700
	Sales	800		Purchases	300
	T Brown	20,100		Payables	12,500
	Loan	3,000		Drawings	5,000
	F Abdul	11,800		Expenses	4,300
				Balance c/d	**17,600**
		———			———
		55,600			55,600
		———			———
	Balance b/d	**17,600**			

Payables

Date	Details	$	Date	Details	$
	Bank	1,200		Opening balance b/d	15,600
	Bank	12,500		Purchases	8,950
	Closing balance c/d	**23,300**		Purchases	12,450
		———			———
		37,000			37,000
		———			———
				Opening balance b/d	**23,300**

Task 2

The trial balance has been prepared with a few balances in the wrong column. The correct trial balance should be prepared as follows, with the corrected account balances included.

Trial balance as at [date]

Account	Debit	Credit
	$	$
Motor vehicles	25,800	
Bank	17,600	
Receivables	45,100	
Payables		23,300
Capital		47,000
Loans		8,000
Sales		41,100
Purchases	21,400	
Expenses	4,300	
Drawings	5,000	
Petty cash	200	
	———	———
	119,400	119,400
	———	———

ACTIVITY 4

1 **B** Purchases is a debit and discounts received (a benefit for paying early) is a credit.

2 **D** Commission received should be a credit, but commission paid is a debit balance so this incorrect posting will be revealed by the trial balance. The two ledger control accounts are overstated by $100 – one is a debt balance and the other is a credit balance. This will not be identified by a trial balance. Omitting the invoice involves omitting both the debit and credit sides of the transaction. Both purchases and inventory are accounts with debit balances so although the wrong accounts are used, the error will not affect the arithmetical agreement between columns.

3 **C** The transaction has been posted to the incorrect class of account.

4 **A** Income from sales is debited to the bank account.

ACTIVITY 5

Total credits exceed total debits by $28,024 ($295,133 – $267,109). The opening balance in the suspense account should therefore be a **debit** balance of $28,024, to make total debits and total credits equal.

Suspense

Date	Details	$	Date	Details	$
	Opening balance	28,024			

ANSWERS TO EXAM-STYLE QUESTIONS

1   **B**   Total of $57,000 divided by two.

2   **A**   Total payables $82,200 – total receivables $53,200 = $29,000.

3   **C**   Of the options, this is the one which leads to a difference between debit and credit columns in a trial balance.

4   **D**   The entry to the purchases account should be debited.

5   **B**   The error is a reversal of entries. Therefore the error needs to be removed, and the correct entries recorded. In effect, the total of the adjustment is twice the value of the original transaction.

6   **C**   The original entry in the suspense account is a debit to match the credit correctly posted to the payables account. To clear the suspense account requires a credit, with the debit recorded in the repairs expense account. It is not a non-current asset as the cost maintains, rather than improves, operational efficiency of the machine.

7   **D**   The correct accounting entries are: Debit purchases $250 ($275 /1.1), Debit sales tax $25 ($275/1.1 × 0.1), and Credit payables $275 (the gross amount). The payables account entry is correct. The correction required is to reduce purchases by $25 with a credit entry and record a debit in the sales tax account for input tax recoverable.

INDEX

A

Account(s), 6
    codes, 204, 240
Accounting
    equation, 53
    estimates, 57
    system, 6
Advice note, 12, 229
Allowance for receivables – specific, 214,
    217, 218, 248
Asset account codes, 240

B

BACS
    payments, 100, 155
    receipts, 257
Bank
    charges, 257
    customer relationship, 88
    obligations, 88
    reconciliation(s), 255, 270
    reconciliation statement, 259
    statement, 257
Banking, 87
Block codes, 46
Bonuses, 134
Book-keeping system, 6
Business transactions, 1

C

Capital expenditure, 240
Cash, 90
    discounts, 194
    handling procedures, 110, 114
    receipts book, 151
    transaction(s), 3, 13
Cash book, 150, 156
    errors, 267
    omissions, 267
Charge cards, 98, 99
Cheque(s), 90, 256
    crossed, 91
    dishonoured, 90, 256
    drawer, 90
    endorsed, 92
    payee, 91
    preparation, 94
    requisition, 15, 276
    signatories, 96

Clearing
    banks, 89
    system, 89, 256
Clock cards, 125
Code number, 44
Commission, 136
Compensating error, 287
Computerised accounting, 39
    advantages, 40
    disadvantages, 41
Confidentiality of accounting, 53
Contract, 230
Correction of errors, 288, 289
Credit card vouchers, 108
Credit cards, 97, 98, 99
Credit
    limit, 16
    note(s), 24, 192, 199, 239
    purchase, 18
    sale, 16, 188
    terms, 16
    transaction, 3
    transaction procedures, 16
    transfer, 93, 94, 256
Creditor, 88
Customer(s), 2
    obligations, 89

D

Data Protection, 28
Data Protection Act 1998, 28
Debit
    cards, 98
    note, 25
Delivery note, 12, 14, 16, 20, 229
Department codes, 138
Direct debit(s), 93, 155, 257
Discount(s), 193
    cash, 194
    settlement, 194
    trade, 193
Dispatch note, 14
Document retention policies, 27